D0576135

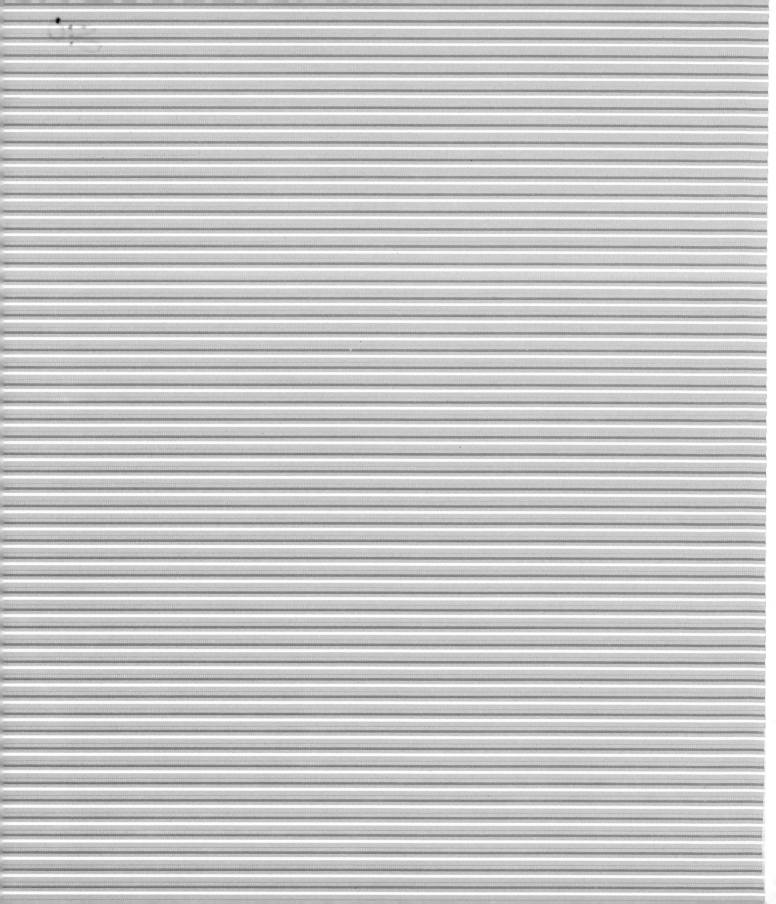

Rick & Lanie's

Excellent Kitchen Adventures

Rick & Lanie's
Excellent Kitchen Adventures

Chef-Dad

Teenage Daughter

Recipes and Stories

Rick Bayless & Lanie Bayless

with Deann Groen Bayless

PHOTOGRAPHS BY CHRISTOPHER HIRSHEIMER

Stewart, Tabori & Chang
New York

To Levita and John, my parents, whose life choices created a place
where my love for food flourished. I sincerely hope that
my life choices, accidental or planned, will create for my daughter
a place where her unique passions can thrive. —RB

� � � � � �

To Fabiola, who has always been there for me
since I was eight months old. —LB

Published in 2004 by
Stewart, Tabori & Chang
A Company of La Martinière Groupe
115 West 18th Street
New York, NY 10011

Canadian Distribution:
Canadian Manda Group
One Atlantic Avenue, Suite 105
Toronto, Ontario M6K 3E7
Canada

Library of Congress Cataloging-in-Publication Data
Bayless, Rick.
  Rick and Lanie's excellent kitchen adventures : recipes and stories /
Rick Bayless and Lanie Bayless ; photographs by Christopher Hirsheimer.
    p.   cm.
  Includes index.
  ISBN: 0-58479-331-7 (hardcover)
  1. Cookery, International. I. Bayless, Lanie. II. Title.
TX725.A1B346 2004
641.59—dc22   2004012627

Designed by Laura Lindgren
Production Manger: Jane Searle

The text of this book was composed in The Mix, The Sans, Beo Sans,
and Instanter.

Printed in China
10 9 8 7 6 5 4 3 2 1
First Printing

LA MARTINIÈRE
GROUPE

CONTENTS

CONTENTS

INTRODUCTION

✦ ✦ ✦ ✦ ✦ ✦

Why We Wrote This Book

Most people know me as that guy who explores the far reaches of the traditional Mexican kitchen—chef of Frontera Grill and Topolobampo in Chicago, author of in-depth, regional Mexican cookbooks, host of a Public Television show on Mexican cooking. Yes, that's the public me, but I'm also an insatiable traveler and student of any culture I come across. I'm a cook whose curiosity and experience extend way past Mexico's borders. I'm the father of a teenage daughter named Lanie (who has literally grown up in our restaurants and been taken on every trip we've made, no matter how exotic the destination). And I'm a guy who cooks a lot at home for my friends and family, partly because I think it's fun and partly because I know how a good meal draws people closer.

I wrote this book from that private side of me: as traveler, culinary explorer, father, home cook. I wanted to tell the story of recipes we *really* cook at home and exactly how our collection came about. Here's how it began. When Lanie was about 7, and her kitchen experiences were growing from arranging smiley-face chocolate chips on pancakes to actually helping make dinner, we discovered that she couldn't eat wheat flour or almost anything made from cow's milk. This led me to start cooking more at home, creating special recipes we could all eat.

At about that same time, we began to travel more outside the United States, meaning we learned about—and fell in love with—a wide variety of delicious dishes we wished we could make back home. This was also the period when Lanie began to ask more about the food from the barbeque restaurant I grew up in, The Hickory House, the long-closed place her grandparents had operated in Oklahoma City for 37 years. Though that food was so thoroughly part of my everyday experience until I left home at 20, I'd never figured out how to integrate that Oklahoma barbeque into the Mexican-focused, Chicago-rooted life we had established.

Lanie's dietary issues soon resolved themselves, and most of the wheat- and dairy-free creations I'd worked out were retired. But my love of home cooking had grown stronger. And the recipes we'd collected in our travels plus the ones I'd written down from my family's barbeque restaurant had taken on an important role in our lives, on our dinner table, in the menus we put together for friends.

As we developed this collection of recipes, we realized there were at least four good reasons to work our material into a book:

1. **It's important for everyone to know how to cook—boys, girls, kids, teenagers, adults—everyone.** Not only does cooking make all of us more independent and better able to take care of ourselves, but it helps us better appreciate the world through flavor and the satisfaction of mastering a simple craft. *And* it helps us make more knowledgeable choices about our nutrition, as well as about political, cultural and environmental food issues. Food is, after all, one aspect of life we all (have to) share in.

2. **Learning about the food of another country helps us push past superficial stereotypes.** I have a passion for *any* travel, but, as a chef, I usually choose destinations where I have culinary contacts—chefs or their families and friends. When we land someplace new, we're often lucky enough to get ourselves invited to dinner at the homes of some of these chef-related families. Which has, in many instances, completely changed our understanding of the place we are visiting. When we've been able to

help prepare the meal (or, better yet, shop *and* help with the cooking), we have found that our relationship to the people, their culture and their surroundings deepens significantly. The everydayness of these food tasks makes us comfortable in their world and gives us a richer understanding of who they are. It reaffirms that, at the core, we all share a common bond. Even *tasting* the food of another culture helps us relate to that culture better.

3. **We all need *simple* recipes for the food we really want to eat.** America is a very multicultural society. We rub shoulders with people from everywhere. We eat Asian one day, Mexican the next, Italian after that. We need up-to-the-minute recipes that reflect our current understanding of how different cuisines influence the way we eat.

4. **Food helps build traditions.** I'm a firm believer in special food served on special plates for special days. This intention to create something meaningful helps us break the dulling sameness of "everyday," so we can completely focus on the "here-and-now." Especially the *people* in our "here-and-now." In our family, for instance, we make a mid-winter barbeque, odd as that may sound. It makes sense for us as a family tradition because, first of all, I come from a barbeque background and it celebrates a long-standing family tradition. It's also our private affirmation that summer will come again. And we get a chance to eat off of Grandma's Frankoma pottery and use my favorite grill (even if it *is* cooped up in a freezing garage). Choose a dish you always make for a special day or prepare with special equipment or serve on special plates and your family and friends will never forget it. That dish will become synonymous with you and that occasion and the people who've shared it with you.

How We Wrote This Book

This cookbook grew into its present shape over many years. First, Deann (my wife, Lanie's mom), Lanie and I traveled to a lot of countries, met a lot of people, cooked with them, ate in a bunch of restaurants, markets and street stalls, and then figured out which recipes to include. As we worked on

the recipes, there were four things we wanted to be sure of: (1) We—and our friends and family—really *liked* and *would make* all the food we included recipes for. (2) We could pretty easily get the ingredients for these recipes. (3) Our dishes came out reasonably close to what we had eaten in their country of origin—in spite of different kitchens and sometimes slightly different ingredients. And (4) our recipes were clear enough that other people could make them successfully.

We brainstormed with our friend and colleague, Kirsten West, to come up with the *easiest* way to authentically make the dishes. Then I wrote out a preliminary "testing" recipe which Kirsten made over and over, changing this or that, until we got them perfect, and, we hope, easy to follow. Finally, Lanie and her friends tested the recipes to make sure not-so-experienced cooks could turn out great dishes. That's when Lanie verbalized all the material that's in the notes before each recipe.

A Note from Lanie

Everybody always says how lucky I am to hang out at the restaurant and have a famous chef for a father and visit families in other countries and all that. Well, there are pros and cons.

PROS
* There's always something to eat—not like sometimes at my friend Jen's house.
* I like charro beans, chips, green salsa, jicama, salmon, pork milanesa, quesadillas capitalinas, ice cream with chocolate sauce, and they are usually on the menu.
* I can usually get a paying job when I need a new CD or accessory.
* I get out of school sometimes for family "research trips."
* I have learned lots about other countries (good for school reports).
* I know lots of different people.
* Sometimes my school friends come into the restaurant with their parents—my friends and I get to hang out in my room at the restaurant—kinda cool.
* There's always stuff going on.

CONS

* I have to taste weird food.
* Some of the food in the foreign countries we visit is so weird I can't taste it or I'm afraid I might you-know-what (like when we were on that train in Thailand and Olivia and everyone was going wild for the catfish in yellow curry with leaves I couldn't pronounce—and all I wanted was a fried egg sandwich).
* Meals at other people's restaurants take a long time; chefs are always sending out extra dishes when *I* want to get home to see *Gilmore Girls*.
* I don't get enough chances to eat my favorites. I'm always having to try something "new."
* My parents have to work evenings; that *definitely* affects sleepovers, shopping, etc.
* There's always too much stuff going on, and *always* until *too late at night*.

Also, writing a cookbook is a lot of work and takes a really long time. Like *years*. I'm not complaining or anything, but I'm glad it's done. Except the parts where we had fun. Like the time when all of Aunt Bonnie's friends showed up when we were making about a thousand potsticker dumplings: Mom trying to remember the "authentic" way she made them when she lived in Taiwan, and Dad trying to figure out the easiest way and (this is *so* him) whether they were best steamed 6 minutes or 7. They all started making potstickers without even being invited, and then we all started laughing, and, well, it was fun. Even though at first I was dreading all the work. That's kind of the way it was everywhere we went. It was fun cooking with all those cool people.

Teens, Cooking

When I was a teenager, I loved cooking dinner (which was a good thing because there were a lot of nights that I had no choice). But I always wanted to cook by myself: organize myself, do everything myself. Okay, I was kind of a control freak. Lanie, on the other hand, doesn't really like to cook alone. For her, it's a lot more fun to cook with friends. Here are a few ground rules that may be useful:

1. *Don't plan too much. (Parents: help with some simple side dishes or dessert.)*
2. *Avoid time pressure. Have some healthy, light snacks on hand so no one starves before dinner gets on the table. (Parents: remember, this kind of cooking is as much about socializing as it is about eating.)*
3. *Check to make sure you have ALL the ingredients before you start cooking. Set them out before your friends arrive and you start working. (Parents: don't meddle.)*
4. *Clean up as you go! (Parents: I know this is going to grate on some of you, but I sometimes hang out in the kitchen helping with the dishes. I like doing dishes, okay? And I like listening to what my daughter and her friends talk about. They're cool kids.)*

MEXICO
{with a side trip to Peru}

❄ ❄ ❄ ❄ ❄ ❄

Rick: The sky was clear blue as we started our descent over the spectacular thousand-year-old ruins of Monte Alban and into the Oaxaca valley. It's always sunny here in December—one reason I've been coming every winter for the past two decades. Another reason is that we've made so many friends here that this small town in the southern highlands of Mexico has become our Mexican home.

Some people tell me I must have been a Oaxacan in a previous life since I feel so at home walking the downtown streets, sitting in the cafés around the square and browsing through shops that sell everything from fantastical wooden creatures to Mexico's finest works of art. I'm totally at home with the food, too. I can slip right into a breakfast of *huevos rancheros* or spicy *chilaquiles* (a crunchy-soft tortilla concoction), then move onto a midday meal of *caldo de gato* (cat's tail soup—a dramatic name for chicken-vegetable soup), chicken in black *mole* (Oaxaca's most famous fiesta dish) with rice and corn tortillas as soft as a chamois rag, and finish with a crunchy-crystalline frozen "ice" made from some kind of tropical fruit.

The food is the main reason I keep coming back. Well, the food and the art. And the generous-spirited people. And the way everyone seems so much calmer and more in swing with nature and the seasons than we are in the United States. That's why, when Lanie was born, I decided I needed to give her Oaxaca once a year. *For Christmas*—America's most important, but most commercial, holiday. I wanted her to know that there are people on earth who can create amazing parties by reaching deep into their spirits—not their pocketbooks. Parties where no one gets a gift (except maybe a little candy from a piñata), but everyone leaves totally satisfied.

We've known Javier Mendez and Toni Sobel (and their four kids) for so long I can't even remember when we met. And for years now, we've shared Christmas dinner at the same outdoor restaurant with its dirt floors, hammocks, an amazing pit-cooked lamb *barbacoa* and a pet monkey. Hours of Christmas dinner that turn into stories and laughs, because we all invite lots of other friends and acquaintances.

But this year I had asked Toni if we could all cook a pre-Christmas dinner together—something I'd been wanting to do for years— Oaxacan recipes she'd learned from her mother-in-law. (She was raised in New York, but came here and married a local 37 years ago.) Really, I asked if we could cook dinner with Andrés, her 15-year-old son. I'd heard stories of his legendary cooking prowess. If he could really cook, I wanted him to make a *mole* with us—one of the hardest (and most special dishes) in Mexico's cookbook.

Coloradito—Oaxacan Red Mole with Chicken, recipe on page 38

That's why, on the 21st of December, a Sunday, Toni, Javier, Andrés, Deann, Lanie and I headed for the nearby town of Tlacolula (though I probably wouldn't have if I'd known how torn up the road was; they're building a new super-highway to the coast). One thing that sets Oaxaca apart from most of Mexico is its markets: each little town throughout the Oaxaca valley has its market day and specialty. Sunday is Tlacolula's market day.

The Tlacolula market has a profoundly rural feel to it. (When I tell you that they sell livestock toward the back of the market, you get what I mean.) Life seems so basic here: stalls of every day clothes (nothing fancy), cooking equipment, tools, simple sundries and decorations, music (cassettes and burned CDs) and mescal (local liquor), all jammed into the streets around the church and food market building.

On Sundays they can't contain all the food in the permanent buildings; it spills out into a concrete-paved square just behind the L-shaped market. Because the area is rural, and quite poor, much of the food is displayed on colored or palm mats on the ground. Not thrown out willy-nilly, but lovingly, beautifully arranged into displays that reflect the people's deep-seated respect for their food. The square is a whirl of colors and smells, punctuated by the staccato chants of sellers calling out prices, quality and selection, sometimes with the aid of an electric megaphone. Dozens of varieties of dried chiles, each giving off a unique, spicy "perfume." Sweet-smelling, deep-red tomatoes. Piles of spinach and other greens. Aromatic fresh herbs. The list could go on almost endlessly.

Because our group was big (and not particularly organized) we wandered this way and that, up and down the aisles, through the front patio and then to the back, until we'd bought everything we needed for our meal. Toni— who knew just what she wanted—kept deferring to me (the *chef*), while I kept deferring to Andrés (because I wanted to see what he would choose). But somehow it all got bought.

My favorite part of the Tlacolula market is the bread building, where they sell large and small rounds of thrillingly delicious bread—much of it baked in old wood-fired ovens. I started buying: first, the little pita-like rounds with coarse, red-dyed sugar; then the chocolate-studded egg bread baked in old sardine cans; then the little streusel-topped buns they call conchas. I didn't want to stop except that I realized we'd all go into sugar overload if bread was all we ate while cooking. Besides, it was already past noon.

That's when we decided to eat goat *barbacoa*. I don't think I've ever been in this market without eating at least one soft taco of slow-cooked goat *barbacoa*: goat meat that is first marinated in a spicy red-chile rub then cooked slowly for a long time with these amazingly aromatic avocado leaves, until meltingly tender. Tacos of goat *barbacoa* are like a brass band of flavors in your mouth. Now, I understand that maybe some people don't want a brass band in their mouths, but you should try it at least once. At least that's what I tell Lanie. One bite. You might find that it's the best stuff on the planet. Especially when you open up that great big white corn tortilla filled with juicy, spicy goat meat, drizzle in a little tangy green tomatillo salsa and then lay in a couple of slices of avocado.

From Tlacolula, Toni and Javier's house is about halfway back to Oaxaca City. It was early afternoon when we turned slowly through their wrought iron gate and made our way to the carport behind the brick, one-story house. They have a big yard—not exactly what you'd call perfectly manicured—filled with a here-and-there collection of fruit trees—orange, lime, tangerine, guava, grapefruit, fig, avocado, native plum. Once we unpacked all our stuff onto the counter that divides their kitchen from the dining and living rooms, there was hardly anywhere to cook. Toni sent Andrés outside to set up the special outdoor stove to toast the chiles and other ingredients for the *moles*.

What are *moles*? Well, that's a little hard to say, at least until you've immersed yourself in Mexican culture. Then you know that when there's a special occasion, you make some kind of meat or chicken (even fish in some places) in *mole*—a sauce, a very special sauce. Usually the sauce is *very* traditional, based on chiles (mild to hot) and lots of other ingredients including nuts, seeds or corn that are blended to give the sauce a wonderful consistency. Some *moles*, made with fruit in addition to other ingredients, are a little sweet. "Special" is the operative word for all *moles*, though.

A note about those chiles: Mexico uses more varieties of chiles than anywhere else on earth. Certainly, cooks there like some of their food to be spicy, but not all the chiles they use are all that hot (what they call *picante* in Spanish). The really hot varieties are typically not used in *moles* and other sauces, only in salsas.

Oaxaca is called the "Land of the Seven Moles" (they range in color from pale green to jet black, with all kinds of earthy colors in between). Andrés was making two of them for us—the easiest ones: the *amarillo* (translates as "yellow" even though it comes out a color we'd call "orange") and the *coloradito* (translates as "brick red"). Both start by dry-toasting dried chiles on a griddle (we used the typical Oaxacan clay griddle), along with onions, garlic and tomatoes. It's a strange step by American kitchen standards, but a step that gives Oaxacan food its particular flavor.

For the *amarillo*, Andrés first soaked some lightly toasted dried *guajillo* chiles (cranberry-red, six inches long, medium-spicy) in hot water until soft. Then he blended them with spices like cinnamon and allspice, plus the griddle-roasted tomatoes, onions and garlic. He put this mixture into a big pot and cooked it until it got darker and thicker. After thinning out the mixture with some chicken broth, he added a little corn tortilla dough to thicken it and then simmered it with the chicken and the huge, aromatic green leaves called *hoja santa*. (I told you *moles* are kind of complex, and they take a while to make.) And that was only one of the *three* dishes he was making with us, cooking in old-fashioned clay pots on a standard gas range in a dead end galley-style kitchen that was better suited to one cook, not four or five. Andrés was unfazed. I was impressed.

The second *mole*, the *coloradito*, was actually a little bit more involved than the *amarillo*. But I like it even better—partly because it's richer with red chile flavor, nuttier and seasoned, as many of the *moles* are, with a little chocolate at the end, adding just a little sweet hint of chocolate woven into the savory flavorings.

So Andrés cooked and cooked, while we pitched in where we could. His mother used her new food processor to blend some black beans to a smooth paste (the way they like beans in Oaxaca) and then fried the paste in a little oil (Oaxacans also use pork lard) until the beans got thick and a little shiny. Andrés loves those fried black beans spread on a tostada (crisp-fried corn tortilla), topped with a little lettuce, some cheese and a salsa he makes out of cooked tomatillos (those slightly sour-tasting, green tomato-looking vegetables that have a papery husk on the outside) whirred in a blender with a special Oaxacan smoky chile and some garlic.

Just as the *moles* were finishing their simmering, Lanie and Laní (Toni and Javier's 19-year-old daughter) were making a dessert I hadn't had for years. I first made it while living in Mexico City, where it is called *isla flotante* (floating island), as it is in France, where most people assume the dish originated. It probably came to Mexico when Maximilian, a Hapsburg emperor, claimed the "throne" of Mexico back in the 1860s and decided he couldn't live without a whole battalion of French chefs. Enough history, though I still wonder how this family came to know the dessert as *huevos nevados* (snowy eggs). They're fun to make and everyone loves them. First Laní and Lanie made a pudding out of milk, sugar, cinnamon, cornstarch and egg yolks. Then they beat egg whites until stiff, scooped them up in rounds and dropped them on top of the simmering pudding to cook. When the egg whites were firm, they transferred them into serving bowls (they used coffee cups) and spooned a little pudding over the top.

The dishes at the Mendez family table couldn't have been more fabulously flavored. They could have been fancier and more elegantly served for sure. In fact, the table itself was very simple: just a spoon at each place to scoop up the sauce of the *mole* and a stack of tortillas to use for picking up the piece of chicken in our bowls. But when we tasted the dishes, it was as if a perfect symphony was being performed.

Now that's true elegance because it's not just about appearance but about something that's from within, something that has taken generations (if not centuries) to get right.

The whole experience turned out to be about much more than the food, of course, as it always does when people enjoy being with others. Whether anyone exactly says the words or not, it's about celebrating a slice of life, and food is the spur that gets it all going. The better the food, the better the time you'll have—if you've surrounded yourself with life-loving people.

As first helpings gave way to seconds, stories and reminiscences started flowing. Laughs spilled out all around. And before we knew it, hours had passed. The sun was descending behind those ruggedly beautiful mountains that hug the valley.

A few days later, on Christmas Eve, all the parish churches paraded their Christmas floats through Oaxaca's main square, followed by the church's brass band, a collection of carolers and—yes, this is true—the church's fireworks master shooting off all kinds of wildness. The whole crowd—whether standing or tucked into the little cafés around the square—seemed to be caught up in celebrating this one instant, this one slice of life. It was that same exuberant love of life we'd experienced at the Mendez table, only on a much bigger scale. That's what I love about Oaxaca at Christmas. That's the kind of Christmas I always want to share with Lanie.

Lanie: I can't believe the road out to Tlacolula was so *bumpy.* I thought I was on one of those horrible Six Flags rides that seems like it's never going to end even though it really only lasts 30 seconds. Thank goodness for air conditioning in Toni and Javier's van. Meant we could keep the windows up even though it's hot. It's dry season—dusty. Dusty and bumpy is not a good combo. In summer it's all green here, but I don't get to see Oaxaca much in summer, since I come for Christmas. Every year since I was born.

We went out with Toni and Javier (known them forever) and Andrew (son—15—real name Andrés) to buy stuff to cook at the market in Tlacolula. It's sort of like all the other big markets in Mexico. Stuff *everywhere:* spread on plastic sheets, hanging on racks, under colored tarps. Jackets, dresses, pants, underwear (like you're going to stand right there and pick it out in front of everyone). Spoons and cooking pots. Tons of CDs and tapes (all being played at the same time, I might add).

Anyway, you get through all the stuff in the streets and then you walk across this big churchyard and you come to the food part. There's one main open place for food—tons of food. But not organized like at the Jewel or Dominick's grocery story. And—let me be honest here—some of it doesn't smell all that great. Especially the d-r-i-e-d f-i-s-h.

Well, it turns out that Andrew, who is supposed to be in charge, really doesn't have a list. Only these recipes folded up and stuck in a pocket. Which means we have to keep reading them over and over and going from stall to stall—and sometimes back again. We finally found the right

tomatoes. And got the dried chiles (now there's a smell). And the fresh cheese. And then we decided we were hungry and couldn't wait to cook all the food. So we went inside this building where there were breads (*beautiful* piles of fresh, fresh breads—some with big sugar crystals on top). That's also where they serve the goat *barbacoa.* Yes, goat.

I don't really *like* goat that much. But at this market that's all you can get besides bread. And my dad said I had to eat more than bread. (Surprise! He says he loves goat!) I chose the goat soup—called *consome.* (Like I was going to choose the goat tacos. . . .) Besides, if you think beef soup and you put enough chopped onion and cilantro in it, you can make it taste okay. It's not like this is a restaurant or anything. There are just tables with benches and chairs around them right there in that big cement building. And the lady who makes the food has a pot sitting on a charcoal fire and a cutting board on a table and a bucket of water to wash dishes. Like camping. Only she has to do it every day.

We got back to Toni and Javier's house—over the same bumpy road—and started cooking outside under the carport. When you prepare dried chiles, you either have to have a great big exhaust fan or be outside or somewhere the chile fumes can blow away. Or you just cough a lot. So we were under the carport browning the chiles (and garlic and onion and tomato and tomatillos) on a portable stove hooked to a gas tank like we use on our gas grill at home.

Then we went inside to their regular kitchen to finish the cooking. We were making *coloradito* out of the dried chiles—a kind of special chile sauce they eat with chicken or on enchiladas here in Oaxaca. And *mole amarillo*—also chile sauce for chicken, but lighter. The little chiles that smelled smoky went in with the tomatillos to make salsa for black bean tostadas that we ate while we were waiting for the other dishes to finish cooking. Oaxacan cooking takes a l-o-n-g t-i-m-e. Especially when all you've had is a bowl of goat soup and it's 4 o'clock.

Till now, Andrew had been showing me and my dad everything (he's kind of cute but seems shy—*amazing* he can cook all these hard dishes). But now Toni told Laní (daughter—19—lived in Indianapolis one year—visited us in Chicago—almost my same name) to help with dessert—this custard with egg whites on top, a dessert from Javier's mother called *huevos nevados*.

Laní was stirring and stirring the custard as it cooked. Andrew was tearing up this huge mound of these leaves called *hoja* (they say O-ha) *santa*. Next thing, the whole kitchen and dining room and living room—really all one big room—smelled like someone had spilled a rootbeer. That's what those leaves smell like. Andrew stuck them *all* in the pot of *mole amarillo*—so what looked like the lighter *mole* I was going to like best now looked like something I'd just be "tasting." Toni said, "We're *hoja santa* freaks." She's lived here for thirty-some years, but I knew she knew what "freak" means to us.

I beat the egg whites all by myself with a whisk (massively painful) until they were all white and stiff and then I turned the bowl upside down and I thought Toni was really going to *freak*. My dad taught me that. When you beat the egg whites completely stiff, you can turn the bowl over and they won't slip out—at least for a few seconds after you stop beating. Fun. We scooped out the whites into sort of balls with a spoon and let them cook on the hot custard. This was my favorite part. Then we put them into coffee cups and spooned custard over them.

So here's what we ate. First: black bean tostadas with lettuce and cheese and salsa. (Very very very good.) Then: *mole amarillo* with a piece of chicken. (Okay.) Then a second main dish!: *coloradito* with a piece of chicken. They don't usually serve two main dishes, but because my dad was interested. . . . (Good—better than *amarillo*.) Then: *huevos nevados*. (Fabulous.)

In Mexico (and at my house), however long the meal takes, that's how long everyone sits around the table afterwards. Sometimes it can be a little boring, but sometimes it's fun. That's what happened when everyone started telling stories about their neighbor, the governor—and how when he came to Laní's school he winked at Laní. And she turned all *red*—I mean at the table when they were telling the story. And everyone laughed. And this turned out to be maybe the best part of the whole day.

Huevos Rancheros

RICK: *No matter where you go in Mexico, everyone knows how to make* huevos rancheros. *They are the Mexican breakfast—tortillas, spicy homemade tomato sauce, eggs. (I don't know why it just has to be breakfast, though. I like them for lunch or dinner, too.) If you want to make them for 8 people, make sure to leave the tortillas in the oven for at least 15 minutes. Double the sauce. And cook the eggs in batches, slide them onto a baking sheet and keep them warm in an oven set at 150° F. Use bacon drippings if you have them—it'll give better flavor than oil.*

✂　✂　✂　✂　✂　✂

LANIE: *Basically, this dish is a flat spicy egg taco that you have to eat with a fork. Personally, I think breakfast should be sweeter. But I do like* huevos *(eggs)* rancheros *(country-style) on Sunday morning when breakfast gets mixed up with lunch—like 12 o'clock.*

| 4 corn tortillas |
| Vegetable oil to brush or spray on tortillas |
| One 28-ounce can diced tomatoes in juice |
| 1 to 2 fresh jalapeño or serrano chiles |
| 3 tablespoons vegetable oil, bacon drippings, or fresh pork lard, divided use |
| 1 medium onion |
| 2 garlic cloves |
| Salt |
| 8 "large" eggs |
| 2 to 3 ounces Mexican fresh cheese (*queso fresco*), goat cheese, salted-and-pressed farmer's cheese, or feta cheese |
| A small handful fresh cilantro leaves, optional |

····· **DO THIS FIRST** ·····

TOMATOES: Tip off and discard liquid.
CHILES: Break off stems and discard. Cut each chile into 4 pieces. (See page 43 for how to work with chiles.)
ONION: Cut off top and bottom and discard. Cut in half from top to bottom. Peel off papery outside layers and discard. Cut halves into thin slices— about ⅛ inch thick.
GARLIC: Peel.
CHEESE: Crumble. (Mexican cheese will crumble finely; goat cheese and feta will make bigger, moister pieces. You need ½ to ¾ cup.)
OVEN: Turn on to 250°F.

1. *Heat tortillas.* Lightly brush or spray both sides of each tortilla with vegetable oil. Stack one on top of the other. Wrap completely in foil and place in oven while you prepare the dish. (It shouldn't take more than 30 minutes.)

2. *Make sauce.* In a blender, combine the drained tomatoes and chile pieces. Cover and blend until smooth. Measure *1 tablespoon* of the oil, drippings or lard into a medium (4- to 6-quart) saucepan. Set over medium heat. When hot, add the sliced onion. Cook—stir frequently—until golden brown, about 5 minutes. Crush garlic through garlic press into pot. Stir well, and raise heat to medium-high. After

1 minute, add the tomato mixture. Stir frequently until mixture starts to thicken, but not as thick as bottled spaghetti sauce—about 5 minutes. Stir in ½ teaspoon salt and remove from heat. Taste and add more salt if you think necessary.

3. *Fry eggs.* Crack eggs into large bowl, being careful not to break any yolks. Set a very large (12-inch) skillet over medium to medium-low heat. (A non-stick is easiest to work with.) Add the remaining 2 *tablespoons* of the oil, drippings or lard. Pour eggs into skillet. Sprinkle with a little salt. Cook 4 to 5 minutes—without flipping them—until they are as done as you like. If the whites don't completely set, then cover pan briefly with cookie sheet or lid.

4. *Finish dish.* Set sauce over medium heat to rewarm. If sauce has become too thick, stir in a little water. Remove tortillas from oven. Unwrap and use tongs or spatula to transfer 1 tortilla to each dinner plate. Use spatula to separate eggs. Transfer 2 eggs to each tortilla. Spoon sauce over eggs, leaving yolks uncovered. Sprinkle with crumbled cheese and cilantro leaves. Serve right away.

SERVES 4

❈ Five Cool Things to Buy at a Mexican Grocery ❈

Baby Lucas: *Little "cans" of flavored powder that you pour out onto your hand and lick off (don't inhale or you'll have a coughing fit). Much better than Lik-em-ade or Pixie Stix. Baby Lucas is a rush (sweet, salty, tangy), especially if you get the chile flavored one. Mango flavor (just a little spicy) is our hands-down favorite.*

Jarritos sodas: *Made in Mexico, in cool flavors like grapefruit (Lanie's favorite), tamarind (tastes like lemony brown sugar) and guava. Made with sugar (rather than high fructose corn syrup) so they're a little healthier. Also look for Sidral Mundet—an apple flavored soda we like a lot.*

Obleas de cajeta: *A candy made of two layers of super-thin crispy rice "paper," with a layer of Mexican caramel sandwiched between. You can also buy bottles of the* caramel (called cajeta, *usually made with goat's milk rather than cow's milk), which is really good on just about anything. Coronado brand is widely available.*

Tamazula Hot Sauce: *Our favorite Mexican hot sauce (there are dozens). Get the one that says "extra hot." It's really not all that hot, but it has the best flavor. When we're looking for something super-hot, we get El Yucateco Salsa Kutbil-ik de Chile Habanero (from the Yucatan part of Mexico), made from the hottest chile in the world. You've been warned.*

Maizena de Chocolate: *You make this powdered drink mix into a wonderful warm drink called atole. It's got a great, comforting texture—think thickish hot chocolate. Great for breakfast, when you're cold, or when you think you're getting a cold.*

Almost Our Restaurant's "Famous" Guacamole

RICK: *Not everyone in Mexico makes the same version of guacamole. Some are very simple (avocado, salt, lime juice, maybe garlic). Others get more elaborate—like this recipe, which is almost like the one our restaurant is famous for. (We left out the fresh chile; if you like spicy, add a fresh chopped jalapeño—see page 43 for how to work with chiles.) The avocados must be soft and ripe so the guacamole will be creamy. After that, the final texture is up to you: I like chunks of avocado in the guacamole, so I don't mash them very much. When Lanie was younger she grated the tomatoes (cut in half) through the large holes of a stand-up grater—rather than chop them with a knife.*

❈   ❈   ❈   ❈   ❈   ❈

LANIE: *Everyone I know LOVES guacamole. It's the perfect snack because—do I really have to say this?—it's creamy and you eat it with chips. I like it on soft tacos, too. I use it like salsa. And what's weird is: I like hardly any of the ingredients on their own. They kind of need each other to taste good.*

....

1. *Prepare flavorings.* With a small knife, cut out and discard "core" at top of the tomatoes where the stems once attached. Stand tomato on side and cut into 1/4-inch slices. Cut slices into 1/4-inch cubes. Place in bowl. Peel garlic. Crush through garlic press onto tomatoes. Cut off and discard the root ends of the green onions. Peel off and discard any withered outer layers. Cut crosswise into 1/4-inch pieces. Add to tomatoes. Bunch the leaf end of the cilantro sprigs together. Use a sharp knife to cut across bunched leaves and stems, slicing them thinly. Stop cutting when you only have stems left. Discard stems. Add to tomato mixture.

2. *Scoop out avocados.* To cut avocados in half, start at their pointy stem end (the top) and circle around pit. Twist sides in opposite directions and pull apart. Use a spoon to scoop out pit and discard. Scoop avocado flesh from skin. Discard skin and add flesh to the tomato mixture.

3. *Add seasonings and mash.* Squeeze lime or lemon. (You need about 1 1/2 tablespoons juice.) Add to avocados. Add 1/2 teaspoon salt. Using an old-fashioned potato masher, the back of a large spoon, or your hand, mash everything together evenly. Taste and season with more salt, or lime or lemon juice, if necessary. Serve with chips or as a "salsa" to put on tacos.

MAKES 2 1/2 CUPS, ENOUGH TO SERVE 6 TO 12, DEPENDING ON HOW HUNGRY THEY ARE AND WHAT ELSE YOU'RE SERVING

6 ounces ripe fresh tomatoes (about 2 medium plum tomatoes or 1 medium round tomato)
2 garlic cloves
2 green onions
15 sprigs fresh cilantro
3 soft ripe avocados
1/2 large lime or lemon
Salt

Avocados

Dark, pebbly-skinned avocados (usually called "California" or "Hass") make great guacamole because they are creamy, don't turn dark (oxidize) quickly once you've mashed them, and once they ripen can be stored in the refrigerator (uncut) for several days without browning. If you buy rock-hard avocados, store them in a closed paper bag at room temperature and allow 4 or 5 days to ripen.

Lime (or Lemon) Squeezing

The absolute easiest way to thoroughly juice a lime is to cut it in half, put one of the halves in the bottom part of a Mexican lime squeezer and press the top part down. Cut side of the lime goes toward the holes. (It looks like you're supposed to put the lime in the squeezer with the cut part facing up, but you're not. In fact, if you do, there's nowhere for the lime juice to go—except right up in your face.) Of course, you can also use one of those cone-shaped juicers you press down and twist on, or you can just stab a fork into the cut half, twist it around a little bit, then squeeze the lime or lemon half hard in your palm until all the juice comes out.

Bayless Family Caesar Salad

LANIE: *This is totally MY SALAD. I've eaten it since before I can remember. We keep a jar of this dressing in the refrigerator all the time—and romaine lettuce, too, which is just about the only kind I really like. My dad says we always have to have salad with our meals, so I guess it's a good thing I like this one. If you don't like salad, you should try this because the dressing and the cheese make it taste REALLY GOOD and it goes with just about anything. You don't have to use the croutons, and you can add some of the Parmesan to the dressing. Hellmann's mayonnaise RULES!*

✼ ✼ ✼ ✼ ✼ ✼

RICK: *Okay, I'll admit it, Caesar salad is kind of a cheap shot (there are a thousand "better," more sophisticated salads), but it sure helped get Lanie started on salad at an early age. Besides, it is really good. Ours is an easy-to-make variation on the original, which was created by Alex Cardini in Tijuana, Mexico, back in the 1930s. It starts with store-bought mayonnaise, rather than a barely boiled egg, into which you whisk olive oil to make a very soft mayonnaise. We don't put in anchovies, for obvious reasons. The dressing makes enough to make this salad 4 times. Store what's left in a sealed jar in the refrigerator.*

FOR THE DRESSING
1 small garlic clove
½ cup mayonnaise (most "lite" mayonnaise works fine here)
3 tablespoons fresh lemon juice
1 tablespoon Worcestershire sauce
⅓ cup olive or vegetable oil
Salt

FOR THE SALAD
1 medium romaine heart (about 8 ounces)
3 or 4 tablespoons grated Parmesan cheese
A generous cup of croutons

····· **DO THIS FIRST** ·····

GARLIC: Peel.
ROMAINE: Cut off and discard root end (1 inch) of romaine. Slice remainder ¾ inch thick. (You'll have about 8 loosely packed cups.)

Crush peeled garlic through garlic press into 2-cup glass jar with lid. Add remaining dressing ingredients, 1 tablespoon cold water and ½ teaspoon salt. Cover tightly and shake well (or stir to combine). Place sliced romaine in a large bowl. Drizzle on ¼ cup of the dressing. Sprinkle on the cheese. Drizzle on a little more dressing, if necessary, and toss to combine. Divide onto salad plates. Sprinkle with the croutons and serve. Refrigerate remaining dressing in closed container for up to 2 weeks.

SERVES 4

Homemade Caesar Salad Croutons

The best croutons are made from firm bread (like French or Italian) or cakey bread (like brioche, challah or Pepperidge Farm white bread). Some people like croutons made from bread that has the crust cut off. If the bread you are using is sliced, the slices should be thick—about 1/2 inch.

4 cups (loosely packed) cubes of bread (about 1/2 of a 1-pound French loaf)
1/4 to 1/3 cup Caesar Salad Dressing (opposite page)
2 tablespoons grated Parmesan cheese
Salt, optional

Position rack in middle of oven. Turn on to 350°F. Spread bread cubes in single layer on a baking sheet. When oven is hot, bake cubes until lightly browned and crisp all the way through—12 to 15 minutes. Remove from oven. Allow to cool 3 to 4 minutes. Drizzle croutons slowly and lightly with dressing, tossing gently and continuously with metal spatula or tongs. Sprinkle croutons with cheese, continuing to toss. Return to oven until browned—about 3 minutes more. Taste finished croutons and sprinkle with salt if you think necessary. Allow to cool before serving. If making ahead, store cooled croutons in an air-tight container at room temperature.

MAKES ABOUT 3 CUPS

Black Bean Tostadas with Smoky Salsa

3 cups cooked black beans
½ medium onion
4 garlic cloves, divided use
1 dried avocado leaf, optional
3 tablespoons vegetable oil or fresh pork lard
Salt
½ pound (5 or 6) tomatillos
2 large dried Oaxacan pasilla chiles OR 2 to 3 canned chipotle chiles (plus 1 tablespoon of their canning liquid)
1 romaine heart or ½ head iceberg lettuce
12 crisp-fried tostadas
4 ounces Mexican fresh cheese (*queso fresco*), goat cheese, salted-and-pressed farmer's cheese or feta cheese

RICK: *Black bean tostadas are one of my favorite things to eat for lunch. They can taste like you're in different parts of Mexico, depending on how you make them. Which is good, I think, because when I taste them made in the Oaxacan way—with beans flavored with anise-scented avocado leaf and salsa made of Oaxacan pasilla chiles—they remind me of how much I miss our friends who made these with us. That's not to say they aren't really good* without *avocado leaf and special chile, too. In fact, we mostly skip the leaf (we have to go to a special store to get it) and use smoky canned chipotle chiles in the salsa instead and we* love *them. Mexican fresh cheese is definitely the best choice here and different from the other substitutions; but if you're stuck, just grate some cheddar or Jack and use that. A final note: In Mexico cooks typically use the bright-tasting* white *onion, rather than yellow onions, in all dishes.*

⁙ ⁙ ⁙ ⁙ ⁙ ⁙

LANIE: *These are the things Andrew made with us in Oaxaca. Nothing complicated—more like a* snack. *I think beans take forever to cook, so I'd make these with canned beans—don't forget to drain them. And I'd buy the already fried tostadas like Andrew did (some people fry them themselves). There's several to choose from at the Mexican grocery near my house. Crispy tostadas, smooth beans, crunchy salad and medium-spicy salsa (it's spicier when left really thick). MMMmmm.*

DO THIS FIRST

ONION: Cut off top and bottom and discard. Peel off papery outside layers and discard. Slice about ¼ inch thick. Chop into small pieces.
GARLIC: Peel. Cut cloves in half.
TOMATILLOS: Peel off papery husks and rinse.
CHEESE: Finely crumble. (You'll have about 1 cup.)

1. *Make fried beans.* Tip off most of bean liquid into a small bowl. Save liquid. Pour beans into food processor. Add chopped onion and *2 cloves* of the garlic. If using avocado leaf, heat skillet over medium heat. Lay avocado leaf in hot pan and turn every few seconds for about a minute until lightly brown and aromatic. Add to beans. Cover processor and run until smooth. Pour oil or lard into a large (10- to 12-inch) deep skillet or Dutch oven. Set over medium heat. When hot,

scrape in bean puree. Stir for 4 to 5 minutes until very thick. Taste and season with salt—usually ½ to 1 teaspoon, depending on how salty the beans are. (If beans were not seasoned while simmering, they will take more.) Remove from heat.

2. *Make salsa.* Put the cleaned tomatillos in a small saucepan. Cover with water. Set over medium heat. If using dried Oaxacan pasilla chiles, heat skillet over medium. Lay chiles in hot pan and turn every few seconds for about a minute, until aromatic. Break off stems and add to tomatillos. Cook until tomatillos turn from bright to olive green—about 4 to 5 minutes of simmering. Drain and let cool. In food processor, place remaining *2 cloves* garlic, tomatillos and chiles. (If using canned chipotle chiles, remove them from can and add to food processor along with 1 tablespoon of canning sauce.) Cover and process until *almost* smooth. Pour into small dish. If thick, stir in 1 to 2 tablespoons water. Taste and season with salt—usually a generous ½ teaspoon.

3. *Finish tostadas.* Slice lettuce ¼ inch thick. Reheat beans over medium heat. If beans are really thick, stir in a little water. Spread hot beans on tostadas. Top with sliced lettuce. Sprinkle with crumbled cheese. Serve right away, passing salsa separately for each person to add to their own taste.

MAKES 12 TOSTADAS, ENOUGH TO SERVE 12 AS A SNACK OR 6 AS A LIGHT MEAL

Mexican garnishing cheese

Peruvian Shrimp Ceviche

RICK: *This is one of the most refreshing dishes you could have on a warm day—perfect for the year-round tropical warmth of Lima, Peru. You start with fresh fish or seafood, steep it in garlicky lime juice, then add fresh cilantro, a little chile, some thin-sliced onions. It's an appetizer or main dish, depending on how hungry you are. Ceviche is an ancient dish which probably got started as a way to preserve fresh fish by soaking it in lime juice. Before refrigeration, "pickling" fish in straight, mouth-puckering lime juice meant today's catch could become tomorrow's dinner. Nothing spoiled; nothing lost.*

For this recipe, it would be easiest to buy peeled cooked shrimp at the grocery store or fish market. (If you can only find large shrimp, cut them into smaller pieces.) If you get raw shrimp, bring a pot of water to a boil, add the shrimp, count to 10, then pour off all the water. Put a top on the pot and let stand 15 minutes. Then uncover the pot and set under cold running water for 1 minute. Drain and peel.

✕   ✕   ✕   ✕   ✕   ✕

LANIE: *When we went to Peru, my friend Bianca (her family went with us), my dad and I cooked with Isabel Alvarez, this chef who my dad had met at some cooking conference. Except that WE didn't really cook because she had most everything already made and she had a chef from her restaurant (Señorío del Sulco—GOOD!) there who would do things faster than we could figure out what he was doing. The ceviche is so simple that she didn't have much to do ahead, so we really learned how to make it. I've liked ceviche for as long as I can remember, which freaks some people out, since the Mexican ceviche we make at our restaurant (yes, they eat ceviche all over Latin America) is made by soaking RAW fish in lime juice. But I still like it. (It doesn't taste raw.) Plus, I like really tangy things—things that make your face all scrunch up when you eat them. This is one of the best.*

¾ cup fresh lime juice

3 garlic cloves

¼ teaspoon ground pepper—they use white pepper in Peru

Salt

1 pound small (30 to 40 per pound) peeled cooked shrimp

½ medium red onion

1 red jalapeño chile—in Peru they use a spicy red chile called *ají limeño*

8 to 10 sprigs of cilantro

Nice-looking lettuce leaves for serving

······ DO THIS FIRST ······

GARLIC: Peel. Cut cloves in half.

RED ONION: Cut off top and bottom and discard. Peel off papery outside layers and discard. Cut into thin slices.

JALAPEÑO: Cut off stem. Cut in half lengthwise. Use knife or small spoon to scrape out seeds and seed pod. Discard seeds and pod. Cut chile into thin strips. (See page 43 for how to work with chiles.)

CILANTRO: Pull off leaves and roughly chop. Discard stems.

In a blender, combine the lime juice, garlic, pepper and 1 teaspoon salt. Blend until smooth. Place shrimp in a bowl. Pour lime juice mixture on top. Add the sliced red onion, chile strips and chopped cilantro. Stir to combine. Lay a lettuce leaf or two on each individual serving plate. Top with a portion of ceviche (including some of the lime juice marinade) and serve.

SERVES 4 TO 6 AS AN APPETIZER

The Truest Peruvian Ceviche

In Peru there are thousands of little eating places that specialize in just one thing: ceviche. Makes sense because Peru has some of the best seafood in the world. (It has something to do with what they call the Humbolt current washing all the good fish up to the Peruvian coast.) When they make ceviche, they take very, very fresh fish—corvina (no translation) or large sole or a type of sea bass—and fillet it. Then they cut the raw fish into cubes and use it just like we use the cooked shrimp in our Shrimp Ceviche recipe. That's right— they use it totally raw—like sashimi or sushi. Some people are a little squeamish about eating raw fish, even when it's perfectly, wonderfully, sweet-smelling fresh. But not in Peru. Or Japan. So, if you want to enjoy the True Peruvian Ceviche—one of the best things in the world—you have to get over that raw fish thing. If you choose to make raw-fish ceviche, make sure your fish is very, very fresh (caught within a day or so), bought from a very reputable fish shop or fish you caught yourself and stored packed in ice. Most fish shops will call fish that is this fresh "sashimi quality."

Another thing: for reasons that can only be understood by those who've been raised in Peru, True Peruvian Ceviche is always served with slices of cooked sweet potato and chunks of boiled corn on the cob (chewy field corn, not tender sweet corn).

Peruvian Potatoes *a la Huancaína*

RICK: *Think of this as a kind of Peruvian "potato salad" with a really delicious creamy-tangy-cheesey-spicy dressing. "Salad," however, doesn't really do it justice, since in Peru anything made with potatoes is a star of the meal, not just a salady accompaniment. Potatoes, native to that country, are the soul of its cooking—the International Potato Institute (yes, it does exist) grows over 5,000 varieties through-out the country from tropical coastlines to frigid elevations higher than anything you'd find in Aspen or Vail. When you eat this dish in Peru, everything about it is distinctive. The potatoes have a yellow buttery flesh that tastes better than any other potato I've ever eaten. The chiles are uniquely sweet and spicy and full of great aromas, all at the same time. The cheese is sweet like cottage cheese but with a fine texture, and there is none of the creamy "dressing" that's always added to potato salad in this country. (Peruvian fresh cheese is similar to Mexican queso fresco, but what we ate in Peru wasn't as salty or tangy as the Mexican version.) This is a recipe that Isabel, our chef-friend in Lima, made at a chefs' conference in California. I thought it was so delicious that we had to visit Peru to taste that cuisine on its own turf.*

✄   ✄   ✄   ✄   ✄   ✄

LANIE: *Delicious—even though the name looks weird. (Pronounced: wan-ki-EE-na.) Nothing weird about the flavor, though. It's just potatoes (FABULOUS) in a creamy sauce made with fresh cheese (could use cream cheese, but would be rich and not taste the same), canned milk (true!), chiles (not too spicy) and soda crackers (for thickening—honest). Really good served with anticuchos—little charcoal-grilled skewers of meat. (They didn't tell me the first ones we had were BEEF HEART. I prefer the "modern" ones made of fish and pork and stuff like that.) You can serve this dish with grilled chicken (the sauce makes a great dip). And you can make it with regu-lar (brown-skin "russet") potatoes, but they're a little crumbly.*

6 Peruvian yellow potatoes
   OR 3 medium-small Yukon gold
   potatoes (about 1 pound)
2 eggs
Salt
¼ cup vegetable oil
1 small red onion
1 large garlic clove
5 Peruvian yellow chiles (*ají amarillo*),
   fresh, frozen or bottled (available in
   Peruvian groceries or by mail, see
   page 225)
   OR 5 yellow banana peppers plus
   1 orange bell pepper
3 salted soda crackers
8 ounces Peruvian fresh cheese or other
   fresh cheese like Mexican *queso
   fresco* or *panela*
1 cup evaporated milk
1 to 2 tablespoons fresh lime juice
6 large lettuce leaves for garnish
A dozen black olives (like the purplish
   Kalamatas), for garnish

······ **DO THIS FIRST** ······

POTATOES: Peel. (If using frozen Peruvian potatoes, they will already be peeled.)
RED ONION: Cut off top and bottom and discard. Cut in half from top to bot-tom. Peel off papery outside layers and discard. Slice ¼ inch thick.
GARLIC: Peel. Cut in half.
CHILES: Break off stem. Cut in half lengthwise. Cut out seed pod and dis-card. Scrape out seeds and discard. Slice ¼ inch thick. (See page 43.)

1. *Cook potatoes and eggs.* Place potatoes and eggs in a medium saucepan. Cover with water. Add 1 tablespoon salt. Set over high heat. When water boils, reduce heat to medium. Let simmer *gently* for 10 minutes. Transfer eggs to a bowl. Set bowl in sink and run cold water over eggs for a couple of minutes. Set aside. Continue to simmer potatoes until tender—about 10 minutes more. Drain water off potatoes. Cool potatoes completely. (If using frozen Peruvian potatoes, simply let them defrost at room temperature—takes about 1 hour. Simmer eggs in salted water for 10 minutes and cool under running water.) Slice potatoes about ¼ inch thick or a little thicker.

2. *Make creamy sauce.* Measure oil into medium (8-inch) skillet and set over medium heat. Add sliced onion, garlic and chile strips. Cook until everything is soft—about 6 minutes. Scrape into blender or food processor. Roughly break up crackers and roughly crumble cheese. Add both to blender or food processor along with the evaporated milk and 1 teaspoon salt. Cover and blend until very smooth. Taste and season with more salt (if you think necessary) and lime juice—it should taste just a tiny bit tangy.

3. *Serve.* Lay a lettuce leaf on each serving plate. Lay a portion of the potato slices over each lettuce leaf, slightly overlapping. (Potatoes are best when at room temperature or *slightly* warm.) Spoon a generous portion of the sauce over the potatoes. Peel eggs and slice each into 6 pieces. Cut olives in half—remove pits if olives have them. Lay 2 egg slices on top of each serving, slightly overlapping. Decorate with the olive halves.

SERVES 6

Lanie's Guide to Peruvian Ingredients

Eating in Peru basically means eating potatoes. Just about the minute I stepped off the plane, I started seeing potatoes and somehow potatoes started almost randomly coming up in conversation. They don't let you forget that Peru is the place where potatoes were first born. And they eat gobs of them—served with things you could never imagine would be served with potatoes. Like ceviche (seafood and lime cocktail) always gets a slice of potato. Sweet potato. I guess sweet potato is kind of a potato. At least as much of a potato as most of what we saw in that gigantic market up in Cuzco. There were dozens of varieties of potatoes—and my dad bought two of EACH ONE. "Research," he kinda barked at me—I mean all I did was ask politely WHAT he was doing. He didn't even seem to care that it took an hour.

Anyway, we found it kind of hard to make a lot of Peruvian food back in Chicago. We couldn't just go to the supermarket and get those special yellow potatoes that everyone thinks are the bomb down there. We couldn't find those long orange peppers that go in practically everything in Lima, either. To make things even more confusing, I figured out that they call those orange peppers "yellow peppers" in Peru. Oh, that wasn't even the half of it.

If you're planning ahead—like when you have to do a country report in school or something—you can order the real Peruvian ingredients (frozen, jarred or dried) online at spiceworlds.com or grantangolandia.com. It'll cost you, though. Otherwise, we stuck with the easier Peruvian recipes to do here at home and worked out these substitutions:

For Peruvian yellow potatoes (papa amarilla) use Yukon gold potatoes.
For Peruvian orange/yellow chiles (aji amarillo) use yellow banana peppers (AKA hot Hungarian wax peppers).

Yellow banana peppers

Creamy Corn Soup with Roasted Chiles

RICK: *When we traveled in Mexico with Lanie as a baby, we always relied on* Crema de Elote *(Creamy Corn Soup, in Spanish) when we went out to eat. Practically every family restaurant had it—mostly in cans with a Campbell's label on it. (Yes, Campbell's is all over Mexico!) Homemade is way better, because you can really taste the roasted chile in it. And if you use* masa harina *to thicken it (instead of cornstarch), there's even more corn flavor. Only difference between here and Mexico is that our corn is sweeter, theirs is starchier. (This recipe is written for our corn, not theirs.) I like to chop up green onion or cilantro to sprinkle on the soup before serving it.*

⌘　⌘　⌘　⌘　⌘　⌘

LANIE: *This may be my very favorite Mexican recipe because I love corn and anything creamy. This is like corn chowder, which I don't think is Mexican. But this recipe really does taste Mexican because it has roasted chiles in it.*

2 medium poblano chiles
  OR 1 large red bell pepper
2 tablespoons butter or vegetable or
  olive oil
1 small onion
2 garlic cloves
3 cups fresh or frozen corn kernels (see
  opposite page for how to cut fresh
  corn from cob)
1 tablespoon cornstarch
  OR 1½ tablespoons *masa harina*
  (Mexican corn "flour" used to make
  corn tortillas—look for it in most well-
  stocked groceries)
3 to 4 cups milk, divided use
Salt

····· DO THIS FIRST ·····

ONION: Cut off top and bottom and discard. Cut in half from top to bottom. Peel off papery outside layers and discard. Slice about ¼ inch thick.
GARLIC: Peel.
CORN: If frozen, let stand at room temperature for 20 to 30 minutes to begin defrosting.

1. *Prepare chiles.* Roast chiles directly over gas flame (no pan), or 4 inches below electric broiler, turning occasionally with tongs until evenly blackened all over. Place in plastic bag. Allow to cool. Peel off and discard blackened skin. Pull out stem and seed pod; discard. Tear open chiles and rinse off seeds and bits of black skin. Cut into ¼-inch pieces. (See page 43 for how to work with chiles.)

2. *Cook onion and garlic.* Put butter in medium (4- to 6-quart) saucepan. Set over medium heat. When melted, scoop in sliced onion. Cook—stir regularly—until the onion is deep golden brown. Crush garlic through garlic press into pot. Stir for 1 minute more. Transfer mixture to blender or food processor. Set aside pot for cooking soup—no need to wash.

3. *Blend soup "base."* Add corn and cornstarch (or *masa harina*) to blender or food processor. Pour in *1½ cups* of the milk. Process until very smooth. If using fresh corn, you may want to strain mixture to get out tough hulls.

4. *Cook soup.* Pour soup into saucepan and set over medium heat. Whisk frequently until mixture boils—about 2 minutes. Add remaining *1½ cups* of the milk (2 cups if using fresh corn) and chile pieces. Reduce heat to medium and simmer gently—stir frequently—for 15 minutes.

5. *Finish, season and serve.* Add more milk if you think soup is too thick. Stir in 1½ teaspoons salt. Taste and season with more salt if you think necessary. Ladle into bowls and serve.

MAKES 5½ CUPS, ENOUGH TO SERVE 4 TO 6

Raw and roasted poblano chiles

An Easy Way to Cut Corn Kernels from the Cob

Turn a small bowl upside down in a very large bowl. Hold the ear of corn by the narrow end and set the base firmly against the bottom of the small up-turned bowl. Use a knife to cut straight down along the cob, cutting the kernels free. Rotate the cob and cut straight down again. Keep going until you've cut all the way around the cob. The small bowl keeps the cob elevated; the large bowl catches the kernels as they fall.

Fideos {Mexican Noodle} Soup

RICK: *This soup is pure comfort food. The noodles get browned before being simmered in the broth, which translates into a rich and flavorful soup. For the most authentic flavor, use epazote, available in Mexican markets or specialty grocery stores, or mint.*

LANIE: *This soup tastes like a cross between Mexican and Italian food. Little skinny pasta noodles in soup with Mexican flavors like chile and tomatoes. Or I tell my friends it's kind of like Mexican ramen. Fabiola, my babysitter ever since I was born, fed me this* sopa de fideos *FOREVER and so did all my Mexican friends' moms.*

Half of a 10-ounce package dried vermicelli, called *fideos* in Mexican groceries (we like the thinnest ones called "angel hair" best)
1 tablespoon vegetable oil, plus a little more for the noodles
One 15-ounce can diced tomatoes in juice
½ small onion
2 garlic cloves
2 quarts (8 cups) chicken broth
1 large sprig fresh parsley, mint or epazote
1 fresh serrano or jalapeño chile
Salt
1 lime

DO THIS FIRST

OVEN: Position rack in middle of oven. Turn on to 350°F.
TOMATOES: Tip off and discard liquid.
ONION: Cut off top and bottom and discard. Peel off papery outside layers and discard. Roughly chop.
GARLIC: Peel. Cut cloves in half.
CHILE: Cut 3 or 4 slits in chile from stem to point. (See page 43 for how to work with chiles.)
LIME: Cut into 6 wedges.

1. *Toast noodles.* Lay noodles on a baking sheet. Brush or spray on both sides liberally with oil. Bake 8 minutes. Turn noodles over. Bake 7 or 8 minutes longer—until golden brown.

2. *Make broth.* In food processor or blender, combine the drained tomatoes, chopped onion and garlic. Process until smooth. Measure *1 tablespoon* of the oil into a medium (4- to 6-quart) saucepan or small soup pot. Set over medium heat. When hot, add the tomato mixture. Stir for 6 to 7 minutes—until it becomes as thick as tomato paste. Add the chicken broth and parsley, mint or epazote. When mixture boils, reduce heat and simmer gently 30 minutes. Taste and season with salt. (Salted broth will need very little. Unsalted broth will need 1½ to 2 teaspoons.)

3. *Finish soup.* Shortly before serving, add chile and noodles to broth. Simmer 8 minutes—stir regularly—until noodles are tender. Remove and discard chile. Ladle into bowls and serve with wedges of lime on the side.

SERVES 4 TO 6 AS A LIGHT MAIN DISH

Toasted vermicelli noodles

Tomatillo Chicken

RICK: *Two things to learn here: (1) Roasted chicken has great flavor—especially on the bone, with skin. That's why we set the chicken on top of the sauce and cook it in a 425°F oven—this allows the chicken to roast while the sauce reduces and intensifies. (2) Tangy things like tomatillos make creamy sauces taste better and creamy things like whipping cream soften the tanginess of tomatillos. You may want to add a little more salt than we use and, if the sauce comes out too tangy for you, stir in a pinch more sugar.*

If you only have boneless, skinless chicken breasts, make the recipe as directed, but pour the sauce base over the chicken breasts and cook them at 325°F for the same amount of time. Remove the chicken breasts to a platter, scraping as much of the sauce as possible back into the pan. Stir in the cream, season the sauce and serve it over the breasts. The recipe will still be good, but the chicken will taste more poached than roasted.

�֍   �֍   ✖   ✖   ✖   ✖

LANIE: *This recipe is totally easy—even for a dish you're making from* scratch. *If you don't know tomatillos yet (say* toe-ma-TEA-yos *not* toe-ma-TIL-os*), you may think they're funky when you peel off that outer, papery husk. They smell a little weird. But they're so delicious when they're cooked, especially with cream.*

1 pound (10 to 12 medium) tomatillos
3 garlic cloves
1 small fresh jalapeño chile (or 1 to 2 fresh serrano chiles)
1 small bunch fresh cilantro
Salt
4 large (about 2 pounds total) chicken breast halves (with bones and skin)
½ cup plain yogurt, heavy (whipping) cream or sour cream
½ teaspoon sugar

> ····· **DO THIS FIRST** ······
>
> **OVEN:** Move one oven rack to highest position. Have second rack in middle of oven. Turn on broiler.
> **TOMATILLOS:** Peel off papery husks and rinse. Spread into 9 x 13-inch metal baking pan.
> **GARLIC:** Peel.
> **CHILE:** Break off stem. Cut into 4 pieces. (See page 43 for how to work with chiles.)
> **CILANTRO:** Separate out a few sprigs of cilantro for garnish. Bunch the leaf end of the rest of the sprigs together. Cut across the bunched leaves with a sharp knife, roughly chopping them. Stop cutting when you only have stems left. Discard stems. You need about ⅔ cup chopped cilantro.
> **CHICKEN:** For pretty appearance, use scissors to trim off the scrawny little rib bones on side opposite breast bone.

1. *Roast tomatillos.* Set baking pan of tomatillos under broiler on highest rack in oven. When soft and splotchy brown/black on one side—about 5 minutes—remove pan. Use tongs to turn tomatillos over. Broil until completely soft and splotchy brown/black on other side—about 5 minutes more. Set aside. Reduce heat to 425°F.

2. *Make sauce.* Turn on food processor fitted with steel blade. Drop in garlic cloves one at a time. When chopped, add the chile pieces. When chopped, stop machine and remove lid. Add the tomatillos and all the juice in pan. Add the chopped cilantro and 1 teaspoon salt. Secure lid and pulse machine a few times. Then process until mixture is as smooth as you can get it.

3. *Bake chicken.* Pour sauce into the tomatillo-cooking pan. Lay chicken on top, skin-side up. Set baking pan in middle of oven. Bake 25 minutes, until chicken is lightly browned and cooked through. To tell if chicken is done, poke a fork into the chicken at the thickest part: if the juice that runs out is clear, then the chicken is done—if pink, then bake longer.

4. *Finish sauce and serve.* Use tongs to move chicken to a serving platter. Add the yogurt, cream or sour cream and sugar to the sauce. Mix well. Taste and add more salt and sugar if you think the sauce needs it. Spoon sauce over chicken, decorate with reserved cilantro sprigs and serve.

SERVES 4

Fresh cilantro

How to Chop Fresh Herbs

All you need to know about chopping herbs is that there are (1) tender herbs, (2) tough herbs and (3) super-tough herbs. Tender herbs (like cilantro, basil and chives) you don't actually chop—they'd just become a mushy green heap. Thinly slice them instead. (With cilantro you can thinly slice the stems along with the leaves—they're very tender; with basil, pull the leaves from the stems before thinly slicing them.) Tough herbs (like thyme, rosemary and parsley) you chop—rocking the knife back and forth quite a few times to mince the leaves into tiny, tiny bits. (Strip the leaves from tough stems before chopping.) Super-tough herbs (like bay) you just put into the pot with other ingredients and remove before serving. Bay is too tough to chop.

Coloradito—Oaxacan Red *Mole* with Chicken

LANIE: *I don't really know what the big deal is with this dish. I know it's hard—my dad said it was the HARDEST RECIPE IN THE BOOK—but when I made it with my friend it wasn't really that bad. It took us less than 2 hours. I'm not going to lie to you: We were proving to everyone that we could make it without anyone's help. And we did!! And they all loved it. Try this for The Real Mexican Experience. One warning: Stand back when you stir the chile puree—it can spatter on your arm and that really hurts. And, yes, there's a little chocolate in the sauce, even though it is sauce for chicken. I know it sounds weird, but it's really good. Chocolate never hurt anything.*

RICK: *Even though Lanie helped Andrés make this* mole *in Oaxaca, I never thought she'd be able to tackle such a complex recipe by herself at 12. Boy was I wrong! She and her friend Nick used this recipe to make one of the best classic Mexican celebration dishes I've ever tasted. I guess it just takes time, dedication, determination and, well, perhaps a little understanding of the ingredients (like how to toast the chiles without burning them) and what the dish should taste like (a little sweet and a bit spicy). And, in both our opinions, it is completely delicious. In fact, I think this dish redefines the word "delicious." I like to serve it with rice and corn tortillas. Andrés made black bean tostadas to start but a simple salad is good, too. And you can eat Floating Islands (page 64) for dessert, as we did in Oaxaca, but strawberries with ice cream is easier.*

FOR THE CHICKEN

8 large chicken breast halves or 8 leg-and-thigh pieces with bone (it needs bone for flavor)
½ medium onion
5 garlic cloves
Salt

FOR THE SAUCE

1 pound ripe fresh tomatoes (3 medium round tomatoes or 6 medium plum tomatoes)
8 ounces (about 16) dried ancho chile pods (look for them in Mexican groceries and many well-stocked supermarkets)
1 medium onion
1 head garlic
¼ cup vegetable oil, divided use
½ cup sesame seeds
1 teaspoon dried oregano
⅛ teaspoon ground cloves
¼ teaspoon ground black pepper
1½ teaspoons ground cinnamon
2 tablespoons raisins
8 whole almonds
3 tablespoons bread crumbs
2 tablets Mexican chocolate (Ibarra brand 3.3-ounce tablets are common)
1 tablespoon sugar
Salt

DO THIS FIRST

ONION AND GARLIC FOR THE CHICKEN: Peel off papery outside layers of the ½ onion and discard. Roughly chop. Peel the 5 cloves of garlic and cut each clove in half.

DRIED CHILES: Pull stems off chiles, tear open and remove all seeds; discard stems and seeds. Tear chiles into large flat pieces. (See page 43.)

ONION AND GARLIC FOR SAUCE: Cut off top and bottom of the onion for the sauce and discard. Cut in half from top to bottom. Peel off papery outside layers and discard. Cut each half into 2 pieces. Break garlic head apart into cloves—don't peel.

MEXICAN CHOCOLATE: On small plate, microwave chocolate for 45 seconds on high (100%) power. Cut each tablet into roughly 8 pieces.

Deann serving Coloradito

1. *Cook chicken.* Place chicken in a large pot. Cover with water. Add the ½ chopped onion, halved garlic cloves and 1 tablespoon salt. Place over high heat. When water comes to a full rolling boil, cover pot and turn off heat. Let sit, undisturbed, for 30 minutes. Then use tongs to remove chicken pieces to large plate. Set aside. Reserve broth to use in sauce.

2. *Pan-roast tomatoes.* Set a large skillet (non-stick skillet is easiest to use) over medium heat. Cover bottom of skillet with aluminum foil, then lay tomatoes on top. Pan-roast about 20 minutes until very soft and blackened in places—turn several times. Watch tomatoes while they pan roast, but continue with the following preparations. When done, remove tomatoes from heat and set aside to cool.

3. *Toast chiles.* Set another large skillet over medium heat. When hot, lay a few chile pieces on the hot surface in a single layer. Press down on them with a metal spatula until they change color and release their fragrance into the kitchen—about 15 seconds. Flip chiles and press down, quickly toasting the other side. (Don't let chiles smoke or they will be burnt and bitter.) Remove to a small bowl. When all are toasted, fill bowl with hot tap water. Let soak about 30 minutes until soft—stir several times—while continuing with the next steps.

4. *Pan-roast onion and garlic.* Set chile-toasting skillet over medium heat again. Cover bottom of skillet with a piece of aluminum foil. Press down so foil is flat in pan. Lay onion quarters and unpeeled garlic cloves on the foil. Roast onions about 8 minutes until soft and blackened in spots—turn several times. Remove onion and set aside. Continue roasting garlic about 7 minutes more (15 minutes total) until soft and blackened in places—turn several times. Set with onion.

5. *Toast sesame seeds.* Remove foil from onion-roasting skillet and set over medium heat again. Pour in *1 tablespoon* of the vegetable oil, then add the sesame seeds. Stir continuously until sesame seeds brown—about 2 minutes. Scrape into large bowl.

6. *Make chile puree.* Use tongs to transfer chiles from soaking water to bowl with sesame seeds. Set soaking water aside. Add the oregano, cloves, pepper, cinnamon, raisins and almonds to the sesame seeds. Mix well. Scoop half of the mixture into blender. Pour in just enough of the chile-soaking water to cover. Cover and blend at high speed until very smooth. Set medium-mesh strainer over a clean bowl. Pour in chile puree and press through with rubber spatula. (Don't

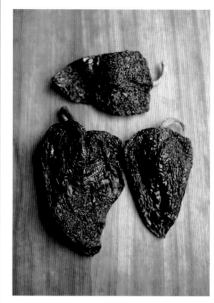

Ancho chiles

wash blender jar since it is used in next step.) Discard the chile skins and sesame seed hulls left in strainer. Repeat blending and straining with remaining sesame seed mixture.

7. *Make tomato puree.* When the roasted tomatoes are cool, peel and discard the skins. Put the tomatoes in a blender with any juices from skillet. Peel the roasted garlic and add to blender. Add the roasted onion. Cover and blend at high speed until smooth. Wash and dry skillet. Set over medium-high heat and add *1 tablespoon* of the vegetable oil. When hot, add the tomato puree. Cook—stir almost continuously—until tomato mixture thickens, 10 to 15 minutes.

8. *Cook chile puree.* Set a large (6- to 9-quart) Dutch oven or heavy pot over medium to medium-high heat. Add remaining *2 tablespoons* of the vegetable oil. When hot, add the chile puree and stir without stopping until mixture becomes very thick—about 20 minutes. Scrape in the cooked tomato mixture, bread crumbs and chopped chocolate. Add 4 cups of the chicken-cooking broth. Stir until chocolate melts. Turn down heat to medium-low and set the lid on the pot slightly askew. Simmer 30 minutes—stir every now and then.

9. *Finish dish.* If necessary, stir in extra chicken-cooking broth to give the sauce the consistency of tomato soup. Add the sugar and 2 teaspoons salt. Stir well and taste. Add more sugar or salt if you think necessary. Lay the chicken pieces in the sauce. Cook 10 minutes more. Use a large spoon to transfer chicken to individual plates. Spoon a generous amount of sauce over each portion and serve.

SERVES 8 WITH LOTS OF SAUCE

Mexican chocolate

Peruvian Chicken and Rice

RICK: *People eat chicken and rice all over the world, but, of course, every culture infuses it with its own uniquely delectable flavor.* Arroz con pollo *is what they call chicken and rice throughout Latin America, and it is more or less the same from country to country—until you get to Peru. There they make the rice delicious smelling (and emerald green) with an infusion of cilantro, garlic and spices. This recipe (which is based on what our chef-friend Isabel taught us in Lima) uses chiles, too, which some recipes don't. Our friend used the dried* mirasol *chile; we use more commonly available fresh chiles, like other Peruvian cooks told us they do. I love this recipe.*

✄   ✄   ✄   ✄   ✄   ✄

LANIE: *How to put this.... This is really good chicken and rice—the browned chicken smells and tastes TOTALLY AWESOME. But...you have to like (really* like*) cilantro to dig the rice. I mean, I really DO like cilantro—in salsa... in small amounts. Some of my friends prefer plainer chicken and rice.*

6 good-sized pieces of chicken—choose either chicken breast halves (with bone and skin) or leg-and-thigh pieces

Salt

2 tablespoons vegetable oil

2 or 3 Peruvian yellow chiles (*ají amarillo*), fresh, frozen or bottled (available in Peruvian groceries or by mail, page 225)
OR 2 to 3 yellow banana peppers

4 garlic cloves

1 medium red onion

½ teaspoon fresh pepper—white pepper is used in Peru

½ teaspoon ground cumin

2¾ cups chicken broth, divided use

¾ cup packed cilantro—cut off large stems before measuring (usually about 1 large bunch)

1½ cups long grain white rice

2 carrots

1½ cups frozen peas

····· DO THIS FIRST ·····

CHILES: Pull off tops. Cut in half lengthwise and scrape out seed pod and seeds. (See page 43 for how to work with chiles.)

GARLIC: Peel. Cut cloves in half.

ONION: Cut off top and bottom and discard. Cut in half from top to bottom. Peel off papery outside layers and discard. Roughly chop.

CARROTS: Peel. Cut off and discard tops. Cut in half lengthwise. Cut each half in half lengthwise. Cut each piece into cubes.

1. *Brown chicken.* Lay chicken on an easy-to-clean cutting board. Sprinkle both sides of chicken generously with salt. Measure oil into large (6- to 9-quart) Dutch oven or heavy pot—should be about 12 inches across. Set over medium heat. When hot, lay in the chicken skin-side down. Cook until brown—about 8 minutes. Turn chicken and cook 2 minutes more. Remove pan from heat. Remove chicken to plate. (Clean cutting board well with warm soapy water.)

2. *Make flavorings.* Place the halved chiles in a small saucepan. Cover with water. Set over medium heat. Cook until very tender—about 10 minutes. Use tongs to transfer chiles to blender. Add ½ cup of the cooking water. Cover and blend until smooth. Pour into a small bowl. Place garlic and chopped onion in blender. Add pepper, cumin, ½ *cup* of the broth and salt (¾ to 1½ teaspoons, depending on saltiness of broth). Blend until smooth. Scrape into small bowl. Place cilantro in blender. Add ½ *cup* of the broth. Blend until smooth.

3. *Cook flavorings.* Return chicken-cooking pan to medium heat. When hot, scrape in chile puree. Stir several minutes until quite thick. Add the garlic mixture. Stir several minutes until quite thick again. Add the cilantro mixture and the remaining 1¾ *cups* of the broth.

4. *Finish dish.* When the liquid comes to a boil, stir in the rice. Slide in browned chicken and cubed carrots. Cover. Reduce heat to medium-low. Cook 15 minutes. Uncover and pour peas on top. Re-cover. Turn off heat. Let stand 5 to 10 minutes. Spoon onto platter or individual plates and serve.

SERVES 6

Chiles— Don't Get Burned

The hot *stuff in chiles is all concentrated in the thin white veins of the chile. So if you're not looking for a lesson in pain management, don't touch them. The* hot *stuff rubs off on your hands, and if your hands touch your eyes or your nose or your . . . well, you get what I mean . . . you'll* know *it. We're talking extreme discomfort. We're talking freak-out* TEARS. *Wear gloves—latex, rubber, gardening, whatever* kind of *gloves you can lay your hands on—so* PAIN of the VEINS *doesn't visit you.*

—Lanie

Simple Mexican *Chilaquiles* {Tortilla Casserole}

RICK: *I've been in love with* chilaquiles *since my first trip to Mexico. Pure soul food. Very comforting. When other people want chicken soup, or oatmeal, or whatever reminds them of Mom when a cold's coming on, I want* chilaquiles. *And I want them to taste exactly like they did when I was 19 in Oaxaca—smoky chiles (like chipotles) and a big branch of epazote (that funky herb that goes into a lot of* chilaquiles *in Mexico). A note about chips: If you can't find thick ones (thicker than Tostitos), only use 2 cups of broth instead of 2½. I sometimes vary this recipe by adding 1 cup shredded cheese (cheddar, Jack, whatever) when I stir the cooked* chilaquiles *just before serving. With cheese, you can skip the sour cream.*

※　　※　　※　　※　　※　　※

LANIE: *I eat these almost every Saturday because they're one of my absolute favorite Mexican breakfast dishes. (And because we only make* chilaquiles *at our restaurant on Saturdays.) They're easy to make from scratch, which I know because we sometimes make them for dinner at home. Meaning that they're not JUST for breakfast. They might sound a little strange, but think about when you eat tomato soup and crumble up a lot of crackers in it. They're like that, but with tortilla chips instead of crackers and spicy tomato sauce instead of soup. And then you pile sour cream and cheese and chicken on top. YUM.*

One 28-ounce can diced tomatoes in juice
2 to 3 canned chipotle chiles
   OR 2 to 3 fresh serrano or jalapeño chiles
   OR a few dashes of hot sauce
2 tablespoons olive oil
3 garlic cloves
2½ cups chicken broth (canned chicken broth is okay)
Salt
8 ounces thick, homemade-style tortilla chips (8 to 12 loosely packed cups, depending on thickness)
½ cup sour cream
1½ cups cooked, coarsely shredded chicken, pork or beef, optional
¼ cup grated Mexican "garnishing" cheese (*queso añejo*), or other dry grating cheese such as Romano or Parmesan
1 or 2 green onions

> ······ **DO THIS FIRST** ······
>
> **TOMATOES:** Tip off and discard liquid.
> **CHILES:** Remove the stems from the chiles (either the canned chipotles or the serranos or jalapeños) and roughly chop them. (See page 43 for how to work with chiles.)
> **GARLIC:** Peel. Cut each clove in half.
> **GREEN ONIONS:** Cut off and discard the root ends. Peel off and discard any withered outer layers. Cut crosswise into ¼-inch pieces.

1. *Make sauce.* In food processor or blender, combine drained tomatoes and chopped chiles or hot sauce. Process until smooth or measure oil into a medium (4- to 6-quart) pot or Dutch oven or very large (12-inch) deep skillet with lid. Set over medium heat. Crush garlic through garlic press into pan. Stir until very fragrant—about 1 minute. Add the tomato mixture. Stir as mixture cooks

Fresh epazote

for 5 minutes. Add broth and $\frac{1}{2}$ teaspoon salt (use more if chips or broth are not salted).

2. *Cook* chilaquiles. When sauce boils, add the chips. Stir to coat chips. When mixture boils again, turn off heat and set cover on pot. Set timer for 5 minutes.

3. *Finish and serve.* When timer goes off, uncover pot and gently stir. Spoon onto plates. Top with dollops of sour cream, optional shredded meat (warmed in microwave) and cheese. Sprinkle with green onions and serve immediately.

SERVES 4 AS A MAIN DISH

❀ Five Cool CDs to Play While Cooking Mexican ❀

There are thousands of Latin CDs, so to narrow the choices to five was a bit tough. Lanie usually likes dance music when she cooks. Sometimes I want something mellow. If we're having a party, I like to mix in a little classic Mexican stuff. The first five have the Lanie seal of approval (I predict that a couple will not be so cool in a couple of years). The final three are my classic (kind of funky) choices.

1.   Amor, Familia y Respeto (Kumbia Kings): A very danceable mix of cumbia (Latin dance rhythm), reggae and rock.

2.   Thalia (Thalia): Straight-ahead pop from a queen of Mexican pop. Danceable. Could be replaced by MTV Unplugged [LIVE] (Shakira). *(She's good, but not Mexican.)*

3.   Chuntaros Radio Poder (El Gran Silencio): Funky rock, cumbia (that Latin dance rhythm again) and rap. The combination may sound strange at first, but it really grows on you, especially the Northern-style Mexican radio announcer interludes.

4.   Cuatro Caminos (Café Tacuba): Great (and varied) rock en español.

5.   MTV Unplugged [LIVE] (Maná): These guys defined classic soulful Mexican rock/pop (since copied by many other Mexican groups). You might also try Lo Esencial de Maná for a larger variety of their songs. Most adults like this, too.

RICK'S THREE BONUS CDs:
6.   Uniendo Fronteras (Tigres del Norte): An old album from this definitive Northern Mexican band (playing umpa style norteño *music with snare drums and accordion. Mostly a funky one-two beat, banging out story-songs called* corridos. *Can be grating, but classic.*

7.   Anniversario 100 (Mariachi Vargas de Tecatitlán): Mariachis singing super-classic Mexican songs you've probably heard if you've ever been to Mexico (or even to a Mexican restaurant). Amazing, almost orchestral-sounding.

8.   La Sandunga (Lila Downs): She sang all through the Frida movie, but her roots are in Southern Mexico. Downs sings gorgeous classic Oaxacan ballads interspersed with funky ranchero songs, in both Spanish and an indigenous language.

Vegetarian {or NOT} Soft Tacos with Guacamole

RICK: *It may sound odd to eat soft tacos filled with potatoes, but, truthfully, all kinds of food get wrapped in soft tortillas in Mexico all the time. The potatoes aren't plain, though. They're mixed with roasted chiles and golden-brown onions... and usually chorizo sausage. Which makes an incredible combination. Go ahead and play around with the recipe, adding more of whatever you like best. You could even try substituting salsa or hot sauce for the guacamole; that would make the whole thing easier.*

✕ ✕ ✕ ✕ ✕ ✕

LANIE: *I know so many potato f-r-e-a-k-s. They love food like this, especially if they're vegetarian. I'm definitely NOT vegetarian, since I like meat and potatoes. So when I make this taco filling, I add chorizo sausage. Regular guacamole is really good, but the one we use in this recipe ROCKS. Definitely limier than the regular one.*

8 ounces (1 cup) Mexican chorizo sausage, optional

3 medium (about ¾ pound) red-skin potatoes

Salt

2 medium poblano chiles—can use red bell peppers or one of each

3 tablespoons vegetable oil

1 small onion

2 soft, ripe avocados

1 large garlic clove

1 lime

10 sprigs fresh cilantro

12 corn or flour tortillas—corn is preferred in Mexico (see page 51 for details on how to heat them)

About 1 cup salsa or a bottle of hot sauce

····· DO THIS FIRST ·····

CHORIZO: With a small knife, slice down the side of chorizo casing. Remove casing and discard.

POTATOES: Peel. Cut in half, then cut halves into 8 pieces.

ONION: Cut off top and bottom and discard. Cut in half from top to bottom. Peel off papery outside layers and discard. Cut halves into slices about ¼ inch thick.

GARLIC: Peel.

CILANTRO: Bunch leaf end of sprigs together. Cut across bunched leaves with a sharp knife, slicing them thinly. Stop cutting when you only have stems left. Discard stems.

1. *Cook chorizo (if using).* Scoop chorizo into medium skillet. Set over medium heat. Cook—stir regularly to break up clumps—about 4 minutes, until thoroughly cooked. If there is lots of rendered fat, tip off and discard excess. Set aside.

2. *Cook potatoes.* Scoop potato pieces into non-metal bowl. Sprinkle with ½ teaspoon salt and toss. Cover with plastic wrap. Microwave on high (100%) power for 4 to 5 minutes, until completely tender.

3. *Roast chiles.* Roast chiles by placing them directly over gas flame (no pan), or 4 inches below electric broiler, turning occasionally with tongs until evenly

blackened all over. Place in plastic bag. Allow to cool. Peel off and discard blackened skin. Pull out stem and seed pod; discard. Tear open chile and rinse off seeds and bits of black skin. Cut into $1/4$-inch pieces. (See page 43 for how to work with chiles.)

4. *Make filling.* Pour oil into very large (12-inch) skillet. Set over medium heat. Add sliced onion and cook—stir regularly—until translucent, about 2 minutes. Add potatoes and cook—stir regularly—until browned, about 5 minutes. Stir in chiles and chorizo (if using). Cook for 2 or 3 minutes more. Taste and season with salt if necessary (if not using chorizo you will need about $1/2$ teaspoon). Keep warm over very low heat.

5. *Make guacamole.* To cut avocados in half, start at their pointy stem end and circle around pit. Twist sides in opposite directions and pull apart. Scoop out pit and discard. Scoop avocado flesh from skin. Discard skin and put flesh in a medium-size bowl. Crush garlic through garlic press into avocado. Cut lime in half and squeeze juice—you need about 2 tablespoons. Add to avocado. Add chopped cilantro and $1/2$ teaspoon salt. Mash together with bean masher, potato masher or back of spoon. Taste and season with salt if you think it needs more.

6. *Serve.* Heat tortillas. (See page 51.) Scoop filling mixture and guacamole into individual serving bowls. Set on table along with salsa or hot sauce and tortillas, and let everybody assemble their own soft tacos.

MAKES 12 TACOS, ENOUGH TO SERVE 4

The Difference Between a Chile and a Pepper

Nothing, really. Everything from a sweet red pepper to the hottest jalapeño is in the same botanical family. But in our country, a lot of us think of the sweet ones (like green and red bell peppers) as "peppers," and the spicy ones (like jalapeños) as "chiles" or "chile peppers" or "hot peppers." So, basically, we divide them up by the way they taste. On the flip side, none of those peppers or chiles has anything to do with the black grains of pepper found in shakers on practically every dinner table in America. That pepper is a ground up spice (a dried berry, actually), called a "peppercorn," less spicy than a hot pepper, grown in countries on the other side of the world.

Fresh Tomato Salsa

RICK: *I love the texture of chopped fresh tomatoes—melting but "meaty" with a wonderful juiciness. And when you mix them with lime juice and crunchy green onion, and then "ignite" them with jalapeño chile and cilantro . . . well, you understand why this is a classic. When Lanie was younger, I didn't let her chop the tomatoes. Instead, she cut them in half and grated them through the large holes of one of those stand-up graters. The salsa was a bit mushy, but grating is an easy way for pre-knife-wielding kids to make this. Lanie still likes to "chop" the cilantro by cutting it up with our kitchen scissors.*

❊ ❊ ❊ ❊ ❊ ❊

LANIE: *Here goes one of those things I don't get: Tomatoes—I don't like them. Tomato salsa—now that's my friend! My dad says it's "illogical"—but they ARE different. One's bland and mealy. The other's tangy and spicy and crunchy—GOOD.*

1. *Chop basic ingredients.* With a small knife, cut out and discard "core" from top of tomatoes where stem once attached. Stand tomato on side and cut into ¼-inch slices. Cut slices into ¼-inch dice. Scoop into bowl. Cut off and discard the root ends of the green onions. Peel off and discard any withered outer layers. Cut crosswise into ¼-inch pieces and add to the tomatoes. Bunch leaf ends of cilantro sprigs together. Cut across the bunched leaves with a sharp knife, slicing them thinly. Stop cutting when you only have stems left. Discard stems. Scoop cilantro on top of tomatoes. Peel garlic and crush through garlic press into the bowl. Cut stem off jalapeño, cut in half lengthwise and scrape out seeds and seed pod. (See page 43.) Then cut the halves into several small pieces. Finely chop the chile pieces by rocking the knife back and forth. (See page 202.) Add chopped chile to bowl.

2. *Season salsa and serve.* Squeeze the lime for its juice (you should have about 1½ tablespoons). Pour over salsa. Add ½ teaspoon salt and mix thoroughly. Taste and season with more salt if you think necessary. It is best served within one hour.

MAKES 1½ CUPS, ENOUGH TO SERVE 4 TO 6 PEOPLE AS A SNACK WITH CHIPS OR 8 PEOPLE TO SPOON ONTO TACOS

12 ounces ripe fresh tomatoes (4 or 5 medium plum tomatoes or 2 medium round tomatoes), the riper the better
2 green onions
10 sprigs fresh cilantro
1 large garlic clove
1 jalapeño chile
½ large lime
Salt

Jalapeño (left) and serrano (right) chiles

Shredded Beef Soft Tacos

RICK: *The only thing there is to say about shredded beef tacos is that some days you've just got to have 'em. They're that good. Stewing beef is easy; it's usually sold in 1-inch cubes. If you can't find any, buy flank or boneless chuck roast and cube it yourself. Everybody eats flour tortillas here in the United States, but in Mexico it's all corn tortillas. Look at the following page and you'll find out how to reheat corn tortillas so they actually taste good.*

☺   ☺   ☺   ☺   ☺   ☺

LANIE: *I could eat these tacos every day, especially when I come home from school and I'm starving. And there—like magic—is the PERFECT TACO. (I know—not everyone goes "home" to a restaurant that has shredded beef tacos. But there's gotta be some perks when your parents have to work nights and weekends.) A warning: When you want to have a perfect shredded beef soft taco moment, you can't be too hungry; you have to boil the meat first, and that takes a whole hour.*

1½ pounds stewing beef

Salt

One 15-ounce can diced tomatoes in juice

1 jalapeño or 2 serrano chiles

4 garlic cloves

2 green onions

12 corn or flour tortillas

About 1 cup salsa (page 54) or 1 cup
    guacamole (page 20)

Fast Ground Beef Filling

In a large skillet, brown 1½ pounds of ground beef in a little oil over medium-high heat—break up large clumps as it cooks. Blend tomato, chile and garlic. Add to beef, along with ½ teaspoon salt and green onion. Cook—stirring regularly—until thick.

⋯⋯ DO THIS FIRST ⋯⋯

TOMATOES: Tip off and discard liquid.

CHILE: Break off stem(s). Chop each one into 4 or 5 pieces. (See page 43 for how to work with chiles.)

GARLIC: Peel. Cut each clove in half.

GREEN ONIONS: Cut off and discard the root ends. Peel off and discard any withered outer layers. Cut crosswise into ¼-inch pieces.

---

1. *Simmer beef.* Put beef in a medium (4- to 6-quart) saucepan. Add 3 cups water and ½ teaspoon salt. Set over medium heat. When mixture boils, cover with lid slightly ajar. Reduce heat to medium-low and simmer until meat is fall-apart tender—about one hour.

2. *Add seasonings.* Uncover pan and raise heat to medium-high. Pour drained tomatoes into blender or food processor. Add chopped chiles and garlic. Cover and process to a puree. Add to meat. Boil until much of the liquid has evaporated—about 15 to 20 minutes.

3. *Mash and "fry" beef.* Add chopped green onions and continue cooking. Mash mixture with back of spoon to break up meat while stirring—until mixture

thickens and darkens, about 8 minutes. (Will begin to sizzle.) Taste and add more salt if you think necessary.

4. *Serve.* Heat tortillas. (See below.) Scoop mixture into a serving bowl. Serve with warm tortillas and salsa or guacamole for everyone to assemble their own soft tacos.

MAKES 12 TACOS, ENOUGH TO SERVE 4

Corn tortillas

How to Heat Tortillas

Corn tortillas: With a microwave oven: *Dribble 3 tablespoons of water over a clean kitchen towel. Wrap tortillas in the towel; slide them into a plastic bag and fold over the top but don't seal. Microwave at 50% power for 4 minutes to create steam around the tortillas. Let stand for 2 to 3 minutes before serving.*

Without a microwave oven: Set up a vegetable steamer (screw off that little post sticking up in the center if using a collapsible steamer). Pour about ½ inch of water in the bottom. Wrap tortillas—no more than 12 at a time—in a (clean!) kitchen towel. Lay them in the steamer, cover and set over high heat. When steam comes puffing out, time 1 minute. Turn off the heat and let the tortillas sit in the steamer for 10 minutes.

If the tortillas are super-fresh (like they've been made that day), people in Mexico turn on the gas burner and just lay the tortillas on the open flame for a few seconds, then flip them over and heat the other side. This doesn't work with an electric burner. They stick!

Flour tortillas: These are easy. Just turn on the oven to 350°F. Wrap tortillas in foil—no more than 8 or 10 in a package. Place them in the oven and bake until hot—10 to 15 minutes.

Green Tomatillo Salsa—Salsa Verde

Even though most everyone thinks salsa has to be made with tomatoes, our favorite salsa isn't. It isn't even red, because it's made with those little green tomatillos—the ones that have the little husks that cover them. The salsa is amazing because it's tangy, as if there were lime or lemon in it. It makes practically everything taste better.

5 or 6 fresh tomatillos (about ½ pound)
1 jalapeño chile or 2 serrano chiles
1 garlic clove
10 sprigs fresh cilantro
Salt
½ small onion

Turn on broiler and adjust shelf to highest position. Peel husk off tomatillos and discard. Rinse tomatillos. Lay on baking sheet (cookie sheet with sides). Slide under broiler. Broil about 5 minutes (tomatillos will be very dark in places). Remove from oven and flip each tomatillo over. Return to broiler and cook 5 to 6 minutes longer. Remove and allow to cool. Scrape into blender or food processor (with all juice from baking sheet). Pull stem off chile and discard. Cut chile into smallish pieces. (See page 43.) Peel garlic and cut in half. Pull leaves from cilantro and discard stems. Add chile, garlic, cilantro leaves and ¼ cup water to blender or food processor. Cover and process until almost smooth. Pour into small serving dish. Taste and season with salt—usually about ½ teaspoon. Peel onion and cut into small pieces. Scoop into strainer and rinse thoroughly under cold water. Shake off excess water. Add to salsa and mix well.

MAKES ABOUT 1 CUP

Fresh tomatillos

Grilled Pizza with Goat Cheese, Green Salsa and Bacon

LANIE: *You read it right.* Grilled *pizza. As in "cook it on the grill." Why in the world would you want to GRILL pizza? Two reasons: (1) Everyone loves pizza, but no one wants to heat the oven in the summer. (2) It's really, r-e-a-l-l-y good. Crispy, a little smoky. O.M.G., I could eat tons of this stuff. (About the toppings: Use whatever you want. We make them like this several times every summer, but I know that green salsa and goat cheese won't sound the SLIGHTEST bit delicious to some of you, even though I really do like it. If you like red salsa but not green, use that—or just use pizza sauce and pepperoni and shredded mozzarella cheese. Whatever.)*

✼ ✼ ✼ ✼ ✼ ✼

RICK: *Sure, everyone loves pizza, but it's not an easy, fast thing to make. And rarely does homemade pizza equal one you'd get from a restaurant. The crust isn't usually as crisp, and the amount of toppings is hard to get exactly right. So here are my secrets: Grill the pizza (rather than bake it), since the strong grill heat will crisp it up from underneath. And don't use too many toppings, since they can weigh down the crust and make it soggy. This recipe transforms a real Italian crispy, thin-crusted pizza into something that seems completely Mexican (salsa) . . . or American (goat cheese and bacon). Anyway, whatever it is, it's r-e-a-l-l-y good, as Lanie would say. Rolling out the dough and laying it on the grill takes a little practice. If your first attempts don't turn out perfect, just keep practicing.*

1½ cups warm tap water (about 110 to 115 degrees—not too hot)

1 envelope (2¼ teaspoons) dry yeast—rapid-rise yeast works best

1 tablespoon sugar

2 tablespoons olive oil, plus more for brushing crust

3⅔ cups all-purpose flour, plus extra for kneading and rolling

⅓ cup cornmeal

Salt

8 bacon slices—thick-cut bacon is best here

1 large red onion

6 ounces creamy goat cheese

½ small bunch fresh cilantro

About 1½ cups tomatillo salsa—use store-bought or make your own (opposite page)

¼ cup grated Mexican *queso añejo* or Parmesan cheese

1. *Make dough.* Measure the water, yeast, sugar and oil directly into a food processor with the steel blade in place. Pulse several times to mix. Measure in the flour, cornmeal and 1½ teaspoons salt. Process until the mixture forms a ball. (If the dough is quite sticky, add 2 to 3 tablespoons more flour, cover and pulse until incorporated. If too dry, add a little dribble of water, cover and pulse until incorporated. The dough should be quite soft, but not sticky.) Remove top of processor and pull out blade, scraping dough back into processor. Scrape dough from processor bowl into large bowl, cover with plastic wrap and let rise while preparing toppings—at least 20 minutes or as much as 1½ hours.

2. *Cook bacon.* Cut bacon slices crosswise into ½-inch strips. Scoop into large (10-inch) skillet and set over medium heat. Cook—stirring regularly—until bacon is browned and crispy—about 10 minutes. Use slotted spoon to scoop crispy bacon out onto plate lined with several layers of paper towels. Discard rendered fat or save for another use. Put bacon into a small bowl.

3. *Prepare grill and other toppings.* Heat gas grill to between medium and medium-high. Cut off top and bottom of onion and discard. Cut in half from top to bottom. Peel off papery outside layers and discard. Slice halves about $1/4$ inch thick. Chop slices finely and place in small bowl. Roughly "crumble" goat cheese and place in small bowl. Bunch leaf end of cilantro sprigs together. Cut across the bunched leaves and stems with a sharp knife, slicing them thinly. Stop cutting when you have only stems left. Discard stems and place chopped cilantro in bowl. Put salsa and *queso añejo* or Parmesan in small bowls.

4. *Form and grill pizzas.* Set the bowls of toppings beside the grill. Press down on the dough to deflate it, then scrape it out of the bowl onto a lightly floured work surface. Cut into quarters. Flour each piece and a rolling pin. Working with one piece at a time, roll and gently stretch dough into a 10-inch oval about $1/4$-inch thick.

Brush or spray rolled out dough oval lightly with oil. Lay oiled side down on grill—needs to be flat, no creases, bunches or ruffles. (This takes practice: I drape the dough over my hand, oiled side up, then touch down one end on the grill and kind of "roll" the rest of the oval off my hand so that it lies flat.) Cover grill for about 3 minutes. Uncover and cook until crust is brown underneath—another minute or two longer. Spray or brush top with oil and carefully turn it over. Spread about $1/3$ cup salsa over pizza crust. Scatter on a portion of bacon, onions and goat cheese. Cook until crisp underneath—about 4 minutes. As each pizza is finished, slide it onto a cutting board. Sprinkle with a portion of the cilantro and *queso añejo* or Parmesan. Use a knife or pizza wheel to cut into serving pieces. Like all pizzas, these are best served as soon as they're cooked.

NOTE: If pizza browns before toppings are warm, adjust one side of grill to medium heat. First, brown crust on medium-high side, then flip dough over onto side heated to medium. Then continue with toppings as described above.

MAKES FOUR 10-INCH PIZZAS, ENOUGH TO SERVE 4 AS AN ENTRÉE
OR 12 AS AN APPETIZER

The Simplest Fried Beans

RICK: *Mashed beans cooked in some garlic and a little oil (or, even better, bacon drippings!) are the perfect go-with for practically every other Mexican flavor—tomatoes, fresh chiles, dried chiles, cilantro, tomatillos. You can make this recipe with whatever bean you like: pinto, kidney, black, white, you name it. By the way, re- in Spanish doesn't mean "do again" as in re-do. It means "well" as in "well made."*

✄ ✄ ✄ ✄ ✄ ✄

LANIE: *I could eat these every day—probably because I HAVE eaten them almost every day since I was born. They're very Mexican—though I'm not (even though it seems like I am because I've been to Mexico so much and eaten so much Mexican food). These beans are just plain regular—basic—so you don't have to think when you eat them.*

2 to 3 tablespoons vegetable oil, rich-tasting pork lard or bacon drippings (use 3 tablespoons for creamier beans)
2 garlic cloves
Two 15-ounce cans beans
OR 3½ cups home-cooked beans (with just enough cooking liquid to cover them)
Salt

Measure oil or bacon drippings into a skillet and set over medium heat. Peel garlic and crush through garlic press into oil. Stir 1 minute. Pour in beans. Mash with bean masher, potato masher or back of a large spoon until almost smooth—about 10 minutes. Cook—stirring almost constantly—until thick enough to *barely* hold shape in spoon. They shouldn't be soupy or thick. Taste and season with salt if you think the beans need more.

MAKES ABOUT 2½ CUPS, ENOUGH TO SERVE 4 OR 5

Basic Beans

Place 1 pound (2½ cups) beans in a medium (4- to 6-quart) saucepan. Measure in 2½ quarts water. Bring to full rolling boil over high heat. Reduce the heat to between medium-low and low. Put the lid on to partially cover. Simmer very gently—look for a gentle rolling on the surface of the liquid—until the beans are very tender, about 2 hours. Stir in 1½ teaspoons salt and let stand 15 minutes.

MAKES 7 CUPS

Charro Beans

RICK: *These are the beans everyone eats in Northern Mexico when they go out for steaks or those fabulous grilled-meat tacos. They're smoky from the bacon and just a little spicy from the chile. I eat these practically every day, with corn tortillas. If you want to feed a big group, go ahead and double or triple the recipe.*

✖   ✖   ✖   ✖   ✖   ✖

LANIE: *I'm not sure whether Charros (that's what we call them at our restaurant) are supposed to be soup or just beans. Maybe soupy beans. We serve them with chicken and skirt steak tacos. They have bacon in them, so they're automatically good.*

1 poblano chile
  OR 1 to 2 pickled jalapeño chiles
4 slices bacon
2 garlic cloves
Half 15-ounce can diced tomatoes in
  juice
Two 15-ounce cans pinto beans
  OR 3½ cups home-cooked pinto
  beans with enough of their cooking
  liquid to cover them (make sure they
  are well seasoned with salt)
Salt
10 sprigs fresh cilantro, optional

····· DO THIS FIRST ······

BACON: Cut into small pieces.
GARLIC: Peel.
CILANTRO: Bunch the leaf ends of the sprigs together. Cut across bunched leaves with a sharp knife, slicing them thinly. Stop cutting when you only have stems left. Discard stems.

1. *Prepare chiles.* Roast chiles directly over gas flame (no pan), or 4 inches below electric broiler, turning occasionally with tongs until evenly blackened all over. Place in plastic bag. Allow to cool. Peel off and discard blackened skin. Pull out stem and seed pod and discard. Tear open chiles and rinse off seeds and bits of black skin. Cut into ¼-inch pieces. If using jalapeños, cut off stems, cut in half lengthwise, scrape out seeds and discard (no need to roast jalapeños). Cut chiles into small pieces. (See page 43 for how to work with chiles.)

2. *Cook flavorings.* Scoop bacon pieces into medium (4- to 6-quart) saucepan. Set over medium heat. Cook—stirring regularly—until bacon is crisp, about 3 minutes. Crush garlic through garlic press into pan. Stir 1 minute. Add chiles and diced tomatoes with their juice. Cook 3 to 4 minutes.

3. *Simmer beans and serve.* Stir beans with their liquid into the tomato mixture. Simmer over medium-low heat for 15 minutes. If broth is thin, mash a few beans with back of spoon or potato masher to make thicker. Taste beans and season with salt if necessary. Ladle into bowls and sprinkle with optional chopped cilantro.

MAKES ABOUT 4 CUPS, ENOUGH TO SERVE 4 AS A SIDE DISH

Mexican Grilled Corn

RICK: *Whole ears of corn—boiled or grilled and slathered with something fabulous tasting—are the street food of Mexico. Grilled is my favorite. The fresh corn in Mexico is different, a little tough and chewy, especially when it's grilled, but I think that's what makes it so captivating. It's all about the toppings anyway: cream, mayonnaise, chile, aged cheese, lime. I like cream (Mexican cream is very thick like the French* crème fraîche*) better than mayonnaise. And it should have enough chile sprinkled on top—arbol chile or cayenne—to make your lips burn a little. You can use paprika or ancho chile powder, if spicy's not your thing.*

�֍   �֍   ✷   ✷   ✷   ✷

LANIE: *Well, I think the NOT-grilled Mexican corn on the cob is definitely THE BEST. Which means there was a "discussion" between me and my dad. And you can see who won. But grilled or boiled is not as important to me as the mayonnaise and cheese smeared all over the corn. (It only sounds strange until you have it.) If you want to do it MY way, just pull off the husk and boil the corn in salted water for about 5 minutes or so. That's how the Mexican* elote *(corn) vendor makes it by my school in Chicago.*

6 ears of corn with husks on
⅓ cup mayonnaise or sour cream
¼ cup grated Mexican "garnishing" cheese (*queso añejo*), or other dry grating cheese such as Romano or Parmesan
1 lime
A little pure ground chile (or paprika if you don't like spicy)
Salt

> ····· **DO THIS FIRST** ·····
>
> **GRILL:** Turn gas grill on medium.
> **CORN:** Place corn in large bowl or pail and cover with water. Soak 15 minutes.
> **LIME:** Cut into six wedges.

1. *First grilling.* Remove corn from water. Shake off excess water. Lay on grill. Cover grill and cook 15 minutes—turn halfway through. Remove from grill and allow to cool.

2. *Second grilling.* Pull the husks all the way back and bunch them together. (It looks pretty to tie husks together with a strip of husk.) If you want corn more tender, brush with oil or melted butter. Lay corn on grill—with husks off grill so they won't burn. Grill 3 to 4 minutes—turning every minute—until lightly browned. Serve slathered with mayonnaise or sour cream and sprinkle with cheese, squeezed lime, powdered chile and salt. Or, let each person doctor their own.

SERVES 6

Corn Tortillas

RICK: *Really good tortillas are like your favorite pair of jeans—totally comfortable as they drape over all the good stuff. Tortillas come in two flavors—flour and corn. Flour is popular in the United States (and a few places in far Northern Mexico, along the U.S. border). Corn is really what everyone everywhere in Mexico eats every day. They're really different (though both are good), but corn tortillas have the authentic flavor that blends perfectly with Mexican dishes. Trouble is, corn tortillas are best when they're fresh—"fresh" as in "just made." For the real experience of Mexico, you just about have to make them yourself. And eat them while they're hot.*

Remember, the dough should not be too stiff, and don't bake your tortillas for more than 30 seconds before flipping the first time. You'll get it right after a few tries. Buy the fresh-ground corn dough ("masa" they call it in Mexico) at a tortilla factory. If that's not possible, use the more accessible dehydrated powdered corn masa ("masa harina" for tortillas is what the package says when you buy it in a Mexican grocery or well-stocked grocery store).

✠ ✠ ✠ ✠ ✠ ✠

LANIE: *My dad MADE me go to the tortilla station in the restaurant—where our fabulous, fast tortilla makers turn out thousands of fresh corn tortillas every day—and I had to practice making tortillas RIGHT IN FRONT OF THEM. Definitely the amusement of the kitchen. Of course I know how to make them. I just haven't practiced much—and they do take practice. Plus, our restaurant's tortilla makers flip them over with their bare hands. Ouch. Anyway, the dough is just a little bit sticky and when it dries on your hands it feels papery. The hardest part is laying them down on the griddle without wrinkles and then flipping them over (I use a spatula). People in Mexico wrap food in them, use them like edible plates and silverware, and eat them three times a day.*

1¾ cups powdered *masa harina* for tortillas (Maseca brand is widely available)
OR 1 pound fresh-ground *masa*

....

1. *Mix dough.* If using powdered *masa harina*, measure it into a bowl and add 1 cup plus 2 tablespoons hot tap water. Mix with your hand, kneading until thoroughly combined. Cover and let stand 15 minutes. If using fresh *masa*, scoop into bowl. Break up and knead a few times until smooth.

2. *Heat griddle or skillets.* Set a large griddle (one that stretches over 2 burners) or 2 skillets on stovetop. Set heat under one end of griddle (or one skillet) at medium. Set heat under other end (or other skillet) at medium-high.

3. *Adjust consistency of dough.* Gently squeeze the dough. If it is stiff (it probably will be), knead in water 1 or 2 teaspoons at a time until the dough feels like soft cookie dough—not stiff, but not sticky. Divide evenly into 16 pieces and roll each into a ball. Cover with plastic.

4. *Press out dough balls.* Cut 2 pieces of plastic bag (plastic wrap doesn't work very well) 1 inch larger than tortilla press. Open press. Lay in one piece of plastic. Lay dough ball in center. Flatten a little. Top with second piece of plastic. Close press. Press gently—enough to mash dough into ⅛-inch-thick disc. Pull off top piece of plastic.

5. *Unmold uncooked tortilla.* Flip tortilla onto right hand (if right-handed). IMPORTANT: top of tortilla should line up with top of index finger. Lay on medium-hot griddle (or skillet) by letting bottom of tortilla touch griddle, then lowering your hand slightly and moving it away from you—the tortilla will stick to the hot surface so you can roll your hand out from under it as it rolls down flat.

6. *First flip.* After about 30 seconds, edges of tortilla will dry slightly and tortilla will release from griddle—before this moment, tortilla will be stuck. With metal spatula (or calloused fingers), flip onto hotter side of griddle (or hotter skillet).

7. *Second flip.* After another 30 seconds, tortilla should be browned underneath. Flip. Cook 30 seconds more—tortilla should puff in places (or all over—a gentle press with metal spatula or fingers encourages puffing). Transfer to basket lined with towel.

8. *Continue.* Press and bake remaining tortillas. Stack each baked tortilla on top of the previous one. Keep tortillas well wrapped in towel to stay warm.

MAKES 16 TORTILLAS

"Floating Islands" in Cinnamon-Orange Custard

RICK: *Though our Oaxacan friends think of this dessert as an old Oaxacan specialty, I've made something like it for years—from the days when I specialized in French desserts. The French call it* Iles Flottantes *(Floating Islands), while our Oaxacan friends call it* Huevos Nevados *("Snowy Eggs"). I taught Lanie to beat egg whites by hand a long time ago and showed her that when they're perfectly stiff, you can flip the bowl over and they won't slide out. It's a cool trick—but you have to know when they're just right or you'll end up with egg whites on the floor.*

✳ ✳ ✳ ✳ ✳ ✳

LANIE: *These are r-e-a-l-l-y, really good—but rich. I don't typically eat a huge portion. It is VERY COOL how you make this custard with the egg yolks and cinnamon, then you beat the egg whites stiff ("meringue") and float balls of the stiff egg whites on the hot custard. And they cook and get even firmer. You don't really need any fancy way to serve these. Lani, our friend in Oaxaca, just served them in coffee cups.*

1 quart milk

One 2-inch piece of cinnamon stick

Two 2-inch pieces of orange zest (use potato peeler to take off strips of colored part of skin only)

1 cup sugar, plus 2 teaspoons more for the meringue

2 tablespoons cornstarch

3 "large" eggs

A few drops lime (or lemon) juice

A little ground cinnamon

····· **DO THIS FIRST** ·····

EGGS: Separate eggs (see opposite page), placing yolks in a small bowl and whites in the bowl of an electric mixer.

---

1. *Flavor the milk.* Pour the milk into a wide, deep skillet, like a 10-inch straight-sided skillet. Set over medium heat. Add the cinnamon stick and orange zest. When milk begins to simmer, regulate heat so it *just* barely bubbles. Simmer gently for 10 minutes. Use slotted spoon or tongs to remove and discard cinnamon and orange zest. Stir in *1 cup* of the sugar.

2. *Thicken milk custard.* Measure cornstarch into small dish and add 2 tablespoons water. Stir to dissolve. Then pour into milk mixture still over heat. Immediately start whisking mixture and continue until it thickens—about 2 minutes. Measure about 3 tablespoons of the hot milk custard into the bowl with the egg yolks. Mix thoroughly, then add yolks back to thickened milk custard. Whisk until thoroughly blended. It is important to do it this way to keep yolks from curdling.

3. *Make egg white meringue.* With an electric mixer, beat egg whites at medium speed until they are very foamy. Add 3 to 4 drops lime juice. Continue beating until the egg white meringue will barely hold stiff peaks when (turned-off) beaters are lifted from bowl. Add the remaining *2 teaspoons* sugar and beat 30 seconds longer.

4. *Cook meringue "islands."* Use a spoon to scoop up a golf ball-size portion of meringue. Using a second spoon, form it into (roughly) an egg shape and drop on top of hot custard. Continue until all meringue is used. (You should have about 16.) Turn off heat and cover pan. Let stand 15 minutes as the hot custard very slowly cooks the meringues. Uncover. (Meringues should be springy—not squishy.) Carefully remove meringues to large plate or baking dish.

5. *Serve.* Whisk custard to make it smooth and silky. Allow to cool. Divide custard among individual serving dishes. Set a portion of meringue "islands" on top of each. Sprinkle with ground cinnamon and serve.

SERVES 6 TO 8

Separating an egg the fun way

Two Ways to Separate an Egg

The Dainty Way: *Working over a bowl, gently crack one side of the egg's shell on the rim of the bowl. Turn the cracked side up and hold the egg with one hand on either side of the crack, thumbs at the crack. Pry open, tipping the egg so the yolk falls into one half of the shell, while the white falls into bowl below. Tip the yolk gently back and forth from shell to shell, allowing all the white to fall into the bowl. Avoid jagged edges. The white must not contain any yolk at all or it will not beat into meringue.*

The Fun Way (Requires Practice): *Hold an egg in your writing hand—thumb and first two fingers around one side, ring and pinky fingers around the other. Working over a bowl, gently crack the egg's shell on the rim of the bowl, aiming at a place that roughly lines up with the space between your middle and ring fingers. Holding the egg firmly, pry the shell apart and let the yolk drop into your other hand, which you are holding over the bowl. The action is this: Thumb and first two fingers grasp one side of the egg, while the ring finger pushes the other half of the shell away. Once the egg has fallen into your other hand—do it gently to guard against breaking the yolk—spread your fingers slightly to let the white drop through. This works best with cold—not room temperature—eggs.*

Lime Zest Ice Cream with Mexican Caramel

RICK: *This is one of the easiest, creamiest, most refreshing ice creams I know. Just mix everything together and freeze it. But you do need an ice cream maker to pull this off. My current favorite is the inexpensive one made by Krups (E358 is the model number). It has a thick bowl you freeze overnight before using. (We just store it in the freezer so it's always ready.) The bowl stays intensely cold, which is what freezes the ice cream, as the motorized paddle turns slowly for about 30 minutes. No need for ice and salt, like in the old-fashioned models. It's not a good idea, however, to store the ice cream in that bowl because it'll become too hard.*

✼ ✼ ✼ ✼ ✼ ✼

LANIE: *Tangy ice cream—sounds a little weird, but it IS really good, especially when you cover it with Mexican caramel. If you don't have that kind of caramel (or any caramel), just use chocolate sauce.*

3 limes
¾ cup sugar
1 cup heavy (whipping) cream
¾ cup yogurt
1 teaspoon vanilla extract, preferably Mexican
An 8-ounce jar of *cajeta* (Mexican goat milk caramel)—available in Mexican groceries or make your own (opposite page)

······ **DO THIS FIRST** ······

LIMES: Using the smallest holes on a grater, grate off the colored rind (aka lime "zest") from 1 lime—leave behind all the white colored pith, which is very bitter. You need about one loosely packed tablespoon—grate zest from another lime if needed. Squeeze the juice from all three limes. Measure 4 tablespoons juice.

In a medium bowl combine lime juice, grated lime rind, sugar, cream, yogurt and vanilla. Mix thoroughly. Pour into ice cream maker and freeze according to manufacturer's directions. Scoop into a freezer container. (The ice cream will be quite soft at this point.) Place in freezer to firm up for several hours or, preferably, overnight. When you are ready to serve, scoop the ice cream into dessert bowls and drizzle a generous amount of the Mexican caramel over the top.

SERVES 8

Cajeta {Mexican Goat Milk Caramel}

2 quarts goat's or cow's milk, or a mixture of the two
2 cups sugar
One 2-inch piece of cinnamon stick
½ teaspoon baking soda dissolved in 1 tablespoon water

In a medium-large (6-quart) heavy pot, combine the milk, sugar
and cinnamon and set over medium heat. Stir regularly until the
milk comes to a simmer. Remove from heat and stir in the dissolved
baking soda—it may foam up. When the bubbles subside, return
the pot to the heat. Adjust the heat to maintain the mixture at a
brisk simmer. Cook—stirring regularly—until the mixture is a pale
golden color, about 1 hour. Stir almost constantly for the next few
minutes as the mixture darkens to caramel-brown and thickens to
the consistency of honey. (Check for proper consistency by pouring a
little on a plate, cooling in the refrigerator for several minutes, then
scooping it up: the *cajeta* should still be no thicker than honey.)
Remove from the heat and pour through a fine-mesh strainer. Cool.
Cover and store in the refrigerator if not using right away.

MAKES 3 CUPS

OKLAHOMA

❈ ❈ ❈ ❈ ❈ ❈

Rick: I was in seventh grade before I recognized that my clothes smelled different from everyone else's. For 12 years, without my knowing it, my clothes had played the role of aromatic advertisement for the barbeque restaurant I was literally growing up in. And by the time I realized this simple but embarrassing fact—and piercing 13-year-old jibes forced me to sniff out and discard my most smoke-saturated shirts—the blood coursing through my veins must have been replaced at least partly with barbeque sauce.

My family has a long and proud history in the food business. My great-grandparents established one of the first grocery stores in Oklahoma shortly after Oklahoma was granted statehood in 1907. My grandfather opened one of the first drive-in restaurants out in Midwest City on the far east side of Oklahoma City, by the Air Force base. One uncle went the grocery store route, the other did the drive-in thing. But my father, John Bayless, who married into the Jones-Potter food family, saw barbeque as his niche. He said it was a calculated choice, though I've never been sure what he'd calculated or how. No one else in our family knew barbeque.

My folks opened the Hickory House in 1952, a little eat-in/take-out place in a small red-brick building at 25th and Southwestern, in Capitol Hill. In those days, it was still a promising neighborhood, although the Capitol building had

been relocated years earlier. They lined the walls and ceiling with aroma-absorbing pine planks and built a massive indoor brick barbeque pit. Its dramatic presence in the one-room restaurant gave the impression that it had somehow been discovered there, and the restaurant constructed around it. Customers ate at swing-arm chair-tables, for which my father had obtained the patent; they were not unlike the swing-arm desks I used years later as a freshman at the University of Oklahoma. And he owned the biggest jukebox Wurlitzer made.

By the time I was old enough to remember, the brick pit had been abandoned (my father said it cooked too unevenly) for a more old-fashioned, trough-type pit out back. It cooked with a smoldering fire about three feet below the grill and had a lid so huge it had to be hoisted with a pulley. That was eventually abandoned for a series of old "refrigerator-pits." For these, my father bought discarded commercial reach-in refrigerators and had his welder friend outfit them with an attached gas-wood firebox to keep the internal temperature of the refrigerator-pit at a smoky 275°F. The last one he built had fans to circulate heat and smoke, and a wide pan at the bottom to collect drippings, adding more moisture to the cooking environment and providing additional flavor for the barbeque sauce.

Hickory House Barbeque Ribs, recipe on page 84

By the time I was 10, the place had grown from a one-room joint with carhop service, a to-go window and nothing recognizable as a dining table, to a legitimate restaurant with three dining rooms. It never forfeited the cafeteria line, though, which all the patrons had to pass through to get their food.

The menu at the Hickory House was more ambitious than many American barbeque restaurants. Everything was made from scratch: seven barbequed meats (pork ribs were the big draw, and the thought of those earthy-tasting hot links still makes my mouth water), seven hot side dishes (folks drove across town for the twice-baked potatoes), and seven cold side dishes (stuffed pickles and sour slaw were big sellers). Plus "French" and rye bread, hot and mild barbeque sauce, olives, peppers, dill pickles and spicy chowchow. The litany of choices we asked every customer to make has worn a permanent, comfortable groove in my brain. This is the brawny, spice-happy, deep-rooted food that molded my young spirit and tastebuds. When I fell in love with Mexico's regional cooking at age 14, it felt like a long-lost relative of my barbeque family.

For 37 years the Hickory House hickory-smoked the meats and stuffed the deviled eggs that provided the Bayless family with a steadfast income and identity. It persevered through bouts of tragedy, tornadoes, alcoholism, quarrels, even my father's passing. We all took our turns at making salads and cooking ribs, catering and bussing tables.

And then one day, the place was gone. I don't think any of us had really seen it coming. The neighborhood hadn't been good for a while; everyone was moving further south. My sister was happy teaching school. I'd moved to Mexico, then Los Angeles, then Chicago to open my (Mexican) restaurant. My sports-writer brother never liked the business. And my mother, Levita, who had been running the place almost entirely on her own for 10 years, was tired. And near retirement age.

When I left home at 20 for graduate school in Michigan, I didn't miss barbeque right away. I was too captivated by all the new food my new home had to offer. Midwest corn roasts, fresh-pressed apple cider and warm donuts, French onion soup at the "gourmet" store and all the European stuff we dragged back from Windsor, Ontario, an hour away. The few times I invited college friends over for traditional barbeque, the ribs from my small kettle grill, the baked beans and the sour slaw didn't turn out like home. Even though I'd made these dishes a hundred times at the Hickory House, I just couldn't get the flavors right in small batches and without familiar restaurant equipment. Besides, the flavors seemed strange in my new home.

Since my mother's retirement, I've only visited my family in Oklahoma City about once a year. We rarely go out for barbeque. Maybe those intense flavors are too packed with memories. Or maybe we all feel that eating another family's barbeque would be disloyal. We just never talk about it.

Nowadays, my sister tells me she occasionally makes Hickory House sweet slaw for her family. My mother says she sometimes takes Hickory House twice-baked potatoes to potlucks. But most of the Hickory House food remained shelved—until Lanie was old enough to start asking about what kind of restaurant Grandma had, and how old I was when I got my first paying job there (I was seven; I filled iced tea and lemonade

cups at a catering job). I resolved to resurrect all the Hickory House recipes for her.

The first step was to go back to the brown photo album-cum-cookbook I'd put together back in high school. Carefully typed out on my electric Smith Corona, the recipes called for bus tubs of this, #10 cans of that and spice mix brands that have long gone out of business. Obviously the recipes needed to be reduced and modernized. After several rounds of small-batch tests (which included replacing garlic powder with fresh garlic—pure personal preference), I was ready to invite my family to our Chicago home for a flavor re-enactment of my youthful memories.

Well, what I'd envisioned as the perfect, harmonious, idyllic cook-together (everyone purring over the perfection of my small-batch recipes) was not perfect, harmonious or idyllic. In fact, it was a comedy of errors. My mother (who's never been much for following recipes) wrestled between the force of habit and the intrusion of my written words. She ended up with a plate of inedibly salty deviled eggs. My sister, LuAnn, normally an excellent cook, was so flustered to be following a recipe for something she knew so well that she turned out twice-baked potatoes so soupy that they ran onto our dinner plates like sauce. Both Mom and LuAnn argued with me about the beans, about whether we put parsley in the sour slaw, about whether it's celery seed or mustard seed in the potato salad. I was so discombobulated by the fracas that I burnt the ribs. And one of my sister's kids, not raised on Bayless family barbeque, delivered the crowning glory by refusing to eat almost *everything*.

What was going on? Why wasn't anyone fitting into the Hickory House Memory Dinner as I had planned?

It wasn't until later, when I thought about my sister's adamant defense of the way *she* had evolved the sweet slaw recipe, that I recognized there really *is* no Hickory House food any more. There are only our individual memories of it. On our own, we'd each re-created the dishes in ways that reflected how we'd grown or, perhaps, how we wished the food had been.

Flavors may be evocative, but they can't re-create the past. I've come to think of traditional flavors—family flavors, regional flavors, cultural flavors—as both part of, and apart from us. Like children, traditional flavors need devotion and the freedom to grow. They thrive when they are reinvented by each individual cook, each generation, as a true expression of the present moment.

So the old Hickory House flavors have been transformed into second generation Bayless Family Flavors. My wife, my daughter and I have developed a family tradition of a Mid-Winter Chicago Bayless Barbeque to remind us that summer will come back. Lanie makes the guest list for that party. I make the snowy path to the garage to tend the ribs.

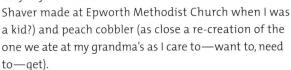

And each year we also put on a more conventional Mid-Summer Chicago Bayless Barbeque with light, crusty biscuits (can I say they're just like the ones Pearl Shaver made at Epworth Methodist Church when I was a kid?) and peach cobbler (as close a re-creation of the one we ate at my grandma's as I care to—want to, need to—get).

And whenever my mother and sister come to visit, *we* make "Hickory House" barbeque for *them*. We cook our own versions of slow-baked beans (I've changed to pintos from the original navys), that wonderfully mustardy potato salad, the garlicky vinegar-and-oil "sour" slaw flecked with aromatic flatleaf parsley, and, of course, the must-have deviled eggs and pimento-cheese-stuffed dill pickles to start off the meal. And now that I've switched from a kettle grill to Oklahoma's pride-and-joy Hasty Bake, I can slow-cook my dry-rubbed spare ribs to a smoky tenderness that rivals our successes in the last Hickory House refrigerator-pit.

The last time my mother was here, she said, "You know, these are the closest thing to Hickory House ribs I've tasted in the dozen years since we closed." I guess the spirit of the Hickory House is alive and well.

Lanie: When my dad says "barbeque" he doesn't mean what most of us mean. Like when you say, "Let's barbeque," and you start making hamburgers.

He's said it to me TONS of times: You GRILL hamburgers. You BARBEQUE ribs and other stuff that takes a long time to cook. You *grill* right over the fire. You *barbeque* with the fire over to the side—so it doesn't burn since the meat or whatever stays on so long. (See, I got it.)

Anyway, barbeque is a bigger deal to him than grilling since he grew up in a barbeque restaurant. I don't really get *why* it's such a big deal, but when he makes BARBEQUE, it's a whole big thing that takes all day and means we're having tons of people over. And he *really* wants it to come out a certain way—which sometimes means he gets a little weird. That doesn't mean I don't like what we make—I like it a *lot*.

My favorites are cheese-stuffed pickles and twice-baked potatoes with the melted cheese on top and deviled eggs. You have to hollow something out to make all three— kind of t-e-d-i-o-u-s, but it can be fun if you do it with someone else. Aunt Lu says that

in order to make sure the yolk stays in the middle of your boiled eggs, you need to stir them some while they're cooking. If the yolk cooks on the side, you just might rip the white when you pry the yolk out—I usually do. Which means some of my stuffed eggs don't look great— but they taste the same.

And—of course—I love ribs (but *he* always gets to make those—a guy thing, I guess). I only *love* them when they come out real tender (not chewy, not burnt). And the barbeque sauce. I like barbeque sauce best on biscuits. *Weird*—I know—but you should try it.

The time my aunt and my grandma came to make barbeque with us was *hilarious*. Shows just how weird my dad can get when it comes to barbeque. He was trying to get them to follow recipes for something they already knew how to make and everybody got confused and there were *several* dishes we couldn't eat. But after everyone got over being weirded out, we started laughing. And my Aunt Lu started telling stories about my dad bringing home all these animals and stuff, and how my grandma used to get all mad. I love it when they tell stories about things he did as a kid that he would NEVER let me do. Like the time he brought home mice or hamsters or something for a science project, and they had babies that got out.

I could go on—about the chameleons and the monkey and the little white sportscar (which he says I can't even *hope* for). And do I have to mention the time my dad—the *chef*—couldn't remember whether it was celery seed or mustard seed in the Bayless Family Hickory House Potato Salad and he had *me* call his mother to ask? (He owes me for that—and I don't let him forget it.)

A couple of years ago, my dad decided I needed to see where he went to junior high and high school, the house where he learned to make peach cobbler (his grandmother's) and where the Hickory House Barbeque Restaurant was. So we went driving all over Oklahoma City with Aunt Lu, my cousins and Grandma. And when we got to the place where Grandma's old restaurant was there were some cars around it, like it was open. I guess someone was using it again—barbeque catering or something—and Grandma went over and started pounding on the door. This guy came over, and she said she'd owned the place for 37 years and wanted to show her grandkids around.

Well, if you know my grandma, you know you don't say no to her. And so there we were *traipsing* all over the place.

And my dad got all weird again and started saying things like "That's where I was sitting when I saw the tornado coming right at us!" and "We used to keep a TV back here so we could watch the Jackson Five on *American Bandstand*." Then he asked me if I knew who the Jackson Five were. *Puh-leeze.*

The place was kind of run down—not at all like the photographs we have hanging at our house. The neighborhood was kind of run down, too. A little depressing.

In Chicago, we always have this big barbeque in the middle of the winter—like, when you're NOT supposed to have a barbeque. Which makes it kind of fun. The first time we did it for our friend Olivia on her birthday. Now I get to invite my friends and their families. Which *can* be fun, except that most of them have never had *real* "Oklahoma" barbeque and so they sometimes act like they're eating FOREIGN food—even though it's American. But that's okay, I guess, because most of them like it and want to come back the next year.

I probably like our summer barbeque better, though, mostly because that got started after a bunch of us went to an N'Sync concert—I can't believe I'm telling you this, since they are *so over.* Anyway, we decided to have a "reunion" party. And we ate barbeque (David, our friend's four-year-old, ate 10 ribs), and we sang N'Sync songs for hours. (I CAN'T BELIEVE I'm admitting this.) That's what I remember about barbeque.

Levita's Egg-and-Cheese "Soufflé"

RICK: *My mom (and her mom) were famous for making this very cheesey "soufflé," which isn't really a soufflé but more of a soft, fluffy bread pudding. Our family had it anytime there was a crowd—weddings, funerals, extended family brunches—because it's easy to make many pans of it and everyone likes it. When Mom sent me the recipe, it had 1961 written on the upper right-hand corner. True to the era, it was very plainly seasoned—no black pepper, only a little dry mustard to bring out the cheese flavor. (I've messed a bit with the recipe below.)*

It's important to cook it slowly for 2 hours (!) so the cheese doesn't get oily and the custard mixture (the eggs and milk) sets slowly, ensuring creaminess. All my growing-up years, we assembled our "soufflés" the night before, covered them and slid them into the refrigerator—that ensures the best texture. Every Christmas morning, we'd pop one in the oven while we opened presents.

❈ ❈ ❈ ❈ ❈ ❈

LANIE: *While I love every ingredient in this dish, I have a few pointers: (1) It's too plain without the black pepper; (2) use Pepperidge Farm white bread if you can (or challah or brioche from a bakery) because whole grain anything is a disappointment here; (3) I added red bell pepper, which I think is an improvement; and (4) it's way better with ham or smoked salmon (my dad says crab, too, but it's third on my list).*

6 "large" eggs

1 teaspoon dry mustard

Salt

½ teaspoon ground black pepper

4 cups milk

12 slices cakey white bread

1 large red bell pepper

12 ounces cheddar, Colby, Monterey Jack or other oozy melting cheese

1 cup (¼-inch pieces) ham, crabmeat or smoked salmon—ends and scraps work perfect here, optional

Oil for baking dish

······ DO THIS FIRST ······

BREAD: Cut crust from bread. Cut each slice into 16 pieces. Measure: you need about 7 cups of cubes.

CHEESE: Shred through large holes of a grater. You need about 3 cups.

---

1. *Make custard and soak bread.* Crack eggs into a large bowl. Add mustard, 1 teaspoon salt, pepper and milk. Beat well until egg is completely incorporated. Stir in the bread cubes. Cover and let stand 1 hour.

2. *Prepare pepper.* Roast pepper by laying it directly over a gas flame (no pan), or on a cookie sheet 4 inches below electric broiler set on high, turning with tongs until evenly blackened all over. Place in plastic bag. Allow to cool. Peel off and discard blackened skin. Pull out stem and seed pod; discard. Tear open pepper, and rinse off seeds and bits of black skin. Cut into ¼-inch pieces.

3. *Add remaining ingredients.* Stir the red pepper, grated cheese, and the optional ham, crab, or salmon into the bread mixture. Smear a little oil over a 9 x 13-inch baking pan. Pour in mixture.

4. *Bake and serve.* Turn on oven to 300°F. When hot, slide in the baking pan. Bake 1³/₄ hours, until browned and set (should look like jello when pan is gently shaken). Let stand 5 to 10 minutes out of oven. Cut into squares and serve.

SERVES 8 TO 10

Bell peppers

Hickory House Sweet Slaw

LANIE: *For me, this is* real *slaw—creamy and sweet and not all chopped into bits. It doesn't take long to make except for cutting the cabbage, which I do in the food processor. And leftovers are good the next day. Add 1 teaspoon vinegar or lemon juice if you want more zing.*

✖ ✖ ✖ ✖ ✖ ✖

RICK: *I like to slice the cabbage with a knife by hand (I almost shave it), but I'm comfortable using a large sharp knife. If you're not, use the thin-slicing blade on the food processor, or use one of those manual flat thin-slicers—they look like a one-plane grater, except they slice. Germans use such a thing to slice cabbage for sauerkraut, the Japanese have their little inexpensive plastic version, and the French have their expensive, more complex stainless steel version called a mandoline. For all versions, you push the cabbage across the blade (can be a little dangerous) and slices come out on the other side.*

> ⸱⸱⸱⸱⸱ **DO THIS FIRST** ⸱⸱⸱⸱⸱
>
> **CELERY:** Cut off leaves. Cut each stalk in half lengthwise. Cut ribs crosswise into ¼-inch pieces.
>
> **CABBAGE:** Cut half head of cabbage in half. Cut out and discard the hard triangular core found on one side of each piece. Slice cabbage crosswise as thinly as possible. You need about 8 loosely packed cups.

Mix chopped celery, pimento or red pepper, sliced cabbage, mayonnaise and sugar in a large bowl. Sprinkle with 1 teaspoon salt. Mix. Taste and add more salt if you think slaw needs it. Cover with plastic wrap and refrigerate until serving time. The flavor and texture are best if slaw is made an hour or two before serving.

SERVES 4 TO 6

3 celery stalks
One 2-ounce bottle chopped pimento OR ¼ cup chopped roasted red bell pepper
½ **medium-small head of green cabbage** (about 1½ pounds needed)
¾ **cup mayonnaise**
1 **tablespoon sugar**
Salt

Roasting a Fresh Pepper

To roast a pepper, lay it directly over gas flame (no pan), or 4 inches below electric broiler and turn it with tongs until evenly blackened all over. Place in plastic bag. Cool. Peel off blackened skin; discard. Pull out stem and seed pod; discard. Tear open pepper and rinse off seeds and bits of black skin.

Hickory House "Sour" Slaw

RICK: *By the time I got to high school, this was my favorite slaw. I still love the garlic and the tangy dressing and the way the cabbage starts to get a little soft if you refrigerate it for a few hours before you serve it. It's not rich, which makes it the perfect accompaniment to ribs and twice-baked potatoes. One suggestion: the thinner you slice the cabbage, the better the slaw will be. Use a sharp knife (if you're good with a knife), a food processor (set up with the thin slicing blade) or a mandoline (with a guard so you don't cut yourself).*

✗　✗　✗　✗　✗　✗

LANIE: *Okay, I'm going to be frank. This isn't my favorite thing, but I know I'm supposed to be polite. So I'll say that you should think of this as a kind of salady slaw—cabbage with vinaigrette dressing. The sweet slaw (page 76), which is more like Caesar salad, is my favorite. It has mayonnaise (like coleslaw should).*

¼ cup vegetable oil

¼ cup distilled white vinegar

1 tablespoon dry sherry

1 tablespoon sugar

2 small garlic cloves

Salt

½ medium-small head of green cabbage (about 1½ pounds needed)

¼ cup chopped fresh parsley (see page 37)

······ **DO THIS FIRST** ······

GARLIC: Peel. Roughly chop.

CABBAGE: Cut half head of cabbage in half. Cut out and discard the hard triangular core found on one side of each piece. Slice cabbage crosswise as thinly as possible. You need about 8 loosely packed cups.

Combine the oil, vinegar, sherry, sugar, chopped garlic and a generous teaspoon salt with 2 tablespoons water in a blender or food processor. Process until smooth. Place the sliced cabbage in a large bowl. Sprinkle on the parsley, drizzle on the dressing and toss to coat. Cover with plastic wrap and refrigerate at least 1 hour before serving.

SERVES 4 TO 6

Hickory House Deviled Eggs

RICK: *My sister Lu's tip for perfect deviled eggs: Stir the eggs gently while you're cooking them to keep the yolks in the center. Removing yolk is much easier when it's NOT all the way on one side—more in the center. Like all dishes that require one-by-one finishing, deviled eggs say, "Hey, you're worth all this work" to whomever you've made them for.*

⚫ ⚫ ⚫ ⚫ ⚫ ⚫

LANIE: *These are classic—best in the book. Any kid, any adult, any PERSON will like these. Or if they don't—I certainly wouldn't understand why. And we always have everything at home to make them (think "emergency appetizer"). Easy. Well, they actually are a little hard, since you have to (1) peel the eggs without gouging them and (2) take out the yolk without breaking the white for beauty's sake.*

1 medium red-skin boiling potato
6 "large" eggs
Salt
1 tablespoon prepared yellow mustard
2 tablespoons mayonnaise
2 tablespoons sweet pickle relish

······ DO THIS FIRST ······

POTATO: Peel and cut into 8 pieces.

---

1. *Boil potato and eggs.* Place potato pieces and eggs in a medium saucepan. Fill with cold water to cover eggs by 1 inch. Add 1 tablespoon salt—a tradition where I come from to keep shells from cracking. Set over medium-high heat. When the water begins to simmer, about 10 minutes, reduce heat to medium-low. Water should stay at a very gentle simmer (so eggs don't come out tough) for 9 minutes. Tip off hot water, use spoon to remove potato to medium bowl and then set pan under cold running water for 3 minutes.

2. *Mix filling ingredients.* Add mustard, mayonnaise and relish to potato, and mash together with a fork. Peel and cut cold eggs in half lengthwise. Then use a small fork or spoon to carefully scoop out the yolks, adding them to the mustard mixture. Set aside the egg white "shells." Mash yolks thoroughly into mustard mixture. Taste filling and add more salt if you want it.

3. *Finish filling and stuff eggs.* Use a fork to fill the egg whites, mounding the filling slightly to cover the whole cut side of each egg white. Drag fork lengthwise down egg to make pretty ridges. Arrange on a platter. (If you like, you can garnish with chopped chives—or purple chive blossoms—or decorate with little pansies.)

MAKES 12 DEVILED EGGS, ENOUGH TO SERVE 6 TO 8 AS AN
ACCOMPANIMENT OR APPETIZER

Hickory House Potato Salad

RICK: *Potato salad means pure summer relaxation to most people, though I ate it year 'round growing up. This version is tangy from mustard and relish, crunchy from celery, and aromatic from celery seed. Make it in February to serve with hamburgers, and you'll almost* taste *summer sunshine.*

✄   ✄   ✄   ✄   ✄   ✄

LANIE: *I like it when we make potato salad with those red-skin potatoes because they're creamy. Second choice: Yukon gold potatoes—not quite as creamy. Third choice: baking potatoes (the sign usually says "bakers" or "russets")—not creamy, almost mealy, mushy. Roasted red pepper has* way *more flavor than the pimentos that come in those little jars. And I guess* any *mustard would work (different FLAVOR, of course), but we use French's because that's what my dad grew up using.*

1½ **pounds potatoes (see Lanie's introduction)**
Salt
1 **garlic clove**
2 **celery stalks**
¼ **cup sweet pickle relish**
2 **tablespoons chopped pimento or chopped roasted red bell pepper (page 76)**
⅓ **cup mayonnaise**
3 **tablespoons prepared mustard**
½ **teaspoon celery seeds**
½ **teaspoon ground black pepper**

····· **DO THIS FIRST** ·····

POTATOES: Peel. Cut into ½-inch-thick slices.
GARLIC: Peel.
CELERY: Cut off leaves. Cut each stalk in half lengthwise. Cut ribs crosswise into ¼-inch pieces.

---

1. *Boil potatoes.* Fill a medium saucepan with 3 inches water. Set over high heat, add potato slices and 2 teaspoons salt. Bring to boiling, then reduce heat to medium. Cook 10 minutes or until potato slices are tender. Set colander in sink. Pour in potatoes to drain. Allow to cool. Scoop potatoes into a large bowl. Use a pastry blender or 2 table knives—one held in each hand—to roughly chop into ½-inch pieces.

2. *Finish potato salad.* Crush garlic through garlic press onto potatoes. Add remaining ingredients to bowl with potatoes. Add ½ teaspoon salt. Stir to combine thoroughly. Taste and add more salt if you think necessary. Cover with plastic wrap and refrigerate until ready to serve. Potato salad gets better if made several hours—even a day or two—ahead.

SERVES 4 TO 6

Hickory House Stuffed Pickles

RICK: *Maybe you've heard of celery stuffed with pimento cheese or peanut butter, but I've never liked celery much. I guess my dad didn't either, because he decided to do dill pickles the way most people do celery. He cut them in half and stuffed them with pimento cheese. Our family restaurant was best known for barbequed ribs, but I have a confession: It's the stuffed pickles I missed the most after my mother sold the place. There, we used huge Kosher dill pickles. In Chicago we use smaller Kosher dills (Classic or Claussen are brands we choose in Chicago).*

✄ ✄ ✄ ✄ ✄ ✄

LANIE: *Even though I couldn't* imagine *eating these when we first started making them, I really like them now. Especially since I like everything about pimento cheese: PIMENTO (really just a kind of red pepper, which I actually prefer even though you have to roast, peel and chop it), CHEESE (I love* mild *cheese) and m-a-y-o-n-n-a-i-s-e (I'm a mayonnaise freak). The only hard thing about these is hollowing out the pickles.*

4 ounces American or mild cheddar
   cheese
3 tablespoons mayonnaise
1½ tablespoons diced pimento or chopped
   roasted red bell pepper (page 76)
Four 3-inch-long dill pickles

····· **DO THIS FIRST** ·····

CHEESE: Set grater in or over a medium bowl and grate cheese through large holes; you need about 1 cup.

PICKLES: Cut pickles in half lengthwise. Cut a shallow V down the center of each one, starting ½ inch from one end and cutting to within ½ inch of other end; discard seedy Vs you've cut out. Turn pickles upside down on paper towels to drain.

To shredded cheese, add mayonnaise and pimentos or roasted red pepper. Mix thoroughly with fork. Use a fork to fill the V in each pickle half with pimento cheese, mounding cheese slightly, covering whole cut side of pickle. Arrange on a platter. (If you want, you can garnish with chopped chives, chopped green onions or chopped parsley.)

MAKES 8 STUFFED PICKLES, ENOUGH TO SERVE 8 AS AN ACCOMPANIMENT OR APPETIZER

Hickory House Barbeque Sauce

RICK: *If the clouds of hickory smoke in my parents' restaurant gave way to rain, this sauce would have poured down. Now, I know you'll see lots of recipes for other barbeque sauces. You've probably bought bottles of secret concoctions sold by barbeque gurus, too. Well, those barbeque sauces aren't this one. This is the simple essence of barbeque sauce. And it starts with ketchup, so it's easy. If you have any meat drippings from your barbeque, stir them in for fabulous flavor.*

✄   ✄   ✄   ✄   ✄   ✄

LANIE: *This kind of barbeque sauce is sorta like soupy, spicy ketchup. Which of course is why it is so good. On anything. I know this may sound weird to some people, but I like it on biscuits. By the way, I say Heinz is THE ketchup to use in this sauce.*

2 garlic cloves

1 cup ketchup

1 tablespoon vinegar—cider vinegar or distilled white vinegar is good

2 tablespoons Worcestershire sauce

⅓ cup dark brown sugar

½ to 1 teaspoon barbeque spice, store-bought or homemade (see below) (you could even substitute chili powder)

¼ teaspoon freshly ground black pepper

Salt

Peel garlic and crush through garlic press into a small saucepan. Add all the remaining ingredients and ¾ cup water. Simmer over medium-low heat for 30 minutes. Taste and season with salt if you think necessary. The sauce is ready to use. It can be stored, refrigerated in a sealed jar, for up to a month.

MAKES ABOUT 1½ CUPS

Barbeque Spice ingredients

Barbeque Spice

2 large garlic cloves

¼ cup plain ground chile (like ancho, New Mexico or *guajillo* chile—available at Mexican markets and well-stocked groceries) or paprika

2 teaspoons ground black pepper

2 teaspoons sugar

2 teaspoons dried oregano (preferably Mexican oregano)

1 teaspoon dried thyme

4 teaspoons salt

Peel garlic and crush through garlic press into a small bowl. Add remaining ingredients. Stir, making sure to thoroughly mix in garlic. If not using right away, store in small jar in refrigerator up to 1 month.

MAKES ½ CUP

Hickory House Barbeque Ribs

RICK: *If you follow this recipe, you'll turn out what I'd call "real barbeque"—pork ribs "marinated" in a dry spice mixture, cooked slowly in a cloud of hickory smoke, and finished with a quick glaze of barbeque sauce. To folks in Texas, however, "real barbeque" usually means barbequed beef brisket, slow-cooked for hours and hours, sometimes served without sauce. In North Carolina, the phrase might mean a whole pig smoke-cooked really slowly and doused with a thin, tangy, clear "barbeque sauce." Or in some places in the Midwest, it means ribs that are boiled until tender, then laid on the grill for a few minutes and smothered with barbeque sauce. You see, to real barbeque geeks like me, barbeque never means quick grilling.*

At the Hickory House, we cooked the larger, juicier spare ribs, rather than the smaller, firmer baby back ribs. Use whichever you like. And we cooked with pieces of hickory, but other woods (like oak, mesquite and cherry) add good flavor, too.

Rather than calling for a specialized smoke-cooker like we used at the Hickory House, I've adapted this recipe for a typical gas grill (it's very easy) or charcoal kettle grill (for those who want to tackle live-fire cooking). Investing in a "rib rack"—it stands the ribs on their sides—is essential when doubling or tripling this recipe.

❈ ❈ ❈ ❈ ❈ ❈

LANIE: *I only have 3 things to say to you when you're making these delicious ribs: (1) Sprinkle dry spice on evenly—you don't want to bite into a clump of it; (2) don't get the temperature so high that the ribs brown too much before they're REALLY tender; (3) watch to make sure that the ends don't burn.*

About 2 cups hickory wood chips
3 large slabs baby back ribs (about 5 pounds total)
  OR 2 medium to medium-small slabs spare ribs (about 5 pounds total)
⅓ cup barbeque spice, store-bought or homemade (page 83)
About 1½ cups barbeque sauce, store-bought or homemade (page 83)

> ⋯⋯ **DO THIS FIRST** ⋯⋯
>
> **RIBS:** At least 4 hours before cooking (or up to 2 days ahead), lay ribs on baking sheet. Sprinkle both sides evenly with barbeque spice. Cover with plastic wrap and refrigerate.
> **WOOD CHIPS:** One hour before cooking, cover chips with water in a bowl.
> **GRILL:** About ½ hour before cooking, if you are using a gas grill, heat *half* the burners on one side to high. (If your grill has three burners, heat two of the three.) Or, if you are using a kettle-style charcoal grill, prepare a charcoal fire, and when the coals are covered with gray ash, bank them on opposite sides.

1. *Set up grill.* Pour 1 inch of water into a 9 x 13-inch baking pan and set over hot (lighted) part of gas grill, or carefully nestle between piles of coals. Drain wood chips. Wrap in foil. Poke 6 holes in foil and either set next to water pan directly over high heat, or set directly over coals. If using charcoal, set grill grate in place over charcoal.

2. *Barbeque ribs.* When the wood chips begin to smoke, lay the seasoned ribs meaty-side up over cooler (unlighted) part of gas grill or in middle of charcoal grill. Close grill. Turn gas temperature to medium. Cook 1¼ hours for baby back ribs, 2 hours for spare ribs, until beautifully reddish-brown and meat is tender when pierced with a fork. (If grill has thermometer, it should stay between 275° and 325°F during cooking. If using charcoal, add more every half hour or so to maintain temperature.) Pour about ⅓ cup of the barbeque sauce into a small dish. Use this to brush ribs. Close grill and cook 10 minutes longer.

3. *Serve ribs.* Remove ribs to cutting board. With a large knife, cut between the bones. Serve with remaining barbeque sauce that has been heated just before serving.

SERVES 6

Ribs in a rib rack ready for cooking

The World's Greatest Chili

LANIE: *My dad and I had a chili cookoff. He made something with lamb and a very strong, very dark chili sauce. I made this recipe: The World's Greatest Chili. So you can guess who won. (At least in my opinion, since I didn't really like his.) The whole chile pods are what make this fabulous, but it's really good with ground chile too. I totally like it better with a combination of pork and beef. You can leave out the beans if you want, but why would you? And about those toppings: you can use cheese and green onions; but also try sour cream, broken tortilla chips, goat cheese—whatever sounds good.*

RICK: *This is classic chili—more-or-less Tex-Mex style. If you make it with the whole ancho chile pods (sometimes called pasilla chile pods on the West Coast), use coarse-ground meat (the classic "chili grind" in the Southwest), brown it well, and add fresh-ground spices; it'll be one of the best chilis you've ever tasted.*

The difference between chili and chile? Chili is the dish; chile is the pod. Why not use regular chili powder? Because it usually contains dried spices (including salt and sugar), which you may not like. If chili powder's all you've got, use 4 tablespoons, leave out the cumin, and go easy on the salt. Chile pods and pure ground chile are available in all Mexican grocery stores.

4 large ancho chiles
OR 3 tablespoons pure ground ancho, New Mexico or California chile (or you can use paprika in a real pinch)
2 tablespoons bacon drippings, vegetable oil or olive oil
1½ pounds ground beef, ground pork, or a mixture of the two
1 medium onion
3 garlic cloves
One 15-ounce can diced tomatoes in juice
1 teaspoon ground cumin
Salt
2 tablespoons corn meal or *masa harina* (flour used to make corn tortillas—available in many grocery stores)
One 15- or 16-ounce can pinto beans, optional
About 1 cup grated cheddar or Monterey Jack cheese
3 green onions

DO THIS FIRST

ANCHO CHILES: Pull off stems. Tear open chiles and dump out seeds. Discard stems and seeds. (See page 43 for how to work with chiles.)
ONION: Cut off top and bottom and discard. Cut in half from top to bottom. Peel off papery outside layers and discard. Slice about ¼ inch thick. Cut slices into ¼-inch pieces.
GARLIC: Peel. Cut each clove in half.
BEANS (IF USING): Drain off liquid.
GREEN ONIONS: Cut off and discard root ends. Peel off and discard any withered outer layers. Cut crosswise into ¼-inch pieces.

1. *Toast and soak chiles.* Heat a very large (12-inch) deep skillet or large heavy pot (like a 6- to 9-quart Dutch oven) over medium heat. When hot, toast chiles one by one: open flat and press down with spatula until chile releases aroma and

toasts lightly—10 to 15 seconds. Flip and toast other side for the same amount of time. Transfer to a small bowl. When all are done, cover with hot tap water and lay a plate on top to keep the chiles submerged.

2. *Brown meat and onion.* Raise heat under pan to medium-high. Add bacon drippings or oil, then the meat and diced onion. Cook for about 10 minutes, breaking up meat with spoon or spatula as it cooks and browns. Remove from heat. If there is lots of rendered fat, tip it off and discard.

3. *Make seasoning.* Drain chiles, discarding water. Place in food processor fitted with steel blade. Add garlic, tomatoes with their juice and cumin. Secure lid and process until smooth. Set medium-mesh strainer over meat pot. Pour in chile mixture and press through. (If processed enough, only chile skins will remain in strainer.)

4. *Simmer chili.* Return pan to medium-high heat. Stir 5 minutes to cook chilé mixture. Stir in 2 cups water and 1 1/2 teaspoons salt. Reduce heat to medium-low. Simmer 45 minutes.

5. *Finish and serve.* Sprinkle corn meal or *masa harina* over chili and stir. Stir in drained beans if using. Simmer 5 minutes more. Taste and season with more salt if you think necessary. Ladle chili into bowls. Scoop cheese and chopped green onions into small serving bowls. Pass separately for guests to add as much as they want.

MAKES 5 CUPS, ENOUGH TO SERVE 4 TO 6

Chicken Pie {aka Chicken 'n' Biscuits}

RICK: *We all have comfort foods—whether it's a burger (Lanie's) or pot roast with mashed potatoes (Lanie's mom). Well, this is one of mine, probably because we ate it at Grandma Potter's a lot when I was growing up. And it has crispy-topped biscuits that get all soft on the bottom, kind of melting into the sauce. You can use chicken breast instead of thighs to make this, but the meat will be a little drier. And don't worry if the sauce doesn't look creamy when you add the first cup of the milk; it comes together as it cooks.*

✽ ✽ ✽ ✽ ✽ ✽

LANIE: *When my friend Stella and I made this together we loved it. She said it was the BEST ONE of these she's ever had. Which made me wonder how many she's had. (I've actually only eaten this a few times—like really only when my dad gets sad or something and wants to make whatever he ate before he became an "adult.") Don't think you have to follow this recipe exactly with the vegetables. Just add what you like—corn instead of peas, for instance. The flavor is mostly chicken anyway—not vegetables.*

FOR THE BISCUITS

1½ cups (7½ ounces) all-purpose flour, plus extra for kneading
2½ teaspoons baking powder
1 teaspoon sugar
½ teaspoon salt
3 ounces (6 tablespoons, ¾ stick) butter
½ cup milk
1 "large" egg

FOR THE CHICKEN MIXTURE

2 tablespoons butter or vegetable oil
1 small onion
¼ cup all-purpose flour
2¼ cups milk
1 pound boneless, skinless chicken thighs
2 medium carrots
Salt
½ teaspoon ground black pepper
1 teaspoon fresh thyme leaves (or ¼ teaspoon dried)
OR 1 tablespoon roughly chopped fresh parsley leaves
1 cup frozen peas

····· **DO THIS FIRST** ·····

BUTTER: Cut butter for biscuits into 12 pieces.
MILK AND EGG FOR BISCUITS: Pour milk into a measuring cup. Crack in the egg and mix thoroughly.
ONION: Cut off top and bottom and discard. Cut in half from top to bottom. Peel off papery outside layers and discard. Slice about ¼ inch thick. Cut slices into ¼-inch pieces.
CHICKEN: On an easy-to-clean surface, cut into 1-inch squares. There should be about 2½ cups. Set aside. Clean surface well with soapy water.
CARROTS: Cut off and discard top end. Cut in half crosswise, then cut each in half lengthwise. Cut across into small pieces.
OVEN: Position rack in upper third of oven. Turn on to 425°F.

1. *Make biscuits.* Measure flour, baking powder, sugar and salt directly into food processor with steel blade in place. Attach lid and pulse 4 times to mix. Open processor, sprinkle butter pieces over top, attach lid and pulse 8 times (1-second pulses). Turn on processor and slowly pour in milk-egg mixture through feed

tube (should take about 4 seconds). Turn off processor. The dough should be a sticky-looking mass; if not, pulse until all flour is moistened and dough "comes together"—it shouldn't take more than a few seconds. Remove processor blade, scraping dough from blade back into processor bowl. Dust countertop heavily with flour. Place dough on the floured surface. Dust dough with more flour. Knead gently 5 times (sprinkling on a little more flour if necessary to keep it from sticking). Pat into a 9-inch round. Use biscuit cutter or drinking glass to cut biscuits—2 to 3 inches in diameter is ideal. Leave on work surface.

2. *Make chicken mixture.* Measure 2 tablespoons butter or oil into a medium (4- to 6-quart) saucepan. Set over medium heat. Add the diced onion and cook—stirring frequently—until it begins to brown, about 6 minutes. Add flour and stir thoroughly. Add about *half* of the milk, and immediately start whisking. Continue until mixture thickens. Add remaining *half* of the milk, and whisk until mixture boils. Add the chicken pieces, diced carrots, 1 teaspoon salt, pepper and thyme or parsley. Simmer over medium-low for 10 minutes. Taste and season with additional salt if you think necessary. Add the peas. Scoop hot mixture into 8-inch square baking pan, and flatten out. Lay biscuits in a single layer on top.

3. *Bake.* Set baking pan on baking sheet to catch any drips. Bake 25 minutes, until biscuits are browned. Best to set baking dish on trivet on table, then scoop out biscuits and creamy chicken mixture onto each plate.

SERVES 4

Hickory House Twice-Baked Potatoes

RICK: *These have a lot more going on than plain baked potatoes, which are so simple you don't really need a recipe. Besides the slow-smoked ribs, my family's restaurant's huge twice-baked potatoes were cause for folks to drive clear across town. There was hardly another restaurant in the area that would tackle these. And, let's face it, when you make them at home, they still spell "special occasion." They aren't complicated—they just take a little time to make. One bite and you'll know it's time well spent.*

✵　✵　✵　✵　✵　✵

LANIE: *"L-O-V-E" is all I can say. They're way better than baked potatoes (which you have to dig at), because these are mashed potatoes inside baked potatoes topped with melted cheese. I mean, what's not to love? The hardest part is scooping out the skins. Scoop too deep and you'll break the skins. But if you don't scoop deep enough, you won't have the right amount of potato to mash. (That's what happened when I made them with my grandmother once, and we added all the milk at once and the potatoes were soupy.)*

4 large (9- to 10-ounce) russet potatoes (these rough brown-skin potatoes are sometimes called "baking potatoes" or just "bakers")
2 tablespoons butter
¼ to ⅓ cup milk
½ teaspoon ground pepper (we used white pepper at the Hickory House)
Salt
About 3 ounces American or mild cheddar cheese

.... **DO THIS FIRST** ....

BUTTER: Cut into 4 pieces.
CHEESE: Shred cheese through large holes of grater. You need about ¾ cup.
OVEN: Position 1 oven rack just above the middle, the second rack just below the middle. Turn on to 425°F.

1. *Bake potatoes.* Use a fork to poke holes in each potato in 4 places. Place in microwave, and microwave on high (100%) power for 15 minutes. Use tongs to transfer potatoes to baking sheet. Slide into oven on upper rack and bake 15 minutes, until a fork slides easily all the way to the center.

2. *Split and hollow potatoes.* Holding potatoes with oven mitt or cloth, cut in half lengthwise. Hold half in mitt or cloth while scooping out hot, soft potato into large bowl. Be careful not to tear the skin—leave about ¼ inch of potato on the skin to keep it firm enough to handle.

3. *Make mashed potatoes.* Add butter, ¼ cup milk, pepper and 1 teaspoon salt to the hot scooped out potato. Use a potato masher or large fork to mash every-

thing together until as smooth as you like it. If mashed potatoes are stiff, stir in a little more milk. Taste and add more salt if necessary.

4. *Fill potato shells.* Lay the 6 nicest shells on a baking sheet. Divide mashed potatoes among shells. Smooth tops, doming slightly. Sprinkle evenly with shredded cheese.

5. *Bake again and serve.* Slide baking sheet into oven on lower rack. Bake until cheese is starting to brown, 20 to 25 minutes. Serve while potatoes are hot.

SERVES 6

※ Five Cool CDs to Play While Cooking Barbeque ※

I don't know how anyone could choose just five country western CDs because the genre's so vast (from old-timey, folksy stuff to bluegrass, western swing, rockabilly and contemporary) that there are many classics. Lanie, on the other hand, would have a hard time choosing five CDs, but for other reasons. Country western isn't really her thing. So this is my list of mostly classic recordings that I think are easiest for every American to love.

1. Essential Bob Wills and His Texas Playboys: *The best Western swing music from back when my mother was a teenager. Totally fun music and lyrics. A great inspiration for Asleep at the Wheel* (The Very Best of Asleep at the Wheel).

2. Down from the Mountain: *A live performance of several groups from the soundtrack to* O Brother, Where Art Thou. *The soul of traditional country music with great*

spirit. If old-timey stuff isn't your thing, you might like bluegrass instead (Appalachian Stomp: Bluegrass Classics).

3. Willie Nelson and Friends: Alive and Kickin: *Willie's a classic. In this live album, he joins other music giants (including Eric Clapton, Elvis Costello, Paul Simon and Norah Jones) to perform his most beloved songs.*

4. Trio: *Divas Dolly Parton, Emmylou Harris and Linda Ronstadt team up with amazing harmonies on old and not-so-old country classics. A close second: Emmylou Harris's* Profile.

5. The Essential Johnny Cash: *This is as good a representation of this icon's decades-long career as you can get— from rockabilly to folk to wonderful duets in the second CD. Second choice: Merle Haggard's* Alive at Billy Bob's Texas.

Goat Cheese Grits

RICK: *Grits are coarsely ground corn meal. And if made from yellow corn, this corn meal "pudding" will have a golden color that's as beautiful as its rich, creamy texture. This is a total microwave recipe because the microwave cooks grits evenly and gently (no scorching on the bottom). The cooking isn't any quicker than on the stove, though. If you want, jazz these up with chopped green onions or chives, bacon or ham. Either nuke leftovers (stir in a little milk to soften them up) or smear a little butter on top and bake them until crusty.*

❈   ❈   ❈   ❈   ❈   ❈

LANIE: *I never remember how much I like these until they're done and I taste them. And they taste* really *good. This is like a REALLY OLD recipe my dad made up for me when I was little and couldn't eat wheat flour or anything made with cow's milk (he used goat's milk). That was a pain. Anyway, they don't taste too much like goat cheese—just a little tangy. And peppery. And creamy. (Yum!)*

3 garlic cloves

Salt

1 cup regular (old-fashioned) grits

2 cups water

2 cups milk

½ teaspoon ground black pepper

4 tablespoons olive oil or butter

4 ounces (½ cup) creamy fresh goat cheese (we also use 1 cup grated cheddar, Monterey Jack or practically any cheese—each will taste different)

······ **DO THIS FIRST** ······

GARLIC: Peel.
BUTTER: Cut into 8 pieces.

Crush garlic through garlic press into a large microwave-safe bowl. Add 1½ teaspoons salt and remaining ingredients *except* cheese. Cover with plastic wrap. Poke 4 holes in plastic for steam to escape. Microwave at 50% power for 10 minutes. Use potholders to remove bowl. Uncover and stir vigorously. Cover again with plastic, poking holes again if you have to use new plastic. Microwave at 50% power for 10 minutes more. Uncover and add cheese. Stir vigorously until everything is smooth. If grits seem very thick, stir in a little milk. They should be as thick as soft mashed potatoes. Scoop into a serving bowl and serve.

NOTE: You can also use quick-cooking grits. Microwave on high power for 5 minutes, stir and microwave on high 5 minutes longer. The texture is very creamy.

SERVES 4 TO 6 AS A MAIN DISH, 8 AS A SIDE DISH

Hickory House Barbeque Baked Beans

RICK: *I do love beans, with their soft texture and sweet, earthy flavor. Once you get used to beans, you've just gotta have 'em. Barbeque beans fill the kitchen with a wonderful aroma, and they're simple to make—you can double or triple the recipe easily if you have a big group. Don't be surprised when they look soupy going into the oven; they thicken as they slow-bake. At my family's restaurant we started with canned pork-and-beans made from tiny white navy beans. Now I use plain canned or home-cooked beans. I like the meatier, fuller flavor of pintos best. (My recommendation: Sneak a taste of the sweet, glazed top when they come out of the oven.)*

⌗ ⌗ ⌗ ⌗ ⌗ ⌗

LANIE: *Barbeque beans should really be called barbeque* sauce *beans. I like them best when they're really saucey (not dry at all). And sticky-crusty on the edges. They're good, but they're not my* absolute *favorite. Really—my favorites are Mexican beans (*frijoles refritos *or* frijoles charros*). I guess that's because I've eaten them almost every day of my life. That's what my dad says about barbeque beans, anyway; he ate them all the time when he was a kid. Maybe that's why WE BOTH LIKE BEANS so much.*

½ **large green or red bell pepper**
Two 15-ounce cans pinto beans or navy beans
    OR 3 to 3½ cups home-cooked pinto or navy beans well seasoned with salt (page 57)
1 cup barbeque sauce, store-bought or homemade (page 83)
½ **cup water or bean cooking liquid if using home-cooked beans**
2 tablespoons dark brown sugar
1 tablespoon Worcestershire sauce

······ **DO THIS FIRST** ······

PEPPER: Pull out seed pod and stem; discard. Rinse out any stray seeds. Cut into small pieces.
CANNED BEANS: Drain off liquid.
OVEN: Position rack in middle of oven. Turn on to 375°F.

In an 8-inch square baking pan, mix together everything except Worcestershire sauce. Stir well to dissolve sugar completely. Dribble Worcestershire over top. Bake until slightly thickened, glazed and browned on top, and bubbling vigorously around the edges, 45 minutes to 1 hour. Let cool slightly before serving.

SERVES 4 TO 6

Crispy-Tender Biscuits

RICK: *I've eaten biscuits since I was born. Biscuits with honey or jam, biscuits on top of chicken pie, biscuits for shortcake, biscuits and sausage gravy for breakfast. (Yes, I'm from the South, and I love biscuits doused with creamy gravy.) There are lots of styles of biscuits, but my favorites are baked in a very hot oven so they're crisp and made from a soft—almost sticky—dough so they're light. These biscuits are rich and special—not something we make every day.*

❌   ❌   ❌   ❌   ❌   ❌

LANIE: *You can get, like, lost in a biscuit. C-r-i-s-p-y, crunchy outside. Soooft, buttery inside. Dreamy. With jelly. Or barbeque sauce.*

4 ounces (8 tablespoons, 1 stick) butter
1½ cups (7½ ounces) all-purpose flour,
    plus extra for kneading biscuit base
2½ teaspoons baking powder
1 teaspoon sugar
½ teaspoon salt
½ cup milk
1 "large" egg

······ **DO THIS FIRST** ······

MILK AND EGG: Pour milk into a measuring cup. Crack in the egg and mix thoroughly.
BUTTER: Cut off 2 tablespoons; set aside. Cut rest of butter into 12 pieces.
OVEN: Position rack in top third of oven. Turn on to 425°F.

1. *Prepare baking pan.* Place 2 tablespoons butter in a 9-inch round cake or pie pan. Set pan in oven for about 5 minutes to melt butter (it can brown a little). Remove from oven.

2. *Prepare biscuit dough.* Measure flour, baking powder, sugar and salt directly into food processor with the steel blade in place. Attach lid and pulse 4 times to mix. Open processor, sprinkle butter pieces over top, attach lid, and pulse 8 times more (1-second pulses). There should still be *tiny* pieces of butter in the mixture. Turn on processor and pour in the milk-egg mixture through feed tube in a thin, steady stream—not too fast, not too slow. Turn off processor. Dough should be a sticky-looking mass. (If not, pulse until all the flour is moistened and dough comes together—it shouldn't take more than a few seconds.)

3. *Pat out dough.* Remove blade from processor, carefully using rubber spatula to scrape dough from blade back in with the rest. Heavily dust work surface with flour. Scrape out dough on top. Dust dough with flour. Knead gently 5 times—sprinkle on more flour if needed to keep dough from sticking to everything. Pat into a 9-inch round. Use a biscuit cutter or drinking glass to cut out biscuits (2½ inches in diameter is perfect). Use a small metal spatula to transfer biscuits one

To Make Biscuit Dough Without a Food Processor

Measure flour, baking powder, sugar and salt into a large bowl. Add the butter pieces to the flour mixture. Use pastry blender or 2 table knives (one held in each hand) to work butter into flour, cutting it into tiny pieces. Dribble half liquid mixture evenly over flour mixture. Use fork to gently mix in. Dribble over second half of liquid. Mix in to form dough.

by one to pan with melted butter, flipping them over in the pan so they have butter on both sides.

4. *Rest biscuits*. Let biscuits stand for 10 minutes before baking. This will help them come out fluffy.

5. *Bake biscuits*. Bake 20 minutes, until browned. Serve warm.

MAKES 11 OR 12 BISCUITS

❈ How to Measure ❈

Until you get to know your ingredients, cooking techniques and classic dishes very, very well, you'll need to follow recipes. Which means you have to measure accurately or things might not turn out the way you want them to. (In baking and pastries, you never graduate from needing to follow recipes and measure carefully.) Here are the basics:

Measuring wet ingredients (such as milk, oil and vinegar): Use liquid measuring cups—usually glass or plastic with a little spout for pouring. These typically come in 1-, 2- and 4-cup sizes. Read from the side of the cup for accuracy; you have to crouch down a little if the cup is sitting on the counter.

Measuring dry ingredients (such as flour or sugar): Use dry measuring cups—usually metal with a flat handle. They typically come in 1/4-, 1/3-, 1/2- and 1-cup sizes. For accurate measuring, fill the cup, then sweep off the excess with a knife or a spoon handle so the top is level. Don't pack the dry ingredient into the cup to make the top level. For ingredients that settle naturally (flour, especially, gets very compact as it sits), stir to fluff it before scooping and sweeping off excess.

Measuring small quantities of wet or dry ingredients: Use measuring spoons—usually metal or plastic. They typically come in 1/4-, 1/2- and 1-teaspoon sizes, plus a 1-tablespoon size (corresponds to 3 teaspoons). If measuring small amounts of dry ingredients (like baking powder), scoop up the ingredient and sweep off the excess as you would when using dry measuring cups. If measuring small amounts of wet ingredients, be sure to scrape out everything (a finger works well for this).

Measuring large amounts of things—especially produce: Most people in America measure produce by pieces (4 apples, 6 potatoes) or by cups (3 cups of chopped tomatoes), which is never very accurate because sizes (or sizes of pieces, if chopped) vary so much. In many countries, ingredients are called for by weight because that's the most accurate way to measure. Even liquids can be weighed (professional bakers do it all the time). All you need is a scale—which, unfortunately, is not a common piece of equipment in American kitchens. If you don't have a scale, you can weigh your produce at the grocery store.

Peach Cobbler

RICK: *Some flavors and dishes are so thoroughly intertwined with a place and a moment that they all become one. That's the case for me with Peach Cobbler. Back in the '60s, my red-headed Grandma Gladys would pile all of her willing grandchildren into her pointy-tail Cadillac and head south from Oklahoma City toward Ardmore to pick peaches (two hours, one stop at Stuckeys). We climbed homemade ladders, hung our quarter-bushel baskets on top of the rails, and followed Grandma's instructions:* Only blushing golden globes, no green at the stem. Mouth-watering aroma, but no soft spots. Not too many in the basket or the bottom ones will get crushed. *A dizzying giddiness overtook me up there in the tree, shaded by its leaves from the blistering Oklahoma sun, breathing air so saturated with peach perfume. That same perfume permeated the car on the trip back, as well as Grandma's house over the next few days as we captured that summer's essence in jars of peach jam, peach butter, pickled peaches and peach halves canned in light syrup. There were more jars of peach halves than anything else, because peaches had come to anchor our family meals. Peaches in an envelope of tender pastry. Peaches in a deep-dish, double-crusted cobbler.*

❊　❊　❊　❊　❊　❊

LANIE: *This fresh peach cobbler is* SO GOOD *you always get tons of compliments from people who eat it. Most people—me included—love desserts and not that many people make them. Which might be why my current favorite "cooking thing" is desserts. Some things I have learned: You have to allow plenty of time— chilling time (both meanings), baking time, cooling time. You have to measure everything EXACTLY. And the easiest way to peel all those peaches (*tedious*) is by pouring very hot (not boiling) water over them in a bowl, letting them stand 1 minute, then pouring off the water. Use a knife to peel off the skin in thin sheets.*

FOR THE CRUST

2⅔ cups (13 ounces) all-purpose flour, plus extra for rolling
¼ teaspoon baking powder
1 teaspoon salt
8 ounces (1 cup, 2 sticks) *cold* butter
Two 3-ounce packages cream cheese, chilled
1 tablespoon cider vinegar
3 tablespoons cold tap water

FOR THE FILLING

5 pounds ripe peaches
1 to 1¼ cups sugar, plus a little extra for sprinkling over lattice crust
5 tablespoons cornstarch
A generous ½ teaspoon grated nutmeg
1½ tablespoons lemon or lime juice
½ teaspoon salt
Milk for brushing over crust
2 tablespoons butter

····· **DO THIS FIRST** ······

BUTTER: Cut all the butter for crust and filling into small pieces. Keep the two measurements of butter separate.
CREAM CHEESE: Cut the cream cheese into small pieces.

1. *Make cobbler crust.* Measure flour, baking powder and salt directly into food processor with the steel blade in place. Pulse to combine. Add the pieces of butter and cream cheese to the processor. Attach lid and pulse 6 to 7 times (1-second pulses), until mixture looks like coarse crumbs. Uncover and evenly drizzle vinegar and water over mixture. Attach lid and pulse about 6 times until mixture begins to clump together—it won't form a ball. Uncover and turn dough out onto a large sheet of plastic wrap. Press pieces of dough together, gather plastic wrap over top, then flatten into a 10-inch square. Refrigerate 1 hour.

2. *Prepare filling.* Peel peaches. Cut peach away from the pit. Cut the peaches into small ($1/2$-inch) pieces. Measure to make sure you have about 6 cups. In a large bowl, mix together peaches, sugar, cornstarch, nutmeg, lemon or lime juice and salt.

3. *Assemble cobbler.* Adjust shelf to middle of oven and heat to 400°F. Remove dough from refrigerator. Unwrap and, using a knife, cut off $1/3$ of dough. Rewrap and refrigerate the "$1/3$" piece. Evenly flour work surface and remaining $2/3$ of dough. With rolling pin, roll into an 14 x 18-inch rectangle. Drape into a 9 x 13-inch ungreased baking dish, easing dough all the way into corners and allowing a little to hang over top rim of dish. (If kitchen is hot, refrigerate dough-lined baking dish.) Re-flour work surface and evenly flour remaining $1/3$ of dough. Roll into 14 x 10-inch rectangle. Cut lengthwise into ten 1-inch strips. Brush top edge of overhanging dough with a *light* coating of milk—just enough to make it sticky. Pour fruit mixture in pan. Dot little pieces of remaining *2 tablespoons* butter over filling. Lay 4 strips of dough at even intervals lengthwise over fruit. Lay the remaining strips of dough at even intervals crosswise over fruit, creating a lattice. Press rim with a fork to seal strips to moistened edge. Trim off any overhanging dough. Brush lattice with milk. Sprinkle with a little sugar.

4. *Bake cobbler.* Bake 15 minutes. Reduce temperature to 350°F. and bake 30 to 40 minutes longer, until fruit mixture is thick and bubbling and crust is browned. Cool 10 minutes before serving, or cool completely and rewarm in a 350°F oven for 10 to 15 minutes.

SERVES 10 GENEROUSLY

Lanie peeling peaches with her grandma

Grandma's Moist Apple Cake {or Muffins}

RICK: *This moist, wonderfully textured, cinnamon-infused apple cake is my mom's specialty—but only as of fairly recently. Odd as it may sound, she didn't cook all that much when I was growing up. I guess that's one of the hazards (or benefits) of being in the restaurant business. Since her retirement, though, she has started trying a lot more stuff. Mom's cake is made with oil, which reveals that this is really a variation on the carrot cakes of the '60s and '70s. Now, I'm evolving it—replacing part of the oil with delicious-tasting butter and decreasing the sugar. I've also discovered that this is versatile enough to be made as a Bundt or layer cake, or even muffins. The cake's texture is best (it slices most evenly) if made a day ahead.*

❈   ❈   ❈   ❈   ❈   ❈

LANIE: *Pure autumn. I connect this cake to Thanksgiving, since we almost always make it then. (Except when we make it into muffins—then you could have it anytime.) Two things: McIntosh apples make the creamiest cake (Granny Smiths are way too firm—they don't mush up when cooked). I like it best with chocolate glaze (opposite page), though sprinkling with powdered sugar is easier.*

1 cup (about 4 ounces) chopped nuts (we mostly use pecans, but it is also good with walnuts, cashews, macadamias, practically any nut)

3 cups (15 ounces) all-purpose flour, plus a little extra for dusting pan(s)

1 teaspoon baking soda

1 teaspoon ground cinnamon

½ teaspoon salt

1¾ cups sugar

¾ cup vegetable oil, plus a little extra for greasing pan(s)

4 ounces (8 tablespoons, 1 stick) unsalted butter
OR an additional ½ cup vegetable oil

2 "large" eggs

¼ cup sour cream, plain or vanilla yogurt or milk

3 medium apples (about 1½ pounds)

····· **DO THIS FIRST** ·····

OVEN: Position rack in middle of oven. Turn on to 325°F.

BUTTER: Unwrap and place in small bowl. Microwave at 50% power for 2 minutes to melt almost completely.

APPLES: Cut apples in quarters down through stem end. On cut side, use small knife to cut out tough core where seeds are. Peel quarters. Chop apples into small pieces—no bigger than ½ inch. You need to have a generous 3½ cups.

PAN: Choose one 10-inch Bundt or tube (angelfood) pan, two 9-inch round cake pans, or two 12-portion muffin pans. Smear bottom and sides carefully with a little oil. Only 18 muffin cups are needed. Sprinkle in a little flour. Tilt around to coat bottom completely. It doesn't have to coat sides. Shake out excess into trash can or sink.

1. *Toast nuts.* Spread nuts on a baking sheet and slide into preheated oven. Bake until toasty smelling—7 or 8 minutes for small nuts or pieces, 10 to 12 minutes for larger ones. Remove nuts from oven and set aside, but leave oven on for baking cake.

2. *Make batter.* Sift flour, baking soda, cinnamon and salt through sifter or wire-mesh strainer into a medium bowl. In another large bowl, combine the sugar, oil, melted butter, eggs and sour cream, yogurt or milk. Beat with a large spoon to mix well. Add the flour mixture and stir to mix thoroughly. Add apple pieces and nuts. Stir to combine thoroughly. (It's easiest to use a clean hand because batter is stiff.) Scoop (or divide evenly) into prepared pan(s).

3. *Bake cake:* Slide pan(s) into oven and bake about 1 hour for Bundt or tube (angelfood) pan or 35 to 40 minutes for layers or muffins, until the cake pulls away slightly from the mold and feels springy in the center. Remove and cool for 5 minutes, then unmold onto a cooling rack to cool completely. The cake is great served as is, or for a special presentation you can glaze it (see below).

MAKES ONE 10-INCH BUNDT OR TUBE CAKE, TWO 9-INCH CAKE LAYERS, OR 18 MUFFINS

Flaky "Mexican" cinnamon sticks

Two Glazes for the Cake

APRICOT GLAZE: In a small saucepan, melt 1 cup apricot jam over medium heat, stirring until runny. Brush or drizzle (from a spoon) over the cake.

CHOCOLATE GLAZE: Microwave 1/3 cup milk in a glass measure until steaming (about 1 minute at 100% power). Break up 4 ounces semi-sweet chocolate, put it in a food processor and process until finely chopped. With the processor still running, slowly pour in hot milk through the feed tube. When the whole thing is smooth, turn off the processor. Measure in 3 tablespoons corn syrup and process to combine. Let cool until thick enough to drizzle over the cake without entirely running off.

THE BEST: Brush the cake all over with apricot glaze. Then make the chocolate glaze and drizzle that on. (Since the cake already has apricot glaze, you'll need only about half of the chocolate glaze; eat the rest.) Sprinkle the top with chopped nuts.

Rick's Favorite Chocolate Birthday Cake

RICK: *I can't say* objectively, definitively *that this is the absolute best chocolate in the world. But since my grandma made it for us all the time, it has to be perfect, right? Still... it's a really good chocolate cake... no matter who makes it. Butter-milk gives it a rich flavor. Hot coffee brings out the taste of the cocoa and gives it a moist texture—edging toward poundcake. Grandma made a frosting with Crisco, cocoa and powdered sugar, but that's not my thing—too gritty and bland. So I make this incredibly creamy chocolate-cream frosting (like what the pastry chefs call* ganache), *based on one I picked up from* Cook's Illustrated *magazine. Very spe-cial, very luxurious. Two notes: To make it easy to remove the cakes perfectly from the pans (especially if they're not non-stick), line the pans with rounds of parch-ment paper or wax paper. For the best flavored cake, use Hershey's Dutch-processed cocoa (or the fabulous Scharffen Berger).*

✕   ✕   ✕   ✕   ✕   ✕

LANIE: *I don't know about you, but chocolate cake—even not-so-great chocolate cake—is ALWAYS worth eating. It's* CHOCOLATE! *And this is so much better than any regular old chocolate cake. It takes a while to make, so be ready for that. First time I made it, I packed the flour down into the cups, which is definitely NOT THE RIGHT THING! (The cake was kind of dry.) Stir the flour, scoop it up and level it off. If the cakes poof up in the middle, cut them off flat with a long serrated knife when cool. I'm not the biggest fan of semisweet chocolate, but it is good in this frosting.*

FOR THE CAKE
¼ cup vegetable oil, plus a little extra for greasing pans
4 ounces (8 tablespoons, 1 stick) unsalted butter
2 cups dark brown sugar
3 "large" eggs
2 teaspoons vanilla extract
2 cups (10 ounces) all-purpose flour, plus a little extra for dusting cake pans
A scant teaspoon baking soda
½ cup cocoa powder
½ teaspoon salt
1 cup buttermilk
1 cup hot coffee

FOR THE FROSTING
1 pound bittersweet or semisweet chocolate
1¼ cups heavy (whipping) cream
⅓ cup corn syrup
¼ cup espresso, very strong coffee or hot water

······ DO THIS FIRST ······

OVEN: Adjust rack to middle and turn on to 350°F.
BUTTER: Melt in a small saucepan over medium heat or in a small bowl in microwave (2 minutes at 50% power).
CHOCOLATE: Chop into roughly ½-inch pieces.
CAKE PANS: Spray or smear a light coat of oil, butter or vegetable shorten-ing over the bottom and sides of two 9-inch round cake pans. Spoon about 1 tablespoon flour into each pan. Tip to coat evenly. Shake out and discard excess.

1. *Make cake batter.* In mixer bowl, combine the vegetable oil, melted butter, brown sugar, eggs and vanilla. Beat with mixer on medium-high speed until homogenous and fluffy, about 1 minute. Into medium bowl, sift together flour, baking soda, cocoa powder and salt. With mixer on medium-low speed, scoop in $\frac{1}{3}$ of flour mixture. When mostly incorporated, add $\frac{1}{3}$ of the buttermilk. Continue with 2 more additions of flour mixture and buttermilk. Beat on medium speed for 1 minute more. Remove bowl from mixer. Pour hot coffee over batter and stir to combine.

2. *Bake cakes.* Divide batter between prepared pans. Slide into oven and bake until cakes have pulled away slightly from side of pans and a toothpick inserted near the center comes out with no sticky batter, about 25 minutes. Remove from oven, and allow to cool 10 minutes. Then, turn cakes out onto wire rack to cool completely.

3. *Make frosting.* While cake is baking, place chocolate pieces in food processor and chop with 1-second pulses until no piece is larger than a pea. In a small saucepan, combine the cream, corn syrup and espresso, coffee or hot water. Heat over medium—stirring regularly—until steaming. Turn on processor and pour hot cream mixture through feed tube. When chocolate is melted, turn off processor, remove lid and blade, then scrape mixture into a bowl. Place in refrigerator and stir every 15 minutes until spreadable, about $1\frac{1}{2}$ hours. (Can be made ahead, covered and refrigerated; let stand at room temperature one hour, then re-beat in food processor or with mixer.)

4. *Frost cake.* Use about $\frac{1}{4}$ of the frosting between the layers. Then spread half of what is left on the sides and the rest on top. (See following page for details.)

SERVES 16

❊ How to Frost a Cake and Make It Dazzle ❊

The easiest way to frost a cake, of course, is just to smear the frosting all over it and call it done. But for special occasions, most of us want the cake to be a show-stopper. Here's what I do:

1. Level the cake layers: *After cake layers have cooled upside down on cake racks, turn them right side up onto individual sheets of waxed or parchment paper. If cakes are domed a little on top, use a long serrated (aka "bread") knife to slice off the rounded tops so that the cakes are level.*

2. Make a cake "sandwich." *Flip one cake layer upside down on to the center of a cake plate or whatever you're serving the cake on. Spread 1/4 of the frosting evenly over the top of the cake, up to the edges. Spreading frosting is easiest to do with a long, narrow metal straight or offset spatula (or use the widest table knife you have—rubber spatulas don't offer enough control for me). Flip the second layer upside down on top of the first. (The layers are flipped over because it is very hard to frost cut cake.)*

3. Frost the sides. *Carefully spread about half the remaining frosting over the sides of the cake. Scoop up some frosting and, holding the metal spatula or knife vertically (blade pointing down), use a gentle rocking, side-to-side movement to work the frosting into an even layer over a small section. Continue until the sides are evenly covered.*

4. Frost the top. *Scoop the remaining frosting onto the middle of the top of the cake. Spread the frosting in an even, smooth layer, starting from the center and working outward in a widening circle, turning the plate slowly as you increase the size of the circle. Spread the frosting out past the edges of the cake so it hangs over a little.*

5. Make it look "pretty." *Holding the spatula vertically as you did when you first frosted the sides, go around the cake again, this time working the frosting that over-hangs the top smoothly down onto the sides. This should create a nice-looking edge.*

6. Make it dazzle. *If you're really good with the spatula, your cake will look like a perfect round box, ready for you to use a pastry bag and fluted tip to create spectacular swirling borders. Most of us aren't that advanced, but we do have plenty of options: (1) Cut a star (or some other bold image) out of waxed, parchment or construction paper. Lay it on top of the cake, and sprinkle the entire top with powdered sugar; remove the star. (2) Using the back of a soup spoon (or something similar), work the frosting on the top into big "waves" (you can do it on the sides, too, if you want). (3) Sprinkle powdered sugar, cocoa powder, white or dark mini chocolate chips (or other candy bits), chopped nuts, candy "confetti" or those little colored (or silvery) balls called nonpareils over the top of the cake (a wavy top is fine); in short, you can sprinkle on anything that goes with sweet. (4) Crush cookies (Oreos, Amaretti, Ferrero Rocher, Pecan Sandies, practically anything crispy) and use to form a border around (or a design on) the top of the cake. (5) Crushed cookies or chopped nuts can be pressed into the sides, either to cover it completely or to make a border at the bottom.*

FRANCE
{with side trips to Italy and Ireland}

❀ ❀ ❀ ❀ ❀ ❀

Rick: Walking out of our hotel on Paris's Left Bank, I was struck by how thoroughly comfortable the French are with beauty. The buildings are beautifully built, as though generations of architects and builders conspired to add to the long-lasting majesty that has been developing in the city for centuries. The fashionable boutiques fill their windows with styles that are up-to-date, yet timelessly beautiful, stately and comfortably sexy. The pastry shops, bakeries and chocolate shops (of which there are many) set out tasty morsels as if they were rings or bracelets at Tiffany. It was clear to me that Parisian craftsmen strive for greater and greater heights, knowing that their customers deeply appreciate their creations, that people from all over the world admire their expertise.

We were in Paris to celebrate an *important* birthday of our close friend Jewel Hoogstoel. The birthday dinner was to take place on one of those barge-like boat/restaurants that navigate the waters of the Seine, the river that divides the right bank of Paris from the left. Floating by those beautifully lit, centuries-old, massive stone buildings in the electric air of a Parisian spring evening is a most memorable way to see the city—or to celebrate a birthday, or just to celebrate life.

But on this day we were on our way to Brie-Comte-Robert, a town 45 minutes outside of Paris where Bob, Jewel's husband, had family. Knowing that Lanie and I love to cook family fare with families wherever we go, Bob had arranged for us to spend a day in Brie, in the kitchen of his relatives, the

Coussements. The oldest daughter, Stephanie, collected us at our hotel and drove us to the historic town her family had inhabited for generations. When we arrived in Brie, Josette, her mother, was waiting to guide us the two blocks through narrow streets to the food market that is set up twice a week right in the middle of the small downtown.

I found Brie's market to be nothing like the earthy, raucous, jam-packed markets I'm accustomed to in Mexico and Thailand. Though set up in the middle of the street, the stalls were attached by a neat canopy that stretched over them all. Each stall was identified by a carefully lettered sign noting the vendor's name, the items they were selling and the prices. There were stalls of hand-crafted cheeses, ice-packed fresh fish from the Atlantic and the Mediterranean, meat (from beef to lamb and rabbit) and poultry (chicken, guinea hens, quail) and, of course, a myriad of delicious, attractive fruits and vegetables.

If it weren't for the absence of walls and a roof, you would have sworn you were in a fancy-food emporium in New York or San Francisco.

Josette kept asking *me* to pick out the ingredients. Because I'm a chef (a very well-respected craft in France), she was deferring to what she assumed was my well-honed expertise in both food quality and preparation. Trouble was, I was hoping to learn from her. And besides, I didn't even know what she was planning to cook. In retrospect, I doubt she herself knew until we'd finished looking over the market's offerings.

French Profiteroles, recipe on page 148

Now, Josette is no wild-eyed gourmet who thinks about food every waking minute. She's just a mom who's been putting tasty, made-from-scratch food on her family's table for many years, like other women in her town. And through the years, she's mastered a slew of different dishes for every ingredient in her market. "What's so hard about cooking?" she seemed to be asking with each of our purchases.

Standing at one of the vegetable stalls, I was eyeing some little radishes for a couple of moments—the really mild ones we call "French breakfast" radishes (the 2-inch-long, bullet-shaped variety that fades from deep red to pale white) when Josette asked if I liked them. *Like* them? I *love* them. So we bought several large bunches, which seemed like a huge amount to me.

Then she asked what cheeses I liked. I haven't found a French cheese I *don't* like (the French are the world's foremost cheesemakers in my opinion), so my answer was stuttering, indecisive. Perhaps that was the moment Josette gave up on my "I love everything" attitude. Happily for me, she took charge, buying first some fresh, light, creamy white cheese called *fromage blanc* and a piece of Coulommiers goat cheese, then a kilo of potatoes, shallots, fresh herb bouquets, several knobby celery roots and baskets of strawberries.

Just across from the street market were a series of small food shops, each smaller than a drink-and-dash Starbucks. We stopped first at a butcher's shop with granite counters and pristine display cases full of prepared dishes, pates and terrines that looked worthy of a magazine cover. Josette picked out a big chunk of head cheese (pieces of briny, cured meat from the . . . yes . . . pig's head, pressed together with herbs and spices from the case). Then, examining the sausage selection hanging above it, she chose several little fresh

sausages. Finally she selected cubes of veal for stewing and meaty salted pork ribs from the fresh meat case. We bought a few long loaves of crackling-crusty French baguette bread at the bakery next door. And we drooled over the Easter chocolates that had just been put on display a couple of doors down as we headed back to Josette's place to start cooking.

The Coussements' house, built a couple of centuries ago, had thick walls and small rooms—more cozy cottage than stately house. The entryway contained little more than an overpiled coat tree, tiny wash room, stairs to the bedrooms above, and enough room to turn around in. But the living room was just about as welcoming a place as I've ever been: The plastered walls were covered with soft cloth and the room was comfortably filled with a beckoning couch, an upright piano, a stone fireplace and a couple of round tables, each draped with a floor-length cloth and covered with family photos and lamps. On the side toward the kitchen, there was a dining room table large enough to seat a dozen people or more. I felt completely, thoroughly at home.

The kitchen was smallish, too, closed off from the living room by curtained French doors. Lanie and I unpacked our purchases on the kitchen table and began preparing the radishes according to Josette's directions: We cut off the leaves, leaving a half inch of the stem, placed the leaves in a large colander for washing, then carefully checked the stem "nub" of each radish to make sure not even one was slightly withered. We still didn't know what we were making.

Josette was busy layering the pork ribs with tomatoes, mushrooms and potatoes in a large enameled cast-iron pot that she'd had for 30 years. In another pot, she melted butter and told me to add the washed radish leaves. When they were wilted, she added a couple of small potatoes and chicken broth (made by dissolving bouillon cubes in water), simmered it all for a few minutes, then got out one of those immersion blenders and pureed the unlikely mixture to a tasty, creamy, pale-green soup. *Radish leaf* soup—which got even tastier and creamier when she added some of that famous French sour cream, *crème fraîche*. I thought it was amazingly good. Josette decided it had too much potato—not silky enough for her.

Around noon, Josette's husband, Thierry, one of the town's physicians, came home to join us for lunch, which started around the fireplace with a glass of Savoie wine, slices of bread and head cheese, little pickles and, as you might imagine, a large bowl of radishes accompanied by coarse salt to dip them into. Before long, Stephanie showed up again, as did her brothers Robin (who attended a nearby college) and Julien (still in high school). It was time to gather at the table.

After we enjoyed the radish leaf soup, ladled into small bowls from a huge white tureen, Josette brought the braised pork rib dish to the table still in its cooking pot. A mouthwatering, meaty aroma flooded the room when Bob lifted the lid, moving the conversation (partly in French, partly in English) from first gear to second. Before long I was writing down the details of how to make tartiflette, the potato-cheese-bacon dish the Coussements love to eat on ski trips to the Savoie. That launched us into further conversation about the specialties of other French regions, which spilled out so fast I could barely keep up. The family suggested I come back to film a television series on the regional specialties of France—which they would direct! Robin would drive our production van, Stephanie and her mom would explain the details of the food, and Julien would help us find cool places to shoot. Thierry would taste everything and let us know if it was good or not.

Dessert was utterly casual. Each of us spooned some fromage blanc onto our plates, then topped it with a sprinkling of sugar and a few small, deep-red strawberries. Nothing fancy, nothing better.

This lovely, homey, perfectly French meal, infused with sporty conversation, was the most I could have hoped for. But it wasn't all that Josette had planned. There was more

cooking to be done. There was dinner.

Except for the dessert, the evening meal seemed to materialize on its own throughout an afternoon filled with a little shopping, sightseeing, lively chatter and the comings-and-goings of family and friends. Lanie had been spirited off to go clothes shopping with Stephanie, returning home with barely enough time for the two of them to make Stephanie's great-grandmother's recipe for the quintessential homey dessert: store-bought butter cookies, dipped in lightly rum-scented syrup and layered with a frothy buttercream. The sweet gets refrigerated until the cookies soften and the whole thing settles into that thick pudding-like texture that practically everyone loves—especially kids. I remember many meals from my own youth that ended with a similarly textured pudding created by layering banana pudding with vanilla wafers.

The sun had set by the time we started eating again. The warm flicker of the candles on the dinner table and the golden glow from table lamps that surrounded it gave the Coussements' dining room the most romantic feel imaginable. Dinner began with soup as had lunch—this time a creamy soup made by simmering the big bulbous root of the celery plant (think of it as a cross between celery and potato), then blending it until smooth with the cooking water. To give that creamy texture, butter and flour were whisked into the simmering soup.

Our main dish was *blanquette de veau*—a veal stew which Josette made by first sautéing veal cubes with garlic and shallots (the small aromatic onion-like vegetable with a taste somewhere between mild onion and garlic—very common in France), then adding herbs, carrots, mushrooms and broth, simmering until the meat was tender. The mixture was thickened to a beautiful creaminess with flour and butter, just as the soup had been. And, to set her veal stew apart from others, Josette added sorrel, the lemony herb/green that's always associated with spring cooking in France.

There we were in France, the place most people consider to be the food capital of the world, sitting around the Coussements' dining table laid with a fine damask cloth and set with *silver* silverware that had belonged to her grandmother. And we were eating stew—good stew, traditionally flavored French stew—but a stew no more complicated to make than what my grandmother used to turn out in Oklahoma City.

Yet, I found myself thinking something was different, and it had to do with art and craft. In France, food is a respected member of the arts community; cooking is a long-treasured craft. Everyday cooks like Josette move in a culture where good cooking is the expectation, just as one might be expected to be conversant with classic literature, or play the piano, or plant a beautiful garden. Over the centuries, it seems that France has decided that it is the arts—from dining to dance—that propel its culture forward. Whether designing a beautiful store window or a high fashion gown for Chanel, whether perfecting an intricately crafted pastry or making a homey French veal stew, the French seem to have collectively bought into the idea that all the arts and crafts are as important as, say, computer technology and factory efficiency are to us Americans.

Our veal stew wasn't the creation of one singularly talented cook, but rather that of a vast culture of talented ranchers, farmers, butchers and, finally, cooks—of which Josette was a shining example. What I tasted that evening, between Thierry's teases, Josette's laughter and the kids' wry pranks, was centuries of harmony created by generations of revered artists and craftsmen. I tasted the love and respect that brings so many to France to eat.

❊ ❊ ❊ ❊ ❊ ❊

Lanie: Of all the places I've been, France was probably my favorite. No, it WAS my favorite. I mean, it's *totally* cool, because the hotel we stayed in had a *fashion channel* on the television! I was sharing a room with my grandmother—we were both visiting Paris for the *first* time—and she let me watch the Fashion Channel whenever I wanted. Models walking that way models walk—I've learned how to do it *really* well since we got back.

And when we walked out of our hotel and down to Rennes Street and then up to the St. Germain des Prés subway stop, we walked right past all these *really cool* pastry shops (French pastries are my absolute favorite) and boutiques. And right past Cartier, which I have known about since I watched Marilyn Monroe (one of my favorites) in *Gentlemen Prefer Blondes*.

But enough about all that, since we were really there for our friend Jewel's birthday, for Easter, and (a little late) for my Grandma's birthday. And to cook with Jewel's way-distant-in-laws—second cousins of Bob (her husband). I was totally psyched about seeing the Champs Elysées (a beautiful big street with Big Name stores) and the Eiffel Tower (*oh yeah*). My dad made sure I saw (1) the Louvre Museum (we got lost . . . meaning lots of wandering, which my grandma did *not* appreciate—but I did see the Mona Lisa and Winged Victory); (2) Nôtre Dame (where we went for Easter service, which would have been cool, except that it was so jam-packed we had to stand through the *whole* service—in French—and we could barely see); (3) those food shops in the Place de la Madeleine—where we bought some amazing flavored macaroons (not the coconut kind) from that famous place called Ladurée; and (4) a bunch of parks and stores and stuff. And restaurants . . .

This is SO my dad: He took me "souvenir" shopping to this very famous, *very old* restaurant cookware shop, Dehillerin (right by the 24-hour bistro where my dad ate pigs feet and I had steak tartare—*okay,* it's *my* weird thing—and orange crêpes like the ones in this chapter). And he told me to pick out something. What was he thinking? A big copper "souvenir" pot? A cast-iron skillet to carry home in *my* suitcase? That was *not* an easy project for me, which I think he figured out, since he finally suggested I get these rubbery molds to bake funny-shape muffins in (which I don't think we've used yet).

When the day came to cook with Bob's relatives, Stephanie picked us up and she was *totally cool.* She decorates the windows for this famous pastry shop (Dalloyau—we went there—*totally awesome*) and works for this guy who organizes Big Name weddings, too. Her parents have this house in the old section of Brie, a small town outside Paris. (She lives in Paris now and is getting married to Laurent.) The house is made out of stone, like all of them around there, and the streets are narrow. And once or twice a week they have a food market set up nearby.

Which is where we went first, guided by Josette, Stephanie's mom. I was in charge of paying for everything in Euros. Markets in the street seem *completely* different from our grocery stores, though this one felt more "regular" than markets we've visited in other countries.

This market would be the kind of place you'd love to have around the corner if you needed to make something to eat in a hurry. The food isn't all wrapped up like what we're used to, so you can just go there and taste a bunch of stuff, then decide what you want to eat and buy it.

My favorite parts were the cheeses (I could taste just about any cheese I wanted) and flowers—definitely not the fish, because they were all whole, lying there on ice right in front of you. That kind of gives me the creeps.

After we bought bags and bags of food, we went back to Josette's house to cook lunch. Stephanie went off to see her friend, which bummed me out, because she left us with all these radishes to clean. (Everyone was really nice, though, so we had fun.) Josette's kitchen was pretty normal looking, meaning I felt comfortable. We did all the prep work for a soup. I was in charge of taking notes about how to make it (a little difficult at first, since we weren't exactly sure what we were making).

Radish leaf soup didn't *sound* very appetizing, but I liked it when we actually sat down to eat it. (During the "appetizers" before lunch, I ate some of the radishes with salt, but avoided the head cheese, mostly because they told me what it was made of—why would they do that?) Even though I didn't know anybody, everyone in the family is really fun at the table. Thierry (Josette's husband) opened the wine bottle with this fancy corkscrew which is called a "rabbit," but which he said *should* be called a "hen" because it plopped out the cork like it was laying an egg—

he clucked when it happened. Which made everyone laugh a lot. Especially our friend Bob, whose name they pronounced something like "Bub," like the inspector would in those old Pink Panther movies. That made me and my parents laugh a lot. Every person at the table was having such a good time that we stayed for a *really* long time.

No one wanted to leave, until Thierry said he had to go back to work. And Stephanie said she wanted to take me to buy clothes. *Awesome!* Well, *almost* awesome, since the place we went turned out to be a little like a French Target with a lot of cool American-style jeans. I couldn't resist buying a pair of "French" jeans, even though they were pretty much what I could get back home.

My parents went out searching for that "hen" corkscrew (my dad's souvenir). And then they went to a chocolate shop to buy an Easter present for Josette, which I told them was totally unfair, because *I* wanted to go with them to buy chocolates. It turned out okay because a little later we all wound up walking back to the place where the market was (gone by this time): My dad found his corkscrew, I found a cool clothes boutique, we all went together to another chocolate shop and we visited the town's old church, which everyone said was way older than our whole country.

After that, we helped cook dinner, which didn't take too long. I didn't like the celery root soup very much—it was just okay. But I did like the veal dish, even though we don't eat veal very much (tastes like chicken), and mushrooms aren't my favorite thing. It had a kind of lemony flavor from this green leaf called sorrel which hardly *anyone* has heard of. But we have some growing in the garden at home, so I know it and happen to like it.

Stephanie and I got to make dessert (this cake sort of thing), following a recipe that was her grandmother's. We had to beat butter, sugar and egg yolks together, then beat egg whites and fold them in. That's when it happened.

I swear it wasn't my fault. My hands were slippery from the butter or something, and I was trying to take a picture of what the mixture looked like, and my dad's digital camera fell into the batter. I was totally shaking on the inside, the way you do when your teacher calls on you to answer and you weren't listening.

It took a while to clean the camera off (I totally learned that sugary things aren't good for electronic equipment)

and get back to the dessert. Which actually turned out pretty good. You layer the fluffy sweet butter mixture (it still tasted okay, even though it had had a camera in it) with butter cookies and sprinkle grated chocolate over the top.

We got back to Paris pretty late—it was a day I'll never forget.

I'll never forget our last meal in Paris, either. We went to this famous old, old café that my Dad knew about (Les Deux Magots), and I ate a *croque monsieur.* Which is basically French for a really good toasted ham and cheese sandwich. Now, I've eaten quite a few *croque monsieurs,* and they're not all alike. My friend Kim's mother used to make *croque monsieur* for her school lunch, because her dad's an international pilot, and they've been to France a bunch of times. And Kim's mother knows I like *croque monsieur,* so she'd always make an extra piece for Kim to give to me.

At the French bistro near our house, the cook lets the cheese run out of the sandwich and into the skillet where it browns. When it comes to the table, it looks like the sandwich has got a stiff lace collar on. And at the French bistro near our restaurant, they coat the whole thing in creamy white sauce, sprinkle it with cheese and bake it—more a full meal than a sandwich, I think.

Well, at that café in Paris, my *croque monsieur* was just the way I like it. Only better. Or should I say "butter"— because that's what I tasted most. They must have used that rich yellow bread and, like, the best cheese and ham. And they must have cooked it slow in lots of butter, until it turned that incredible brown color.

I love Paris.

Eggs on the Eights

LANIE: *No brainer here. Eggs. Bacon. Potatoes. Easy. I mean,* what's not to like? *It only took me one try to get it right. Now I make it a lot on Sunday mornings. You should, too. P.S. All this "eights" business is because my dad was trying to teach me how to make this when I was* really little. *Easy to remember and all that.*

×　×　×　×　×　×

RICK: *I say "ditto" to Lanie's love for eggs, bacon and potatoes. But if you've ever been the one to fry bacon, cook eggs over easy and make hash browns for six people, you know it takes a while. This dish is a big, oven-baked omelet—they call it a* fritatta *in Italian, though the Italians would think this one tastes American because of our smoky bacon (they'd use unsmoked pancetta or bits of prosciutto ham). And it combines all those delicious ingredients in one easy, impressive-looking preparation. Like she says, perfect for Sunday morning.*

3 to 4 bacon slices

4 medium (1 pound total) boiling potatoes (red skins or Yukon golds are our favorites)

2 garlic cloves

Salt

8 "large" eggs

······ **DO THIS FIRST** ······

BACON: Cut crosswise into 1-inch pieces.
POTATOES: Peel. Cut each one in half, then cut halves into four equal-sized pieces. Place in a microwave-safe bowl.
GARLIC: Peel.
EGGS: Crack eggs into a bowl and beat with a fork to break up yolks.
OVEN: Place rack in middle of oven and turn on to 350°F.

Set 10-inch non-stick skillet with ovenproof handle over medium heat. Lay bacon in pan, spreading into single layer. Cook 8 minutes—stirring occasionally—until it begins to brown. While bacon is cooking, cover bowl containing potatoes with plastic wrap and poke a hole in the plastic. Microwave on high (100%) power for 5 minutes, until potatoes are almost tender. Add potatoes to pan with bacon and cook another 8 minutes—stirring occasionally. Crush garlic through press into skillet; stir in thoroughly. Sprinkle 1/2 teaspoon salt over the eggs. Add the eggs to the skillet. Stir slowly 8 times. Place in oven and bake for 8 minutes. Loosen around the edges and slide onto a serving platter. Cut into wedges and serve. (Chopped chives or fresh thyme or parsley sprinkled on top makes this look really appetizing.)

SERVES 6

Bob's Dutch Baby

LANIE: *Bob is our friend who took us to visit his family in France, and he taught us how to make Dutch Baby. My mother's Dutch, and she says this dish is NOT Dutch. And it definitely doesn't look like a baby. So I'm CLUELESS about everything but Bob. Anyway, it's good and cool-looking—a puffy-crispy BOWL! (It's cool to watch the sides rise up as it bakes.) We fill the edible bowl with fruit and drench the whole thing with syrup. Powdered sugar sprinkled over the top (put a spoonful in a little strainer and shake it on) is essential.*

✂ ✂ ✂ ✂ ✂ ✂

RICK: *If you've ever had a great big puffy skillet full of apple oven pancake, this is similar. Since the apples aren't baked into it, the whole thing comes out crisper. About fruit, I suggest you change with the seasons: use strawberries (green leaves removed) in early spring, blackberries and raspberries in early summer, peaches and nectarines (peeled and pitted) in mid-summer, and apples and pears (peeled and cored) in fall and winter. (Citrus fruit like oranges and grapefruit are really too juicy to use.) For an over-the-top experience, dollop some lightly sweetened whipped cream (or not-so-over-the-top yogurt) on the fruit before sprinkling with sugar.*

2½ ounces (5 tablespoons) butter
¾ cup flour
3 "large" eggs
¾ cup milk
½ teaspoon salt
3 cups fruit (see Rick's note)
A little powdered sugar
Syrup (we use maple or blueberry, but any syrup will do)

······ **DO THIS FIRST** ······

OVEN: Adjust rack to upper third of oven. Turn on to 450°F.
FRUIT: Cut fruit (except small berries) into small pieces about ½ inch.
SYRUP: Warm syrup over low heat or in a microwave at 50% power for 1 minute just before serving.

---

1. *Melt butter.* Put butter in very large (12-inch) skillet with oven-proof handle. Set in oven for 5 minutes to melt butter completely—okay if it begins to brown.

2. *Make batter.* While butter melts, measure flour into large bowl. Add eggs, milk and salt. Beat until smooth, using a whisk, large spoon or hand-held electric mixer.

3. *Bake and serve.* Pour batter into hot pan. Return to oven and bake 15 to 20 minutes, until sides are puffed up and dark golden brown. Remove from oven. Loosen from sides and bottom of skillet, then slide onto serving plate. Pile fruit in center and sprinkle with powdered sugar. Cut into wedges. Pass warm syrup to pour on top.

SERVES 4 TO 5

French *Gougères* {Cheese Puffs}

LANIE: *These are just like the cream puffs you make for the profiteroles on page 148 (my favorites), except you put cheese in the batter and you don't serve them with ice cream and chocolate sauce. In fact, you don't fill them at all. They're like something you put out at a party and just pick up. Really good—especially if the Swiss cheese isn't too strong.*

❊　❊　❊　❊　❊　❊

RICK: *Just as when you're making profiteroles, keep in mind two things: Let the cooked base cool for 5 minutes before adding the eggs, and make sure the oven is completely up to temperature before sliding in the baking sheets. They're delicious both warm and at room temperature. You can also make them ahead, wrap them well and freeze them for up to three months. When you want to make a party or meal something special, pop these, frozen, into a 350°F oven for 5 to 10 minutes to warm and crisp. Pile them on a big platter and top with a snowy sprinkling of grated Parmesan. I think it's worth getting imported (stronger tasting—sorry, Lanie) Gruyère or Emmenthaler cheese.*

Salt

4 ounces (8 tablespoons, 1 stick) butter

1 cup (5 ounces) all-purpose flour

5 "large" eggs

4 ounces Swiss cheese

······ **DO THIS FIRST** ······

BUTTER: Cut into 8 pieces.

FLOUR: Measure out and set by stove.

EGGS: Break into a large measuring cup. Beat with a fork until smooth. Pour off and discard anything over 1 cup.

CHEESE: Grate cheese.

BAKING SHEETS: Spray or lightly brush 2 baking sheets with oil or line them with parchment paper.

OVEN: Position racks in upper third and lower third of oven. Turn on to 400°F.

1. *Cook cream puff base.* Measure 1 cup water and ½ teaspoon salt in a small (3- to 4-quart) saucepan. Add the pieces of butter. Set over medium heat. When mixture begins to boil, stir continuously until butter melts. Just when butter is melted, add the flour all at once, and stir until the mixture becomes a rough-looking ball and comes free from the sides of the pan. Continue to stir over heat for 3 to 4 minutes. As you stir, smear out paste slowly over bottom of pan; then collect it into a ball and smear it out again. Repeat until paste looks quite shiny.

2. *Add eggs and cheese to base.* Scrape mixture into food processor with metal blade in place. Let cool 5 minutes. Secure top and turn on. Pour beaten eggs slowly through feed tube in a steady stream—should take about 45 seconds. Run machine until mixture becomes smooth—about 15 seconds longer. Add grated cheese and pulse just until well combined. Remove bowl. Pull out blade. Use rubber spatula to scrape mixture off blade and back into processor bowl.

3. *Form puffs.* Use a tiny (1$\frac{1}{4}$-inch wide) ice cream scoop or 2 soup spoons (one to scoop up batter, the other to scoop batter off spoon) to scoop out 48 one-table-spoon mounds. Place mounds about 2 inches apart on baking sheet. (Dip a clean spoon in water and use to smooth top of mounds if they are ragged looking.)

4. *Bake puffs.* Place 1 sheet on each rack in the oven. Bake 8 minutes. Have potholder in hand, then open oven and quickly reverse upper and lower sheets. Bake 8 minutes longer. Turn off oven and set timer for 10 minutes. When timer goes off, prop open oven door slightly with a metal spoon or spatula and set timer for 15 minutes more. Remove puffs from oven and serve.

MAKES 48 PUFFS, ENOUGH TO SERVE 12 TO 18 AS AN APPETIZER/SNACK

French Warm Goat Cheese Salad

RICK: *This salad has become such a popular French export that quite a few American restaurants, even those that don't serve French food, have it on the menu. I'm a fan: warm soft cheese, coated with crunchy crumbs, next to the tangy salad. It's easy, and filling enough to make a light meal. Start with dried bread crumbs rather than fresh (fresh will never crisp). The best are panko crumbs (inspired by the Japanese). Or use day-old rustic bread, such as sourdough or a very crusty baguette: Tear it into pieces, pulse in a food processor until you have coarse crumbs, then dry them out for a couple of minutes on a baking sheet in a 300°F oven. About the vinegar: We prefer wine vinegar but most any will work. And about lettuce: Look for the "variety" mix of small leaves often sold as mesclun lettuce, but small heads of Bibb lettuce taste good too.*

※　※　※　※　※　※

LANIE: *I first ate this at a French restaurant in Chicago near our restaurant—the one with such slow service that we call it the "thank you for your patience" restaurant. (Which may be the reason I liked this salad so much—I was* starving *by the time I got it.) Then, we ate it in France at this café my Dad said was famous because famous old people had eaten there. Which kinda made me yawn, though I would have thought it was pretty cool if Beyoncé had walked through the door. Anyway, it's a really, really good salad because the goat cheese tastes really good warm. Only problem is, in France they make it with salad mixture that has a lot of that curly frisée lettuce in it, which feels to me like you're eating live spiders. At home we make it with a lettuce mix that doesn't have frisée.*

¼ cup plus 1 tablespoon olive or vegetable oil, divided use

¼ teaspoon ground black pepper

1 tablespoon French-style mustard (use smooth or coarse—like Poupon—or practically any mustard except yellow ballpark mustard)

1 teaspoon vinegar

Salt

One 4-ounce log creamy fresh goat cheese

½ cup coarse bread crumbs

6 cups (about 3 ounces) loosely packed small young salad greens (like what's sold as mesclun at well-stocked groceries)

> ······ **DO THIS FIRST** ······
>
> **GOAT CHEESE:** With a thin-bladed knife, cut *cold* log crosswise into 8 disks. If disks crumble, reform into balls and pat into disks—or try cutting with dental floss.
>
> **SALAD GREENS:** Wash. Dry thoroughly with salad spinner or on towels.
>
> **OVEN:** Position rack to 4 to 6 inches below broiler. Turn on to broil.

1. *Make dressing.* In a small jar, combine ¼ cup of the oil, pepper, mustard, vinegar and ¼ teaspoon salt. Secure top and shake to combine thoroughly.

2. *Set up goat cheese for broiling.* In a small bowl, drizzle *1 tablespoon* of the oil over bread crumbs. Use fingers to work oil evenly into crumbs. Spread crumbs onto a plate. Lay goat cheese disks in a single layer over crumbs. Sprinkle crumbs over top. One by one, pat crumbs into disks on all sides, then lay disks on a baking sheet.

3. *Dress salad.* Place salad greens in a large bowl. Shake dressing to mix thoroughly. Drizzle over greens (you may not need all). Toss with tongs to coat evenly. Divide onto 4 salad plates.

4. *Broil goat cheese and serve.* Set cheese under broiler. Cook—watch very carefully and don't walk away—until crumbs are browned and cheese is soft—about 1 minute. Use spatula to turn cheese disks over. Broil until browned. Transfer 2 pieces of goat cheese to each plate. Serve.

SERVES 4

Five Cool CDs to Play While Cooking French

We asked some French teenagers what cool music they listened to and this is what we got: The Beatles, The Kinks, David Bowie and Al Green, plus a little Britney Spears. "No," I said, "I mean cool French music." To which they replied, "We listen to The Beatles, The Kinks . . ." The full list did include some French nationals, though they're not exactly what we'd call "pop" or "rock"—and certainly not hip-hop. (Try Googling "French Pop Music" and you'll see what I mean.) So here is some forever "cool" music that might expand your horizons, plus some very French current stuff.

1. Room with a View/Chambre avec Vue *(Henri Salvador)*—For that smooth, it-could-only-be-French classic sound, you could go for Charles Aznavour (Aznavour: Ses Plus Grands Succès *is a good starter album), but my heart is with Henri Salvador. (The French claim him, even though he was born in French Guyana.) Maybe it's that swaying Bossa Nova beat that infiltrates the French crooner's songs. He's "Buena Vista Social Club" old, but he sounds like he's just getting started.*

2. Du Jazz dans le Ravin *(Serge Gainsbourg)*—My *favorite by the very famous French hipster songwriter of the '60s. Listening to this cool stuff (he's influenced many of today's hot bands), you get a glimpse of how we got* from beatnik cool to techno-lounge—especially his Comic Strip *album.*

3. United *(Phoenix)* or Moon Safari *(Air)*—Phoenix and *Air are two French duos (from Versailles, Julien, my French friend, says) that do some pretty cool, loungy electronic stuff.* Face *magazine called* Moon Safari *the "best post-French house, Seventies California, country-rock concept album of modern love songs." Which means a little of everything or a lot of nothing. I like* United *by Phoenix better (a little more rock-oriented). To me, both sound a lot like "sound track" music, which is why Sofia Coppola used them in her movie.*

4. Tourist *(Saint Germain)*—This group takes the French *techno thing (what Europe's calling the "French Touch") in a jazzier direction by incorporating some Latin rhythms, making for a cool album of groovy dance music—emphasis on the "groovy."*

5. Discovery *(Daft Punk)*—kinda house, kinda derivative, *totally wacky album that I love. So all-over-the-place that it sounds like a different group from track to track. But who cares? Most all of it's danceable.*

Potato-Leek Soup with Bacon

RICK: *This is a European classic that has traveled all over the world—seems like everybody loves it. I based this version on one from our friend Patricia Wells' cookbook* Bistro Cooking, *because it's simple, delicious and classic. She calls for lean slab bacon which typically isn't smoky like regular bacon. I like the taste of smoke so that's what I've called for. Two pounds of Yukon golds are a good alternative to redskin potatoes; they add an almost buttery taste.*

✳   ✳   ✳   ✳   ✳   ✳

LANIE: *I LOVE this soup. Massive comfort food, especially with the bacon which is always a big time comfort food for me. Only one thing: It takes a while to cut up all those leeks and potatoes, so you can't be in a big hurry. Or you can get someone to help—which is usually my plan.*

4 ounces (4 thick slices) bacon
2 pounds (6 medium) leeks
2 pounds potatoes (red-skin are best—
    you need about 9 medium)
½ teaspoon ground black pepper
Salt

Leeks

> ······ **DO THIS FIRST** ······
>
> **BACON:** Cut slices crosswise into ¼-inch strips.
> **LEEKS:** Cut off and discard roots. Cut off all but 3 inches or so of tough dark
>   green top leaves; discard tops. Cut leeks lengthwise from end to end. Rinse
>   carefully to get all dirt out of layers. Cut leeks crosswise into ¼-inch strips.
> **POTATOES:** Peel. Slice ½ inch thick. Cut slices into ½-inch cubes.

1. *Brown bacon.* Set a small (5- to 6-quart) soup pot over medium heat. Add sliced bacon. Cook—stirring frequently—until bacon browns, about 8 minutes.

2. *Cook leeks and potatoes.* Add sliced leeks. Cook—stir frequently—until soft, about 10 minutes more. Add diced potatoes and 1½ quarts water. Bring to a boil. Set lid on pot slightly to one side to allow steam to escape. Simmer—stirring occasionally—for 30 minutes more.

3. *Season and serve.* Check consistency: If thicker than a typical potato soup, add more water. Stir in the pepper and 2 teaspoons salt. Taste and add more salt if you think necessary. Choose soup texture you prefer: chunky-brothy, chunky-smooth or smooth. **For chunky-brothy,** the soup is ready to serve. **For chunky-smooth,** ladle a portion of soup into a food processor (no more than half full) and process until smooth. Pour back into pot. **For smooth,** process all of soup *in batches* as described above and pour into a new pot. Ladle soup into bowls and serve.

MAKES 8 CUPS, ENOUGH TO SERVE 8 TO 10

Creamy Radish Leaf Soup

LANIE: *I know this soup sounds strange (and I didn't say "Oh my gosh!" the first time I tasted it), but I've really gotten to like it. Think potato soup, then add this other mild flavor—like a cross between radishes and lettuce. (No, it's not like eating soup and salad in one bowl!) Josette, our friend in France who showed us how to make it, taught me two things: (1) Put out the radishes left over after you make the soup with salt and* butter *(weird, but good) for a snack before dinner. (2) Using one of those blenders on a stick is really cool. (That's what she used to blend the soup into a puree.)*

❈　❈　❈　❈　❈　❈

RICK: *Honestly, I don't think people would be able to tell what was in this homey, satisfying soup if you didn't tell them. They'd just think it was really good. When Josette made it for us, she added the very rich, not-very-sour French "sour" cream called* crème fraîche. *That's Lanie's favorite, but it's expensive here. I actually like the taste of yogurt better in this soup. Josette used yellow-fleshed charlotte potatoes, but we don't have those in America, so we make our version with the similar textured Yukon golds. Josette surprised me by using water and chicken bouillon cubes in place of broth and it came out tasty. As with most things in cooking, you've got lots of options.*

3 tablespoons butter

2 large bunches radishes with fresh-looking leaves

1⅓ pounds potatoes (Yukon golds are best—you need about 5 medium)

5 cups chicken broth, plus a little more if needed

½ teaspoon ground white pepper

Salt

⅓ cup *crème fraîche*, sour cream or yogurt

⋯⋯ DO THIS FIRST ⋯⋯

RADISHES: Cut leaves off radishes right where stem joins radish. Refrigerate radishes for another use. Sort through leaves and discard any wilted or yellow ones. Wash leaves and dry in salad spinner or on towels. You need about 6 cups lightly packed.

POTATOES: Peel and cut into 1-inch pieces. You need about 3½ cups.

---

1. *Wilt radish leaves.* Set a medium-large (5- to 6-quart) saucepan or small soup pot over medium heat. Add the butter. When melted, add the radish leaves. Cover and cook—stirring every once in a while—until completely wilted, about 15 minutes.

2. *Simmer soup.* Uncover pot. Add potato pieces and broth. Set lid on pan, slightly ajar to allow steam to escape. Simmer until potatoes are fall-apart tender—about 30 minutes.

3. *Blend and serve.* Turn off heat under pot. Use an immersion blender to blend soup until smooth. (If you don't have an immersion blender, use a regular blender— fill blender jar *only half* full. Remove center from blender top, secure top, cover with a kitchen towel and blend until smooth. When soup is blended, pour into a bowl and continue with another batch. Return soup to pot.) Stir in pepper, about 1 teaspoon salt (depending on saltiness of the broth) and *crème fraîche,* sour cream or yogurt. Add more broth if you think the soup is too thick. Taste and add more pepper and salt if you think necessary. Ladle into soup bowls and serve.

MAKES ABOUT 6 CUPS, ENOUGH TO SERVE 6 TO 8

Radishes with their leaves

Chicken in Mustard Sauce

RICK: *When I was in my early twenties, I took my first trip to France and tasted my first bite of creamy French mustard sauce—over rabbit browned in butter. Mustard sauce with rabbit, chicken or some other meat is a classic in French bistros (the casual-but-nice restaurants that offer homey, traditional cooking). When I took Lanie to France, I ordered kidneys in creamy mustard sauce. She loved the sauce, but I couldn't get her to try the kidneys. (Not something she's been raised with, I know, but cactus and hominy and crackling pork skins—traditional Mexican foods— don't seem to bother her.) This is a dish for special occasions. Everyone loves it, even Lanie's friend Nick who swears he doesn't like Dijon mustard.*

⌗   ⌗   ⌗   ⌗   ⌗   ⌗

LANIE: *It's the little browned bits you scrape up in the pan that make the sauce soooo good. You have to get the* heat *right in the pan, because (1) if it's too low, there won't be any browned bits, or (2) if it's too high, the bits will be* black—*which tastes really awful. When you put the chicken in the pan, don't walk away. I did, and our friend Kirsten who was with me (she was raised in Germany and ate this dish, like, every Sunday for years) started* freaking. *You're supposed to stand there and make sure the chicken browns right. (BTW, Kirsten also thinks the chicken should have the bones and skin for flavor, which I think makes it hard to eat. You decide.)*

Four 5- to 6-ounce boneless, skinless chicken breast halves

Salt

Ground black pepper

About ⅓ cup flour

1 tablespoon butter

1 tablespoon vegetable oil

½ cup chicken broth or white wine (wine makes the dish taste very French)

3 tablespoons French-style mustard (smooth or whole-grain is okay)

¾ cup *crème fraîche* or heavy (whipping) cream

3 tablespoons chopped fresh chives or parsley

Smooth and grainy mustards

----

1. *Season chicken.* Pat chicken dry on paper towels. Sprinkle both sides of each piece with salt (takes about 1 teaspoon to season all of them) and pepper. Spread flour on a plate. Lay chicken in flour, then flip pieces over to coat completely.

2. *Fry chicken.* Set large (10-inch) skillet over medium to medium-high heat. Add butter and oil. When butter melts and just begins to brown, quickly and gently pat chicken between palms to distribute flour evenly, shake off excess and lay chicken in pan in a single layer. When brown underneath—about 3 minutes— turn with tongs and cook the other side until brown outside and cooked through—about 5 minutes more. The chicken should be juicy, but not pink inside—cut into the center with a small knife to make sure. Remove chicken to a clean plate. Reduce heat under pan to medium.

3. *Make sauce.* Immediately pour in broth or wine. (Pour from side to minimize spattering.) Use a spatula to scrape up any sticky bits from bottom of pan. Boil until almost syrupy looking—about 2 minutes. Add mustard and *crème fraîche*

or cream. Boil until sauce has thickened slightly, 3 to 5 minutes. Taste and add as much salt as you think necessary.

4. *Serve.* Place chicken breasts on dinner plates. Spoon sauce over each one. Sprinkle with chives or parsley and serve.

SERVES 4

Kirsten's Roasted Potatoes for Four People

3 tablespoons butter

6 garlic cloves

6 (about 1½ pounds) medium boiling potatoes (red-skin or Yukon gold potatoes are our favorites)

A little ground black pepper

Salt

Position rack in middle of oven. Turn oven on to 400°F. Put butter in an 8-inch square baking pan. Peel the garlic and add the whole cloves to the butter. Slide into oven. Cut the potatoes into roughly 1-inch cubes. When butter has melted, add the potatoes to the pan. Sprinkle with the pepper and ½ teaspoon salt. Stir to coat potatoes evenly with butter. Roast in oven—stir every 15 minutes—until browned outside and tender within, about 45 minutes.

Poached Salmon with Irish Butter Sauce

LANIE: *I refuse to be embarrassed: butter's one of my FAVORITE things. And butter in Ireland—well—that's GOOD butter. No, it's better than good! I don't know why—are Irish cows different? Our Irish friend Darena Allen says they love their cows more. Feed them really well. Anyway, my dad can sometimes buy Irish butter here. And it's true—it's better than our butter, at least the butter I've tasted. And, when you use it to make this sauce—it feels like pure SILK in your mouth—you've got the most awesome thing in the world. I like salmon, always have. Favorite dish.*

✄　✄　✄　✄　✄　✄

RICK: *Salmon seems to be Ireland's favorite fish. For centuries they ate the wild salmon caught off Ireland's coast, though now the demand has exceeded the supply. So they farm-raise a lot of salmon, but its flavor isn't as good as the wild fish. And some of the salmon farmers aren't feeding their salmon good stuff and are polluting the waters they raise their fish in. In the United States, I mostly eat salmon during the summer, when I can buy beautiful wild salmon caught in Alaska. (They manage their fisheries well there.)*

Irish butter sauce is really that classic sauce called hollandaise (like you'd put on eggs benedict). Most people think it's tricky to make. Darena's method of making it is easy, almost foolproof—as is my method for poaching the fish. With very little time in the kitchen, you can turn out an impressively special meal. (I like to serve the fish with boiled red-skin potatoes and green salad.)

Salt

2 pounds (or a little more) salmon fillets (fillets that are shiny—almost translucent—are freshest)

3 "large" eggs

6 ounces (¾ cup, 1½ sticks) butter (unsalted butter tastes freshest)

1 tablespoon lemon juice

A small handful fresh chives

····· **DO THIS FIRST** ·····

SALMON: Cut into 6 pieces of equal size. If you see little white "pin" bones, pull them out with tweezers.

EGGS: Separate, putting yolks and whites into separate small dishes (page 65). Cover and refrigerate whites to add to scrambled eggs or fry for sandwiches.

BUTTER: Cut into 12 pieces.

CHIVES: Holding long chives tightly bunched, slice crosswise into tiny pieces.

1. *Poach salmon.* Fill a skillet (large enough to hold the fillets without overlapping) with 1 inch of water. Add 2 teaspoons salt, stir to dissolve, set over high heat and bring to a boil. Slide salmon skin-side up into the water. When water begins to *gently* simmer, turn off and set timer for 8 minutes (10 minutes if you want your fish well done).

2. *Make sauce.* Pour egg yolks into medium (3- to 4-quart) saucepan (with heavy bottom is best—heats yolks slowly so they won't scramble). Add 2 tablespoons water and whisk to blend completely. Set over low heat and whisk continuously at a pretty rapid pace. Add 1 piece of butter at a time, letting each one melt before adding the next—this will take about 5 minutes. If sauce ever starts to look curdled or oily, remove immediately from heat and whisk in another piece of butter to cool sauce. Lower temperature a little, return pan to heat and continue. When all the butter has been whisked in, remove pan from heat and whisk in the lemon juice and ½ teaspoon salt (use less if using salted butter).

3. *Serve.* When salmon timer rings, use spatula (with holes if possible to let all water drain off) to gently remove fillets one at a time from water and place on dinner plates. With your fingers, carefully peel off and discard skin. Flip fillets over after removing skin—they're prettier on the other side. Spoon sauce over each fillet. Sprinkle with chopped chives and serve immediately.

NOTES: The sauce has to heat very slowly or the yolks will scramble and the butter will separate out. If you use a *heavy* pan set over low heat, the cold pieces of butter will keep the sauce at the right temperature as they melt—right for turning out a silky, foamy sauce, rather than one that is either filled with bits of scrambled egg yolk or has butter separating out. The sauce is best served as soon as it is made, though it can be kept warm for 20 to 30 minutes by setting the pan in a larger pan filled ¼ full with hot (*not* boiling) water.

SERVES 6

Tartiflette—French Potato-and-Cheese Supper

RICK: *Our abiding, personal relationship with* tartiflette *may strike some people as odd, since we've actually never tasted a real one—that is, one made by a French person. We've prepared a few in Chicago, and we're convinced they're authentic because we sent pictures to our friends who have eaten them made by their French cousin, and they said ours looked right.*

The real story starts with us sitting at the dinner table with the Coussement family near Paris enjoying a very French dinner. And, like many folks who love to eat, everyone kept talking about their favorite dishes. And the favorite of favorites for the Coussements was tartiflette, *which made the whole table light up with stories of going snow skiing in Savoie and eating from earthenware dishes filled with this amazing, rich, cheesey layering of potatoes and bacon. They told me the recipe in meticulous detail, which is what's here. It's all about the cheese—a brie-looking cheese called* Reblochon—*that melts down over everything.*

❅　❅　❅　❅　❅　❅

LANIE: Tartiflette *IS all about the cheese. The first* Reblochon *we got was kind of dried up with orangey m-o-l-d all over the outside that we had to scrape off. And it hardly melted. And the rind—and the cheese—was WAY TOO STRONG for me. I wished we'd just made it with* raclette *or* Gruyère *or maybe even just Muenster from Wisconsin. Which, by the way, are all pretty delicious possibilities, but I guess not very authentic. The dish is rich, so serve it with a lettuce salad or a fruit salad.*

6 ounces (6 thick slices) bacon

2 tablespoons butter

2 medium onions

Salt

2½ pounds (about 10 medium) white- or red-skin boiling potatoes

One 1-pound Reblochon cheese (a 6-inch round), fresh and kind of soft at room temperature with no orangey mold on its white rind

OR 1 pound Gruyère, *raclette* or brick cheese

····· **DO THIS FIRST** ·····

BACON: Cut crosswise into ¼-inch strips.

ONIONS: Cut off top and bottom and discard. Cut in half from top to bottom. Peel off papery outside layers and discard. Slice halves about ¼ inch thick.

POTATOES: Peel. Cut into ¼-inch slices. You should have about 7 cups.

CHEESE: Holding knife perpendicular to the face of the Reblochon cheese, scrape across cheese until any spots of dark orange and white "bloom" disappear. The cheese will be golden yellow. Split in half as you would an English muffin. If you wish, cut about ⅛ inch of rind off *edge* of each half to encourage cheese to melt more evenly. If using Gruyère, *raclette*, or brick, shred through large holes of grater (you need 3 to 4 cups).

OVEN: Place rack in middle of oven and turn on to 400°F.

1. *Cook bacon, onions and potatoes.* Set very large (12-inch) skillet over medium heat. Add the bacon pieces. Cook—stir regularly—until bacon begins to crisp, about 5 minutes. With slotted spoon, remove bacon to paper towels. Pour off half of bacon fat and set aside. Add butter and sliced onions to pan. Cook—stir regularly—until onions are deep golden brown, about 10 minutes more. Add 2 teaspoons salt, ½ cup water and the sliced potatoes. Stir well. Cover pan (use a cookie sheet if necessary) and cook—stirring several times—until potatoes are almost soft, about 15 minutes. Add bacon and mix well.

2. *Layer dish.* Spread a teaspoon or two of reserved bacon fat over bottom of a 9 x 13-inch baking pan. Spread potato and onion mixture in an even layer in the dish. Lay the disks of *Reblochon* skin side down on top without overlapping—feel free to cut disks to fit. If using grated cheese, sprinkle it on top of potatoes.

3. *Bake and serve.* Place in oven and bake until cheese has melted and begins to brown—30 to 35 minutes (25 to 30 minutes if not using *Reblochon*). Let stand 3 to 4 minutes until bubbling stops. Then scoop portions onto plates and serve.

SERVES 6 (OR 8 IF NOT HUGE EATERS)

Reblochon *cheese*

Balsamic Green Beans

RICK: *This recipe is deceptively simple—and exceptionally good. It offers everything green beans need: enough cooking to mellow their flavor, garlic to give them a tantalizing aroma, and balsamic vinegar's dark syrupy sweet-sour glaze to draw you back bite after bite.*

❈ ❈ ❈ ❈ ❈ ❈

LANIE: *This was the* first *vegetable I actually* wanted *to eat. (Unless you count Caesar Salad.) We make it every year at Thanksgiving, and I'm in charge of d-r-i-b-b-l-i-n-g on the balsamic vinegar. That's what they did when we ate at this inn in Italy. So it's what we do. Balsamic is expensive . . . so we dribble.*

12 ounces (4 cups) green beans
Salt
2 tablespoons olive oil
1 large garlic clove
1½ to 2 teaspoons balsamic vinegar

> ······ **DO THIS FIRST** ······
>
> **GREEN BEANS:** Break off and discard the stems and little tips.
> **GARLIC:** Peel.

1. *Blanch beans.* In a large (6- to 8-quart) saucepan, bring 4 inches water to boil over high heat. Add 2 teaspoons salt. Add cleaned green beans and cook 7 minutes (5 minutes for the little French green beans). Drain and spread out on large plate to cool.

2. *Sauté and serve.* Pour oil into large (10-inch) skillet. Set over medium heat. Crush the garlic through a garlic press into the oil. Add the green beans and cook 3 to 4 minutes—stirring continuously—until beans are hot. Sprinkle with about ¼ teaspoon salt. Stir to season evenly. Scoop onto a platter. Slowly and evenly pour vinegar over beans. Serve right away.

NOTES: The green beans can be regular ones, yellow ones, or the skinny little French ones called *haricots verts.* Or they can be snow peas or sugar snap peas. Everyday balsamic vinegar is available in the grocery store, but you can find very special "artisanal" balsamic in specialty stores. Some of it is so expensive you'll want to call it black gold. We think it's worth the extra cash.

SERVES 4

❉ Four Steps to Growing Three Herbs (on the Windowsill) ❉

For most of us, it's possible to find basil and chive plants in the produce section of the grocery store. So you should start your windowsill herb "garden" with them. (If there are no basil plants, buy some fresh basil, put 3 or 4 stems in a glass of water and set in the window. Within 2 or 3 weeks roots will form. Plant stems in potting soil and keep moist.) To those, add a thyme plant (you'll probably have to buy it at a plant nursery), because thyme is delicious and you can potentially keep the plant alive longer than the other two (for years if you know what to do).

If you follow these guidelines, you'll be able to snip a few chives, a few basil leaves and a few sprigs of fresh thyme regularly from your own fresh herbs.

(1) Set the plants on old plates or plant saucers in the sunniest window you have—*preferably a window that faces south.*

(2) Every day or two, *water the plants a little bit—less in the winter (when it's cooler and plants grow less), more in the summer (when it's hotter and plants grow rapidly).*

(3) Once a week, *fertilize plants. Buy liquid fertilizer (preferably organic like Neptune's Harvest—available at* many garden centers or at neptunesharvest.com). In a quart jar with lid, mix up a quart of diluted fertilizer according to directions on the bottle. Set the plants in the sink and slowly pour diluted fertilizer on until it runs out the bottom.

(4) When the night temperature stays above 40°F, set the plants outside for the warm months (then bring inside again when the weather gets cold). Water every day if the weather is very hot. Continue fertilizing once a week.

Basil likes the most water, chives the second most and thyme the least. All like lots of sunshine. They all will grow bigger if you replant them into larger pots in the spring with fresh soil. (Chives planted in the garden will survive winters in most every U.S. climate; they die back in below-freezing conditions and re-sprout in spring, which doesn't solve the need for chives in winter.) Even if you don't have perfect growing conditions and the plants only last a couple of months, you've had more fresh herbs to use than you otherwise would have had. Bottom line: Some windowsill herbs are better than none.

Tuscan Pasta with Tomato Sauce

RICK: *Italians eat pasta in a different way than we do. They'd choke if you served them a big pile of plain spaghetti with a cupful of marinara sauce on top and a shaker of Parmesan on the side. They want a small plate of pasta that has less sauce with lots of lively flavor. And they want it* before *the main course—not as* the *main course. Here's how this very Italian recipe became one of the favorites at our house: When Lanie was five, we were invited to lunch at the apartment of a fellow cookbook writer, Faith Willinger, in Florence. In Lanie's honor, she boiled some spaghetti, made a very simple, smooth, garlicky tomato sauce that she cooked with the drained pasta for a few minutes. Amazingly, it absorbed most of the sauce, and gave it wonderful flavor. She freshly grated Parmesan on top and stirred in fresh basil, and I went into the stratosphere. It was incredibly delicious. In our house, the favorite canned tomato choice is Muir Glen Fire Roasted Diced Tomatoes.*

❆ ❆ ❆ ❆ ❆ ❆

LANIE: *Well, it's not the first time. He said it all before I could get started. And why on this dish? I mean, it's* supposed *to be a "kid's dish." Anyway. It IS really good. Everybody thinks so. I like to add sausage. Corkscrews "grab" the sauce and are easier to dish up than spaghetti.*

3 tablespoons olive oil, divided use

2 garlic cloves

2 cups tomato pulp (we like Pomi brand strained tomatoes)
OR one 28-ounce can diced tomatoes in juice
OR 1½ pounds ripe cherry, round or plum tomatoes

½ teaspoon ground black pepper

Salt

1 pound dried pasta (corkscrews, penne and spaghetti are our favorites—use about 14 ounces if you choose spaghetti)

1 small bunch (12 to 15 leaves) fresh basil (or other fresh herbs like parsley, thyme or savory)

½ to ¾ cup grated Parmesan or Pecorino cheese (fresh-grated has more flavor)

⋯⋯ DO THIS FIRST ⋯⋯

PASTA-COOKING WATER: Measure 4 to 5 quarts water into a very large (8-quart) pot. Cover and set over high heat until boiling, then reduce heat to keep water simmering.

GARLIC: Peel.

TOMATOES: For tomato "pulp," simply measure 2 cups. For canned tomatoes, drain and pour into food processor. Secure lid and process until quite smooth, but with a little texture left. Measure 2 cups. For fresh tomatoes, cut into 1-inch pieces. Place in food processor. Secure lid and process until almost smooth, as described above. Pour through medium-mesh strainer into a bowl to get out the bits of skin. Measure 2 cups.

BASIL: Stack 3 leaves on top of each other. Roll up from pointy end. Thinly slice roll (cutting basil this way keeps it from browning). Repeat with remaining leaves. Finely chop (page 37) other herbs if using—you need 2 to 4 tablespoons.

1. *Make sauce.* In a wide, medium (4- to 6-quart) pan, heat *1 tablespoon* of the olive oil over medium heat. Crush garlic through garlic press into the oil. Stir for 1 to 2 minutes, until the garlic begins to brown. Raise heat to medium-high. Add the tomato pulp. Cook—stirring regularly—5 to 7 minutes, until most of the tomato liquid has evaporated and it looks like medium-thick tomato sauce. Season with pepper and ½ teaspoon salt if using unsalted tomatoes. Stir in the remaining *2 tablespoons* of the olive oil. Keep warm over low heat.

2. *Boil pasta.* Return the heat under the pasta-cooking water to high. Uncover and add 2 tablespoons salt and the pasta. Boil—stirring occasionally—until pasta is just ¾ done (still crunchy raw inside)—7 to 10 minutes. Scoop out ½ cup pasta-boiling water and set aside. Set colander in sink. Drain pasta through colander.

3. *Finish dish.* Turn heat under sauce to medium. Add the pasta and reserved pasta-boiling water. Cook—stirring gently all the time—until the pasta is done (not too soft—should have a nice "bite") and has absorbed a good amount of sauce, about 3 minutes or so.

4. *Serve.* Taste and season with more salt if you think necessary. Divide among the plates. Sprinkle with chopped basil (or other herbs) and cheese. Serve immediately.

SERVES 4 AS A MAIN COURSE, 6 TO 8 AS AN ITALIAN "PASTA" COURSE

Basil, thyme and chives

Bayless Family Pasta with Pesto

LANIE: *My dad said that the pesto for pasta is supposed to be just basil, nuts, garlic and olive oil blended until smooth. You toss it with boiled pasta and Parmesan. And I don't really like it. At least not done that way. Too strong. So we made a compromise: We add cream cheese or goat cheese to kind of m-e-l-l-o-w out those "classic" flavors.*

✻   ✻   ✻   ✻   ✻   ✻

RICK: *Yes, this recipe is a cross between what'll appear to be Italian tastes and American ones. Here, the classic Italian version Lanie described above is balanced with more cheese. But we brightened the flavors again with a little lemon or lime. It's our favorite pesto.*

¼ cup **pine nuts or walnuts**

3 **garlic cloves**

2 cups (1½ ounces) **fresh basil leaves**

¼ cup **lemon balm, optional**

⅓ cup **olive oil**

¼ cup **cream cheese or fresh goat cheese**

1 tablespoon **lime or lemon juice**

Salt

1 pound **dried pasta (we like fusilli—corkscrews—best, but spaghetti is good, too)**
OR 1 recipe homemade fresh pasta (see opposite page)

½ to ¾ cup **grated Parmesan cheese**

······ **DO THIS FIRST** ······

PASTA-COOKING WATER: Measure 4 to 5 quarts water into a very large (8-quart) pot. Cover and set over high heat until boiling, then reduce heat to keep water simmering.
GARLIC: Peel.

1. *Toast nuts.* Scoop nuts into a small skillet. Set over medium heat. Stir until nuts release toasty aroma into kitchen—about 3 minutes. Remove pan from heat and let nuts cool.

2. *Blanch garlic.* Place peeled garlic in microwave-safe cup and barely cover with water. Microwave on high (100%) power for 1 minute. Scoop garlic out of water with spoon. Allow to cool.

3. *Make pesto.* In a food processor, combine cooled toasted nuts, basil leaves, lemon balm if desired, olive oil, cream cheese or goat cheese, lime or lemon juice and ½ teaspoon salt. Cut each garlic clove into 3 pieces and add to processor. Secure lid. Pulse 5 or 6 times, then run machine until mixture is smooth—about 1 minute. Leave pesto in food processor.

4. *Boil pasta.* Return heat under water to high. Uncover and add 2 tablespoons salt and the pasta. Stir thoroughly. Boil until pasta is done—usually 9 to 12 minutes for dry pasta, 3 to 4 minutes for homemade fresh pasta—until kind of soft but still firm when you bite it (what Italians call *al dente*). Scoop out ½ cup pasta-boiling water and set aside. Set colander in silk. Drain pasta through colander.

Fresh basil

5. *Finish pasta and serve.* Turn on food processor. Pour reserved pasta water through processor feed tube. Turn off, remove lid and blade (scrape pesto from blade back into bowl). Dump drained pasta back into pot. Scrape pesto from the processor bowl onto pasta. Sprinkle on *half* of the grated Parmesan. Use tongs or a large spoon or fork to stir, evenly coating pasta with pesto and cheese. Divide onto plates and garnish with basil leaves if you have extras. Serve immediately, passing the remaining Parmesan for everyone to add to their own liking.

SERVES 4 AS A MAIN COURSE, 6 TO 8 AS AN ITALIAN "PASTA" COURSE

Making homemade pasta

Homemade Egg Pasta

Our absolute favorite homemade pasta—super light and tender—is made with white spelt flour. If you can get it, use 2¼ cups (10 ounces).

2 cups (10 ounces) all-purpose flour, plus a little more for rolling the dough
3 "large" eggs

1. *Make dough.* Measure flour directly into food processor with the steel blade in place. Secure top. Crack eggs into a liquid measuring cup and beat with a fork until smooth. Turn on food processor. Slowly pour eggs through feed tube into the flour. Run processor until mixture forms a firm ball, about 1 minute. (If it doesn't form a ball, sprinkle a couple teaspoons of water over the dough and process until it comes together.) Remove top, then remove dough, being careful of the blade. Lay dough on countertop. Sprinkle generously with flour. Knead (see page 138) for 9 full minutes, adding more flour if dough is sticky. (This should be a very stiff dough.)

2. *Roll out and cut dough.* Clamp pasta machine securely onto countertop. Open to widest setting. Cut dough into 4 equal pieces. (Cover with towel or plastic wrap to keep from drying out.) Flatten one piece and flour both sides. Roll through machine. Fold into thirds. Roll through again. Keep folding and rolling until dough

feels silky—about 6 times. Adjust machine to one setting narrower. Roll pasta through machine. Adjust machine to one setting narrower. Roll pasta through machine. Continue until you've reached the next-to-thinnest setting—dough gets thinner and longer with each pass. If sheet becomes too long to handle, cut it in half and roll each half separately. Move handle to cutter attachment of pasta machine. Roll pasta sheets through the cutter attachment. (The ¼-inch fettuccini size is easier to work with than the thin linguine size.) Loosely gather pasta strands as they come out of the cutter. Place in a heap on the countertop. Fluff periodically to make sure no strands stick together. Repeat the rolling and cutting for each of the remaining pieces of pasta dough. Pasta can be boiled right away or made ahead, dried completely and stored for several days in a plastic bag at room temperature.

SERVES 4

How to Knead Dough

To knead dough like you mean it, you have to become "one" with the dough, feel it as if it were part of your body. Lightly flour your work surface, hands and dough. Then flatten the dough slightly, fold the top half (the part away from you) over the bottom half. Use the heels of your hands to press the two parts together. Then in one fluid motion rock your hands over the top, pressing the dough out into a shape similar to the one you started with. Rotate the dough ¼ turn. Continue this process for as long as described in the recipe. It's all about rhythm and pressure and getting to know the feel of the particular dough. Bread or pasta dough is most frequently kneaded, though you occasionally have to lightly knead biscuit and pie dough.

Yogurt Cheese, Served French Style

RICK: *This is one of those simple French desserts that makes everyone happy: fresh-tasting cheese with fruit and a little something sweet. And it's totally flexible, since you can buy the French fresh cheese (called* fromage blanc—*literally "white cheese") or make yogurt cheese (as we've described here). You can use or skip the sour cream or* crème fraîche *(French sour cream, but richer and less sour than ours). And you can choose practically any fruit you want—any kind of berry or chopped apple, pear, papaya, mango, peaches, nectarines. (Peel or pit or de-seed, whatever's appropriate.) Even a mix of chopped dried fruit is good in winter, though Lanie doesn't like it very much. Look for cheesecloth in the grocery store in the area where cooking equipment is sold. Or skip the strainer lined with cheese cloth and use a yogurt cheese "maker" like the Donvier one in the photo.*

✄　✄　✄　✄　✄　✄

LANIE: *This cheese tastes as fresh as plain milk, but it's almost as creamy as cream cheese. The first time I ate it, we bought it with our French friends in Brie-Comte-Robert. But you can't find it much here, so if you want it, you'll have to make it. All it takes is yogurt, a strainer, a refrigerator and 12 hours. Just about as good as the French stuff, just a little tangier. And everybody gets to spoon sour cream on top of their own portion and then sprinkle sugar on that,* that *which I thought was pretty cool.*

1 quart plain yogurt (whole, low-fat or no-fat is okay)

¼ cup *crème fraîche* or sour cream

3 cups berries (strawberries, raspberries, blackberries or blueberries—if using strawberries, cut them in half)

Sugar, for serving

Yogurt cheese "maker"

1. *Make yogurt cheese.* Rinse a 2-foot piece of cheesecloth (or clean, light-weight, flat weave kitchen towel or handkerchief) and squeeze. Fold cloth in half and use to line small colander or medium-large strainer. Set colander or strainer in a deep bowl. Scoop yogurt into colander, stirring gently with each scoop. Lay plastic wrap over top. Place in refrigerator for 12 to 24 hours to drain out clear whey. What's left is yogurt cheese.

2. *Serve.* Scoop a portion of cheese onto dessert plates. (To make it look nice, scoop cheese into biscuit cutter to mold it round, then lift off mold.) Stir *crème fraîche* or sour cream until smooth. Spoon some on top of each portion. Place fruit around sides. Serve, passing sugar for all to sprinkle on top to their liking.

MAKES ABOUT 2 CUPS, ENOUGH TO SERVE 4

Hot Chocolate Soufflés

RICK: *Everyone thinks soufflés are hard to make because you have to fold in beaten egg whites and serve the soufflé directly from oven to table (before it sinks, which it does as it cools). Don't be too concerned. Honestly, this is the second recipe I taught Lanie to make (after oatmeal in the microwave—she was 7 or 8).*

Three notes: (1) If you only have one mixer bowl, put the whites in another kind of bowl. Make the soufflé base and transfer it to another bowl. Then wash and dry your mixer bowl before using it for beating the egg whites. (2) If you don't have individual molds or custard cups, bake the soufflé in a large mold (one that holds about 8 cups—we've even used a heatproof 2¼-quart mixing bowl). Bake for 40 to 45 minutes. (3) Use semisweet (not sweet) chocolate. Regular semisweet baking chocolate is fine, but really good chocolate like Lindt, Valhrona or Scharffen Berger will make truly amazing soufflés.

※ ※ ※ ※ ※ ※

LANIE: *This dessert is one of the coolest things ever. Number One awesome thing about it: it's chocolate. Number Two: it's warm + fluffy. Just make sure you beat the egg whites right—not too runny, not too firm. And fold them into the chocolate GENTLY so your soufflé is fluffy, not heavy. And most important: Make sure everyone is at the table when the soufflés are ready. Last time I made it, my dad walked away (he should know better)—when he got back his had already sunk. (Still tasted good, though—just not as fluffy.)*

6 ounces semisweet chocolate

6 "large" eggs

⅔ cup sugar, divided use

¼ teaspoon salt

2 tablespoons heavy (whipping) cream or milk

1 teaspoon vanilla

A little powdered sugar for sprinkling on top

······ **DO THIS FIRST** ······

SOUFFLÉ MOLDS: Set out eight 6-ounce individual soufflé dishes or custard cups. Spray inside of each mold with oil or cooking spray, or smear with butter. Sprinkle inside of each with a bit of sugar, tipping to coat evenly. Set on baking sheet.

CHOCOLATE: Break or chop into small pieces and place in medium-size glass or ceramic microwave-safe bowl.

OVEN: Place rack in middle of oven and turn on to 350°F.

1. *Melt chocolate.* Microwave chopped chocolate on high (100%) power for 1 minute. Stir and remove spoon. Microwave 1 minute more and stir again. If not completely melted, microwave another minute and stir.

2. *Make soufflé base.* Separate eggs (page 65), placing yolks in one mixer bowl and whites in another. Add ½ *cup* of the sugar and the salt to the egg *yolks*. Beat with mixer on medium-high speed until very light, fluffy and thick—about 3 minutes. (Mixture should be so thick that when you lift turned-off beaters, an egg yolk "ribbon" falls that takes 3 to 4 seconds to dissolve.) Set aside. Stir cream or milk and vanilla into the melted chocolate. Stir in ⅓ of the egg yolk mixture. Fold (opposite page) in remaining egg yolk mixture in 2 additions. Set aside.

3. *Beat egg whites.* Beat egg whites with mixer on *medium* speed until fluffy but not at all stiff—3 to 4 minutes. Sprinkle in remaining *1 tablespoon* of the sugar. Beat 1 minute longer on medium speed—until whites are shiny and firm but not stiff. (Beaten whites should form a soft peak—looks like top of a Dairy Queen ice cream cone—when turned-off beaters are lifted out.) Stir ⅓ of egg whites into chocolate base. Gently fold in remaining egg whites in 2 additions. Divide evenly among prepared soufflé molds. At this point you can refrigerate the soufflés for several hours before baking, but then they will need to bake longer (20 to 23 minutes).

4. *Bake and serve.* Place molds on baking sheet in middle of oven and set timer for 15 minutes. Don't open oven during baking. When timer goes off, soufflés should be puffed and cracked on top. When you gently shake the baking sheet, soufflés should jiggle only slightly (when you spoon out the center to eat, it should be creamy). If soufflés are really jiggly, quickly close oven and bake 2 to 3 minutes longer. Remove from oven, sprinkle with powdered sugar and serve *immediately*—before the soufflés start sinking.

SERVES 8

Definitions 101: Whisking and Folding

Sure, you can use a spoon or a fork to whip or mix different ingredients together, but a whisk—with its 6, 8 or 10 wires curved into a loop—can do those two things very efficiently.

If "whipping" is your goal (like whipping egg whites or cream), a whisk will do it quicker than any other tool. And it will beat in more air, too.

If "mixing" is what you want to do (as for salad dressing or pancake batter), a whisk will usually do it thoroughly and quickly. And if you're gentle, the whisk won't beat up the stuff you might want to keep in small pieces. On the other hand, if the ingredients are thick and heavy, like cookie dough, a whisk doesn't work at all. The ingredients will just stick in the middle of the whisk and won't combine.

"Folding" has one major definition in the kitchen: to gently, but thoroughly, combine two mixtures, usually with different textures. For instance, we often fold light-textured beaten egg whites or whipped cream into heavier-textured chocolate or batter. The goal is to keep all the air in those fluffy beaten whites (or cream) while incorporating them evenly into a mixture that threatens to flatten them.

*Here's how to do it: **Step 1:** Stir about one-quarter of the light stuff into the heavy stuff (just to lighten it—you'll lose the air but that's okay). **Step 2:** Scoop about one-third of the remaining light stuff on top of the heavy stuff. Using a rubber spatula, cut straight down through both the light and heavy stuff (to the bottom of the bowl), then draw the spatula toward you—slightly flattened out—across the bottom and up the side of the bowl, "folding" the heavy mixture up over the light one. (It's like drawing a circle in front of you—perpendicular to your body.) Continue until the light and heavy stuff are almost completely combined. **Step 3:** Turn the bowl about 90 degrees and repeat Step 2 with half of the remaining light stuff. **Step 4:** Repeat Step 3 with remaining light stuff.*

French Crêpes

½ cup milk
2 "large" eggs
1 cup (5 ounces) all-purpose flour
½ teaspoon salt
3 tablespoons butter
crêpes

RICK: *Most of us think of French crêpes as something fancy (don't we think of most anything French as fancy?)—when, truth be told, they're mostly street food in their homeland. I learned to make crêpes when I was ten years old, watching Julia Child on her first television show. They became "my specialty"—I made them for the family each year on Christmas morning, rolled up with sweetened cream cheese and baked with buttery raspberries. As a kid I made crêpes in my mom's old 7-inch cast-iron skillet. I still think it is the best, though now I sometimes use a low-sided French crêpe pan or a non-stick skillet.*

✕   ✕   ✕   ✕   ✕   ✕

LANIE: *Now I understand why my dad gave me a CRÊPE PAN as my first piece of kitchen equipment. A nostalgia thing. I do love crêpes, though, and they're really pretty easy. Make sure to get the temperature of the pan right so the batter coats the pan evenly. I find it a little hard to swish the batter around and make them round. Once I made a square crêpe. Without trying.*

1. *Make batter.* Put ³/₄ cup water, milk, eggs, flour and salt in blender. Place butter in small microwave-safe bowl. Microwave at 50% power for 1¹/₂ minutes to melt almost completely. Add to blender and process for 30 seconds. Scrape down sides and process 30 seconds more. Let stand 1 hour or refrigerate for later use.

2. *Cook.* Lay a double layer of paper towels on a baking sheet. Set 7-inch crêpe pan or small (7- to 8-inch) "well-seasoned" cast-iron or non-stick skillet over medium heat. If pan is NOT non-stick, pour in a little oil and rub around with a paper towel. When pan is hot enough to make a drop of water pop around happily, pour in about 2 tablespoons batter. (A 1-ounce ladle works well.) Very quickly tilt pan to coat bottom evenly with batter. It is okay if there are a few holes— don't add more batter, or crêpe will be doughy. Cook until crêpe browns around edges and pulls away from sides of pan—about 45 seconds. If crêpe browns more quickly, turn heat down a little. If it browns more slowly, turn heat up. Run table knife around sides to ensure it's free, then carefully slip knife under crêpe, pick it up and flip it over. Cook until lightly browned underneath—about 30 seconds more. Shake pan gently to ensure crêpe isn't sticking, then slide onto paper towel on baking sheet. Make rest of crêpes the same way. As crêpes cool on paper towels, stack one on top of another on one side of baking sheet. If not serving within one hour, cover with plastic wrap and refrigerate.

MAKES EIGHTEEN 6-INCH CRÊPES

Nutella Crêpes

RICK: *If you haven't had Nutella, go out and get some. The flavor of chocolate and hazelnut whipped to the consistency of peanut butter is a crowd pleaser.*

⌘ ⌘ ⌘ ⌘ ⌘ ⌘

LANIE: *Every time I have these, I think, "This is definitely the best thing I have eaten all day." You can use more (or less) Nutella than we do. Or you can add a scoop of ice cream or whipped cream making them HEAVENLY. In the summer we sometimes replace the Nutella with sweetened yogurt cheese (page 139) and fresh berries.*

1½ **tablespoons butter**
About ½ cup Nutella
12 crêpes (see opposite page)
A little powdered sugar, for dusting crêpes

1. *Melt butter.* Place butter in small microwave-safe bowl and microwave at medium (50%) power for 2 minutes to melt. Lightly brush bottom of a baking sheet with butter.

2. *Fill and bake crêpes.* Turn on oven to 400°F. Spoon about 2 teaspoons Nutella in center of each crêpe. Fold in half, lightly brush top with butter. Fold in half again (making a quarter) and press lightly to spread Nutella through crêpe. Brush top lightly with butter. Lay filled crêpes in two rows in buttered pan, slightly overlapping. Bake crêpes until lightly crispy—about 10 minutes. Use metal spatula to transfer crêpes to dessert plates. Scoop some powdered sugar into small strainer. Sift over crêpe. Serve.

SERVES 4

Another Way to Make Crêpes

I like to make crêpes this way (in fact, I taught this method to Lanie first), because they come out thinner. But it takes a little practice. First, heat the pan (oil it if necessary) as described in the recipe. Pour in a scant ¼ cup batter, quickly tilt the pan to distribute the batter evenly over the bottom, then pour any excess (any that doesn't set) back into the container. When the crêpe is brown underneath, trim off the "lip" formed where you poured the batter out. This will give you a round crêpe. Then flip and cook the other side as described in the recipe. If the crêpe "peels" off the pan when you're pouring out the excess (threatening to plunk into the batter container), you know the pan is too oily or too cool. If the crêpe comes out too thin, the pan is too cool. If the crêpe comes out too thick, the pan is too hot. Like I said—it takes a little practice to get this one right.

❈ Dateline, Chicago: Flowers Garnish Food at Bayless Home ❈

Okay, I know flowers in your food may sound as odd as gummy bears on your pizza. But you may already be eating flowers without knowing it. Think about it: The top of broccoli is a huge unopened flower. And so is an artichoke. And saffron (reportedly the most expensive spice in the world) is the deep-orange filaments (they look like short, colored threads) from inside a flower. The blossoms of zucchini plants are stuffed with cheese and other ingredients and eaten by the thousands every day in countries like Mexico and Italy. Violets are candied to decorate the most exquisite pastries in France.

To become an experienced flower eater, buy a pot of chives at the grocery store, set it in a very sunny window and don't forget to water it. Snip off a few pieces every once in a while, chop and sprinkle on lasagna or a casserole (wherever you want to taste that mild green onion flavor). Then, in spring or summer, your chives will bloom purple. You can break the flowers apart and sprinkle them on salad, pasta or pizza, or whatever you like, really. They taste like chives but are prettier.

Pick violets in the spring if you live where violets grow (it's our state flower here in Illinois—they're everywhere). They don't taste like much, but they look cool on chocolate-covered profiteroles or sprinkled on goat cheese salad.

I love to put the spicy-tasting round leaves and blossoms of nasturtiums in salads. If you plant the variety called "whirlybird," the blossoms are multicolored and beautiful. Calendula (it looks like an orange marigold) has been a favorite edible flower for centuries, traditionally used to flavor puddings, make home remedies and decorate desserts. Plant the variety called "alfa" if you want blossoms early, or the one called "erfurter orangefarbige" if you want a really beautiful deep orange blossom. Seeds for all of these flowers can be ordered from Johnny's Select Seeds (johnnyseeds.com).

A gentle word of warning: Only eat flowers grown organically or for food purposes—without poisonous chemicals, and be sure to eat only flowers known to be edible, like the ones described above.

Sticky Orange-Butter Crêpes {Flamed or Not}

RICK: *This is an easy, showy version of Crêpes Suzette, an old recipe that a French chef named Henri Carpentier invented for a nobleman over a hundred years ago. I remember the first time I flamed something—I was 12 and I was cooking crêpes like these. (I think my folks were a little scared.) You have to be very careful, since you're setting what is, in fact, a very controlled fire. But it's pretty cool if you do everything just right. Let the alcohol cook to a count of exactly five before igniting—no longer—and if you're using a match, keep your match hand as far away from the sauce as possible so you don't get burned.*

✼ ✼ ✼ ✼ ✼ ✼

LANIE: *For me, the taste of the orange marmalade is kind of strong, so if you're like me, use the all-orange juice version. The flaming is kind of cool, but a little* freaky. *(And definitely* not *a little kid thing—I need to have my dad around.) It's not all that big a flame, so don't get your hopes up—you* pyromaniacs.

RICK'S VERSION OF SAUCE
2 ounces (4 tablespoons, ½ stick) butter
  (salted butter tastes best here)
½ cup orange juice
½ cup orange marmalade

LANIE'S VERSION OF SAUCE
2 ounces (4 tablespoons, ½ stick) butter
  (salted butter tastes best here)
1¼ cups orange juice
½ cup sugar

12 crêpes (page 144)
3 tablespoons orange liqueur, optional
  (Cointreau or Grand Marnier are
  best—most Triple Sec doesn't have
  enough alcohol to flame)

1. *Make sauce.* Turn oven on to 400°F. Set large (10-inch) skillet over medium heat. Cut butter into four pieces and add to skillet. When butter begins to brown, add the orange juice and marmalade or sugar. Stir well. Let come to a simmer and boil gently, until mixture becomes lightly syrupy—8 to 10 minutes (little bubbles turn into bigger bubbles that are slower to burst). Reduce heat under skillet to medium-low.

2. *Coat crêpes with sauce.* Lay a crêpe in the sauce, pretty side up. Use 2 large spoons to flip crêpe over, then fold in half, then in quarters. Use spoons to lift crêpe out of pan—drain as much sauce as possible back into pan—and transfer to a 9 x 13-inch baking pan. Continue dipping, folding and transferring remaining crêpes, laying finished crêpes slightly overlapping.

3. *Flame crêpes and serve.* Slide baking pan with crêpes into oven. Heat until crêpes are bubbling, 6 to 7 minutes. Remove pan from oven. Return skillet with remaining sauce to medium heat. When sauce is bubbling slightly, remove from heat. If using liqueur, pour it into pan, swirl several times and pour over crêpes in baking dish. Hold a **long** lit match or gas "clicker-lighter" near side of dish and catch sauce on fire. Shake dish until all flames subside. The edges of crêpes will brown and crisp. (If not using liqueur, drizzle remaining warm sauce over crêpes.) Lay three crêpes slightly overlapping on each dessert plate, spooning sauce over top. Serve right away.

SERVES 4

French Profiteroles

RICK: *The recipe for these little pastry puffs (often called cream puffs), filled with ice cream and drizzled with chocolate sauce, was one of the first I ever mastered. We were on vacation in Colorado Springs visiting my aunt and uncle—I was ten or eleven years old—and we went to Michel's ice cream parlor. (As his name suggests, Michel was French, same as the cream puffs.) Michel coaxed these puffs into all sizes and shapes; he built them into rockets and atomic bombs (this was the '60s)—even a model of Pike's Peak. Inspired by these architectural flights of fancy, I went home and taught myself to make the simple cooked dough and watched it bake into golden hollow puffs.*

This recipe is for the classic vanilla-ice-cream-and-chocolate-sauce version you find at many French restaurants—many of which don't feature very crispy puffs. I like them crispy and that's what you'll get with this recipe.

※　※　※　※　※　※

LANIE: *We* did *eat these in France, and they* were *really good, but mostly I eat them at a little French restaurant near our house, where they are* not *drizzled with chocolate sauce, but, well, drenched. (I'm not complaining.)*

When I first made these, they didn't turn out so good. Who knows *what went wrong, but they didn't rise enough (not much of a hollow in them). My dad said I didn't measure accurately. (I've hung around pastry chefs enough to know that measuring is* everything *when you're making desserts.) So be* patient *and* precise. *(The truth: we split ours, filled them and drizzled them and no one really noticed they weren't perfect.)*

FOR THE PUFFS
¼ cup milk
1 tablespoon sugar
½ teaspoon salt
5 ounces (10 tablespoons, 1¼ stick) butter
1 cup (5 ounces) all-purpose flour
5 "large" eggs

FOR THE CHOCOLATE SAUCE
1 cup heavy (whipping) cream
¼ cup corn syrup
1 tablespoon molasses (can replace with extra tablespoon corn syrup)
8 ounces bittersweet chocolate
¼ teaspoon ground cinnamon
2 teaspoons vanilla extract

FOR FINISHING THE PROFITEROLES
1 quart ice cream (we like vanilla, mocha or coffee)

····· **DO THIS FIRST** ·····

BUTTER: Cut into 8 pieces.
FLOUR: Measure out and set by stove.
EGGS: Break into a large measuring cup. Beat with a fork until almost smooth. Pour off and discard anything over 1 cup.
CHOCOLATE: Chop into small pieces.
BAKING SHEETS: Spray or lightly brush 2 baking sheets with oil or line them with parchment paper.
OVEN: Position racks in upper third and lower third of oven. Turn on to 400°F.

1. *Cook cream puff base.* Measure ³/₄ cup water, milk, sugar and salt into a small (3- to 4-quart) saucepan. Add the pieces of butter. Set over medium heat. When the mixture begins to boil, stir continuously until butter melts. Just when butter is melted, add the flour all at once and stir until the mixture becomes a rough-looking ball and comes free from the sides of the pan. Continue to stir over heat for 3 or 4 minutes. As you stir, smear out paste slowly over bottom of pan; then collect it into a ball and smear out again. Repeat until paste looks quite shiny.

2. *Add eggs to base.* Scrape mixture into food processor with a metal blade. Let cool 5 minutes. Secure top and turn on. Slowly pour beaten eggs through the feed tube in a steady stream—should take about 45 seconds. Run machine until mixture becomes smooth—about 15 seconds longer. Remove bowl. Pull out blade. Use rubber spatula to scrape mixture off blade and back into processor bowl.

3. *Form puffs.* Use a tiny (1¹/₄-inch wide) ice cream scoop or 2 soup spoons (one to scoop up batter, the other to scoop batter off spoon) to scoop out 48 one-tablespoon mounds. Place mounds about 2 inches apart on baking sheets. (Dip a clean spoon in water and use to smooth top of mounds if they look ragged.)

4. *Bake puffs.* Place 1 sheet on each oven rack. Bake 8 minutes. Have potholder in hand, then open oven and quickly reverse upper and lower sheets. Bake 8 minutes longer. Turn off oven and set timer for 10 minutes. When timer goes off, prop open oven door slightly with a metal spoon or spatula and set timer for 15 minutes more. Remove puffs from oven. Set aside.

5. *Make chocolate sauce.* In a medium (4- to 6-quart) saucepan, combine cream, corn syrup and molasses. Set over medium heat. Let come to a simmer—stirring occasionally. Add pieces of chocolate and remove from heat. Stir frequently until all chocolate has melted. Stir in the cinnamon and vanilla. (If not using right away, rewarm over low heat before serving.)

6. *Assemble profiteroles.* Cut cream puffs in half crosswise and set 3 or 4 of the bottoms on each dessert plate. Scoop a small ball of ice cream onto each base. Set top of puff over ice cream. Spoon, ladle or pour warm chocolate sauce over each puff. (Store extra cream puffs in the freezer. Crisp them in a 350°F oven for 5 to 10 minutes before serving.)

SERVES 8 (WITH ENOUGH CREAM PUFFS TO SERVE ABOUT 6 AGAIN)

Rustic French-Style Fruit Pie

Blueberry, Raspberry, Blackberry, Cherry, Peach, Apricot, Apple, Pear or Practically Any Other Fruit

RICK: *This French approach to fruit pie is the easiest pie I've ever made. It's the easiest dough to make (not tricky to put together, a dream to roll out, always flaky) and the easiest to form (no difficulty shaping into a pie pan, no fancy crimping). This is really a free-form rustic fruit tart rather than a deep fruit pie, meaning it won't come out runny since there's less fruit to thicken. It also has a high crust-to-fruit ratio—which Lanie and I both love. At Poilâne, the internationally famous bakery in Paris, they make individual rustic tarts (6 to 7 inches across) filled with apples and baked in an old wood-burning oven. I would eat one every day if I could.*

✄　✄　✄　✄　✄　✄

LANIE: *Working with dough IS a little tricky—no matter what my dad says. And it takes a little time. But once you've done it a couple of times, it gets a lot easier. You can make this tart with lots of different fruits, but my favorite is blueberries. I love the way they taste and you don't have to peel them or cut them up. Definitely serve this pie with ice cream—vanilla's good—it won't cover up the flavor of the pie.*

FOR THE DOUGH

- 1¼ cups (6¼ ounces) all-purpose flour, plus a little more for rolling out the dough
- ⅛ teaspoon baking powder
- ⅛ teaspoon salt
- 4 ounces (1 stick) unsalted butter
- 3 ounces cream cheese or creamy fresh goat cheese
- 1½ teaspoons vinegar

FOR THE FILLING AND FINISHING

- 3 cups *prepared* fruit (see Step 3)—start with *one* of the following:
    - ✳ 1 pound blueberries, raspberries or blackberries
    - ✳ 1¼ pounds cherries
    - ✳ 2 pounds peaches, nectarines or apricots
    - ✳ 1½ pounds apples or pears
- ½ to ¾ cup sugar (depending on the tartness of the fruit) plus a tablespoon to sprinkle on pie before baking
- 2½ tablespoons cornstarch (2 tablespoons for less-juicy fruits like blueberry, apricot and apple)
- 1 tablespoon lemon or lime juice
- Powdered sugar, for sprinkling on finished pie

····· **DO THIS FIRST** ·····

BUTTER: Cut into 8 pieces.
CHEESE: Cut into 6 pieces.
VINEGAR: Measure into a small dish and add 1½ tablespoons cold water.

1. *Make dough.* **Food Processor method:** Measure flour, baking powder and salt into food processor with a metal blade. Add pieces of butter and cheese. Attach lid and give mixture 6 or 7 one-second pulses. Mixture should look like coarse crumbs—small bits of butter visible—no bigger than the size of a pea. Uncover and evenly drizzle vinegar and water mixture over flour mixture. Attach lid and give mixture 6 more one-second pulses, until mixture *begins* to form a dough. Stop machine, uncover and remove blade. **Hand method:** In large bowl, whisk together the flour, baking powder and salt. Mix the pieces of butter and cheese into flour with a large fork or pastry blender. Mixture should look like coarse crumbs. Evenly drizzle the vinegar and water mixture over the flour mixture. Use fork or pastry blender to work liquid thoroughly into mixture. (You should be able to press rough bits of dough together and see them hold; if too dry, work in one more tablespoon cold water.)

2. *Refrigerate dough.* Cut large piece of plastic wrap and lay on counter. Dump out dough onto plastic. Gather edges of plastic to cover, pressing dough into a circle 1/2 inch thick. Refrigerate one hour while preparing fruit.

3. *Prepare fruit.* Pick over **blueberries, raspberries** or **blackberries** for stems and leaves. Or, cut **cherries** in half; remove and discard pits. Or, peel **peaches** or **nectarines**; cut in half—start where stem was and cut down to pit, then cut around fruit until you reach your starting point; pry halves apart; remove and discard pits; cut into 1/2-inch pieces. Treat **apricots** like peaches and nectarines—just don't peel them. Or, cut **apples** or **pears** into quarters right through where the stem was; peel quarters; cut out the core and cut fruit into 1/2-inch pieces.

4. *Roll out dough.* Adjust shelf to middle of oven and turn on to 400°F. Dust work surface with flour. Unwrap dough and place on flour-dusted surface. Dust top of dough with flour. Roll into 12- to 14-inch circle. (Roll dough from *center* of disk away from you, then rotate a quarter of a turn and roll again—from center away. Continue rotating and rolling until dough is desired size.) Set ungreased cookie sheet (baking sheet with no sides) beside dough (if you don't have a cookie sheet, using a baking sheet—the one with short sides—turned upside down). Lay rolling pin on one side of dough and gently roll dough around pin. Unroll onto sheet. Place in refrigerator until you are ready to form pie.

5. *Mix filling.* Measure sugar, cornstarch and lemon or lime juice into the bowl with the fruit. Mix thoroughly.

6. *Form pie.* Scoop fruit into center of rolled out dough. Spread the fruit into a *level* 8-inch circle in the center of the dough. Gently fold uncovered dough toward center, pleating dough as you go, to contain the fruit. Make certain there aren't any cracks around side (juice will run out through cracks). Pinch any cracks together to seal. Sprinkle fruit and crust around edges with sugar.

7. *Bake pie.* Set pie in middle of preheated oven. Bake 30 minutes. Reduce temperature to 325°F and bake 10 to 15 minutes longer, until crust is richly brown and fruit juices have thickened. Cool 10 minutes or more. Slide from cookie sheet to a decorative cutting board or platter, sprinkle with powdered sugar and serve.

NOTES: You may want to add cinnamon to apples or pears. Mix McIntosh and Granny Smith apples for an interesting texture. Dough made with cream cheese will hold its shape a bit better than dough made with goat cheese. There is not a noticeable flavor difference.

SERVES 6 TO 8

Classic Chocolate Truffles

8 ounces chocolate
6 tablespoons heavy (whipping) cream
1 cup unsweetened cocoa powder or
    powdered sugar (or some of both)

RICK: *One of life's greatest pleasures is a bite of an ultra-creamy, ultra-chocolatey chocolate truffle. If all you've had is Hersheys, M&M's and Snickers, these chocolates will definitely wake up your tastebuds. My absolute favorite is made from good* bittersweet *chocolate (like Lindt or Scharffen Berger). Lanie likes sweeter chocolate or milk chocolate. If you like milk chocolate, use 12 ounces rather than the 8 in the recipe. We say thanks to Elaine Gonzalez, our "Chocolate Queen" friend, for this recipe.*

✕   ✕   ✕   ✕   ✕   ✕

LANIE: *We make these for presents sometimes because EVERYONE LOVES THEM. They do require "delicate hands" and a lot of patience. Which sometimes I don't have. Chocolate truffles are a massive reward for the work you have to do. (I always eat a couple when I'm finished, even when they're for presents.) Rolling truffles in cocoa powder adds a bitter taste, so I usually go for the powdered sugar (except when the truffles are made with really sweet chocolate).*

> ⋯⋯ **DO THIS FIRST** ⋯⋯
>
> **CHOCOLATE:** Break or cut chocolate into smallish (about ½ inch) pieces.
> **COCOA OR POWDERED SUGAR:** Shake through sifter or fine strainer onto large
>   flat plate.

1. *Make chocolate "filling."* Place chocolate pieces in food processor. Secure lid and pulse until finely chopped. (It should look dusty—like cocoa.) Measure the cream in a microwave-safe cup with handle. Heat in microwave on high (100%) power until steaming—about 1 minute. Turn on processor and slowly pour in cream. Run machine until completely smooth—about 1 minute. Scrape chocolate mixture into pie pan or similar dish and flatten to about ³/₄ inch. Cover with plastic wrap and refrigerate until *barely* firm—30 to 45 minutes.

2. *Form truffles.* Set baking sheet on counter. Use small spoon to scoop out a rough-shaped "ball" of chocolate about ³/₄ inch in diameter—about 1¹/₂ teaspoons chocolate. Use another spoon to scoop chocolate off first spoon and onto baking sheet. Don't let balls touch—they'll stick together. Continue until all chocolate is used. One by one, roll chocolates into balls. If balls seem soft, refrigerate a few minutes. Then roll in sifted cocoa or powdered sugar to evenly coat. Store in single layer in sealed container in refrigerator. Let warm to room temperature before serving.

MAKES ABOUT 30 CHOCOLATE CANDIES

Crispy Meringue Shells with Ice Cream and Fruit "Salsa"

RICK: *I'm wild about meringue. I have a hard time keeping my fingers out of a bowl of egg whites beaten with sugar into a frothy white marshmallow gooeyness. And when you bake the sticky stuff, it gets this cool crispy crunchiness. This foolproof recipe was the first thing Darina Allen served us when we went to visit her in Ireland. (The Irish are really into meringue.) The only difference between this recipe and hers is that she made her meringues like two big crispy cake layers with fruit and whipped cream sandwiched inside. We make little shells to fill with ice cream and fruit.*

✄   ✄   ✄   ✄   ✄   ✄

LANIE: *Patience . . . patience. You need patience here, because you have to beat the egg whites f-o-r-e-v-e-r. And then bake the meringue for h-o-u-r-s. But it's TOTALLY worth it. Pretty. Yummy. One of the first desserts I learned to make by myself. But just get prepared—the stuff is sticky. You get sticky. The kitchen gets sticky. Hey, it's not my fault. It's meringue. When they are cooked, be careful—very fragile. (Once we had leftover meringues in this zip-top bag and I accidentally dropped them. They broke into like a hundred pieces so we served them on top of the ice cream and fruit.)*

2 "large" eggs

1¼ cups (4 ounces) powdered sugar

2 cups fresh or frozen fruit chopped into small pieces, if necessary (we like raspberries, blackberries, blueberries and strawberries)

A little regular sugar, if necessary

1 pint ice cream, frozen yogurt or sorbet

Mint sprigs for garnish

····· **DO THIS FIRST** ·····

EGGS: If eggs are cold, place in a bowl of warm tap water for 10 minutes. Separate eggs (page 65).

POWDERED SUGAR: Sift through mesh strainer or sifter, then carefully measure. (If you don't sift it first, you'll get too much sugar.)

BAKING SHEET: Smear oil *lightly* on a large baking sheet. Sprinkle with flour, shake around a little to coat all of surface, then shake off excess into trash can. Or, cover baking sheet with parchment paper.

OVEN: Place rack in middle of oven and turn on to 250°F.

1. *Make meringue.* In bowl of mixer, combine egg whites and powdered sugar. Beat on high speed for *15 full minutes.*

2. *Make fruit "salsa."* Use an old-fashioned potato masher or the back of a large spoon to roughly crush fruit, making it look juicy. If fruit is not juicy, add a little fruit juice. Taste, and stir in a little sugar if the fruit is too tart—but don't make it too sweet. Cover and refrigerate.

3. *Form shells.* Use ice cream scoop or large spoon to scoop out 6 (or 8 if you have enough) portions of meringue, spacing them 3 inches apart on the baking sheet. Use back of a large spoon to make a deep well in each meringue "ball."

4. *Bake shells.* Bake 1½ to 2 hours, until completely crispy and very lightly browned. Allow to cool for 15 minutes. If you're making these ahead, store them in an air-tight container—like Tupperware—just as soon as they have completely cooled.

5. *Serve.* Half an hour before serving, move ice cream from freezer to refrigerator to soften slightly. Place meringue shells on dessert plates. Fill well with a scoop of ice cream. Spoon fruit "salsa" on top. Decorate with mint sprigs.

SERVES 6 (OR 8 IF YOU MAKE THEM SMALL)

MOROCCO
{starting in southern Spain}

❊　　❊　　❊　　❊　　❊　　❊

Rick: The weekend Deann and I fell in love, New Year's 1979, we sat on my cheap, off-white Haitian cotton couch and listened to Jackson Browne sing a song about the mysteries of Morocco. The song was pressed into vinyl and the old record player was set to repeat. And it did for hours as Deann and I talked on and on, exploring the mysteries we were each bringing to this newly sprouted relationship.

For two decades after that fateful weekend, I harbored hopes of my own Moroccan adventure. I'd made Moroccan couscous and preserved lemon chicken from Paula Wolfert's enthralling *Couscous and Other Good Food from Morocco*. I'd read her meticulous directions for making paper-thin *warka* pastry (the same technique we'd seen for making egg roll wrappers in Taiwan and Thailand). And I'd completely fallen in love with the exotic Moroccan "pie" called *bastilla* with its many crispy layers of *warka* sandwiching sweet-and-savory cinnamon-and-saffron–scented chicken.

It was the mystery of Morocco's complex spices that fueled my imagination, though. I didn't understand how or why Moroccan cooks offered such a distinctive face of flavor. Tasting Moroccan food at home only emphasized its mystery. Tasting it in Morocco, I dreamed, would bring an "ah-ha!" that'd allow me to cook Moroccan dishes from the heart—not from the measurements of a recipe.

Turning on the television at 10 a.m. on September 11, 2001, I watched the World Trade Center crumble. My mysterious Moroccan dreams turned to fear. Though I'd always strived to be culturally sensitive, I knew so little—far too little—about the Muslim cultures with which we share so much of our planet. Eventually the fear evolved into an urgent desire to experience Moroccan flavors first hand. Overstated as it may seem to some, I believe that the soul of a culture is revealed in its flavors. When you have the opportunity to share those flavors with the folks who created them, there's potential for real understanding.

So, it was decided: that year's vacation would include Morocco. But it would begin in Spain which, oddly enough, is a great place to learn about the culture and refinement of Morocco. For the nearly 800 years that spanned Europe's dismal medieval period, Spain—especially southern Spain—was the thriving intellectual capital of the Arab/Muslim world. It was more a part of North Africa's cultural empire than Europe's.

We started at the Alhambra, that perfectly restored Moorish relic in Granada, in southern Spain. When we arrived, I discovered even more remnants of Moorish culture than I'd expected. Flamenco-like "gypsy music" drifted from cafés and clubs and bedroom windows. Market stall–filled streets twisted and turned like those I'd seen in pictures of Morocco, and restaurant menus read like Moroccan cookbooks. And the Alhambra reigned over the town in a language ancient and complex. It was one of the most glorious places of its day: the perfectly

Paella, recipe on page 178

proportioned rooms, the rhythmical designs in tile and woodwork, the framing of nature through the horseshoe-shaped windows, and, in the most important chambers, the dramatic ascension that leads the eye toward cupolas of heavenly stained glass. I could understand why European nobles sent their kids to Granada for "finishing school."

Our days in Southern Spain included several meals at tapas bars, each one featuring numerous small dishes of pure, uncomplicated Spanish flavor. We've included recipes for our favorite tapas dishes in this chapter. Then we headed down to the coast for two days of beaches and paella (that wonderful collection of rice/seafood/meat dishes). I highly recommend our "starter" paella recipe.

From the coast, we flew across the Straits of Gibraltar to Casablanca, and then headed out for Marrakech by car. Arriving that afternoon, our first glimpse of the city was the ancient, 30-foot-high, earth-and-stone ramparts that surround the old part (the medina) of Marrakech. Matching the color of the surrounding earth, the ramparts glowed rusty orange in the afternoon sun. Unflinching and unadorned, they seemed almost to be a natural geological formation. Within the gates, the houses were not much more welcoming: expressionless walls, occasionally punctuated by a small high window, each house abutting another. They lined both sides of the streets, forming narrow ways that twisted and turned like sections of a maze. And people were more physically reserved than I'd expected. Men wearing *djellabas* (loose hooded, long sleeved robes) and women in long kaftans with headscarves (some women also wore a

face veil, leaving only their eyes visible) walked down the street with people in typical western dress.

When Bouchra Benjelloun picked us up at our hotel, she looked anything but traditional. The cousin of chef-friend Rafih Benjelloun (Imperial Fez in Atlanta, Georgia), she was dressed in very fashionable black pants and a brilliant red bolero jacket. Bouchra had invited us to go marketing with her, then back to her house to cook. She was spry and slight, with lively eyes. When she turned on the ignition of her Volkswagen Jetta, Algerian dance music called *rai* blared through the radio. She apologized and shot me a quick grin. I knew that this was going to be fun.

In a thousand years, I could never have pictured Bouchra in the Marrakech wholesale food market. She had to jockey her car into a space between donkey carts (donkeys still attached), then carve a path for us on foot through a haphazard arrangement of produce. The market was spread over a dusty open field, with men (no women) selling wooden crates or heaps of fruits and vegetables from the backs of carts or flatbed trucks, or simply from tarps spread on the ground. It was impressive, but not beautiful. It had an impermanent feel, as if a modern-day caravan had just stopped and spread out its wares, offering a slim variety of produce with which cooks could just about make do. Red onions, spinach and mallow greens, pumpkins, fava beans, tomatoes, peppers, eggplant, celery-like cardoon, parsley and cilantro. And lots of oranges; Morocco is famous for its oranges.

Our second stop was to a food market renowned for quality, in the old Jewish quarter just outside the medina. It was filled with small stalls of all of the foods that a good Moroccan cook needs: vegetables, fresh and dried fruit, fresh and salted seafood from the Atlantic and Mediterranean, dried goods (spices, chickpeas, lentils, couscous, vinegar, paper towels), a few dairy products, and lamb and beef, both fresh and made into sausage. (Muslim and Jewish dietary restrictions forbid pork.) Most impressive, though, were the massive, beautiful stalls that sold the famous Moroccan preserved foods: olives in a variety of earthy colors, lemons, peppers and hot sauce (*harissa*).

Standing among those stalls, it made sense to me that before modern-day refrigeration and easy long-distance transportation, cooks of this desert climate dealt with the sporadic harvests by preserving whatever they could for times of scarcity. And the Arabs, prominent traders who traversed a territory that stretched from southeast Asia all the way to the east side of north Africa, were famous for the spices they brought from far-off lands, spices they wove into their food to remind (or boast) of their thriving exotic trade routes.

Bouchra's house is in a very modern section of town. It welcomed us with its rather austere, grand entry that opened into large rooms with spare furniture pushed to the walls, as is typical in Morocco. When I saw the kitchen, I felt completely at home: It looked very much like the one in the "modern" '60s ranch home of my childhood. This was a modern Moroccan house.

After showing us around and sequestering her dogs, Bouchra ushered us onto her backyard patio, a tiled area with an overhead canopy and billowing curtains on all sides to block the intense sun. On the patio table was a plate of traditional nut sweets and cookies along with small colored glasses waiting to be filled with Morocco's famous mint tea (sweetened green tea infused with fresh mint leaves) poured from the classic Moroccan silver teapot. It was the first time I'd experienced this legendary, gracious North African mint tea-and-sweets welcome. It was so delectable, so gracious, that I felt we could have lingered for hours. But Bouchra had other plans: We would cook a dozen dishes with her by nightfall.

There were six of us in the kitchen: Lanie, Deann, Bouchra, her mother and a genial old Berber woman—the family housekeeper for many years—who moved stealthily around the kitchen, showing up in exactly the right place to take care of whatever was needed. We jumped into cooking the first seven dishes at once.

Bouchra's mother, a master of the stuffed flaky pastry *bastilla*, walked us through the preparation of the complexly spiced filling made from poached chicken, ground almonds and eggs that she wrapped in hand-made sheets of *warka* pastry dough. Then it was on to couscous, the cornerstone of Moroccan meals. Few of us in the United States understand that couscous is *pasta*—thousands of tiny "grains" of pasta. To become soft and appealing, the grains

must be transformed by slow, careful moistening and steaming. The quick-and-easy couscous available in our groceries bears about as much resemblance to what we were about to experience as instant mashed potatoes bears to the real thing.

Bouchra started lamb simmering with tomato, turmeric, ginger and pepper in the bottom of a large two-part *couscousier* (a couscous-cooking pot consisting of a deep pot, a shallower, perforated steamer that fits over the pot and a lid). This would create the steam needed to cook the couscous and, eventually, the aromatic, brothy stew that's served with it. Over the next hour, with the help of her housekeeper, Bouchra transformed the dry grains into fluffy deliciousness: First she moistened them with water, then steamed them for 15 to 20 minutes over the simmering lamb in the perforated top of the *couscousier,* and finally turned them out to fluff with her fingertips, breaking up any clumps. She repeated the whole procedure two more times, adding salt and, at the end, olive oil and butter. Mounded on a beautiful platter and topped with the slow-simmered lamb (and vegetables she'd added along the way), it was a beautiful sight.

For Lanie, she demonstrated a couscous variation her three boys—ranging in age from mid-teens to early twenties—loved: Warm buttered couscous sprinkled with cinnamon and sugar.

Before 3 o'clock came around, we had rolled two versions of beef meatballs (our favorite were seasoned with hot paprika, cumin, parsley and garlic) and cooked them nestled in tomato sauce in a *tagine,* an earthenware pot with a cone-shaped top. Bouchra had cut up a chicken, mixed it with saffron, ginger, onion, olive oil and preserved lemon, then cooked it

until meltingly tender; she piled it on a serving platter and garnished it with purplish olives. Another classic earthenware *tagine* was filled with lamb, prunes and spices. Yet another was layered with beautifully arranged vegetables topped with salted sardines that had been coated with mashed garlic, paprika, lemon, cilantro and parsley.

It had all begun to blur until we sat down again at the patio table and enjoyed each distinctly flavored, complexly spiced bite. From my years living in Mexico, I'd become accustomed to a complex array of spices singing in unique harmony. The spices in these dishes weren't just singing new tunes, they were singing a new style of music for me.

That afternoon, we took a break in the cooking marathon to search out a well-known spice stall in the market section (*souk*) of the medina. This section of the medina's jumble of twisting streets is about one mile square—the largest *souk* in Morocco. Rather than being mostly filled with food vendors, as I'm accustomed to in Mexico, this market is both a workshop and outlet for Morocco's famously accomplished craftsmen. In fact, the *souk* sells very little food—dried fruits and spices are the big draw.

When we got to the stall, there was more fragrant cumin there than I'd ever seen in one place. And cardamom, ground ginger, deep orange turmeric root, cinnamon and black pepper. I tried to write it all down but eventually gave up and started buying. We'd been taken to this particular stall for its *ras al hanout,* the house "all purpose" spice blend. Inhaling deeply, I experienced the promise of a flavor I'd never known. How had they created this unique blend that smelled like a single, newly discovered spice?

That evening, back at Bouchra's home, we prepared four simple "salads" (imagine vegetable dishes, served cool): spinach-like mallow, tomatoes and peppers, pumpkin, and eggplant. In Morocco, salads like these start both family meals and big celebrations. We shared them with the Benjelloun family—a sophisticated lot who had traveled through much of the world. But as they tasted the traditional dishes of their homeland, scooping up mouthfuls of roasted pepper salad with torn pieces of traditional flatbread, I watched an inimitable look of proud satisfaction creep across their faces. This was the ancient nourishment for their Moroccan bodies and souls.

Morocco is a spectacle of wind-swept deserts, oases, earth-colored fortresses, labyrinthine marketplaces and exotic storytellers. Of everything we saw and tasted, there are two things that will always stay with me from this initial experience of the country. The first is the way in which the aesthetic of the Arab culture reflects the peoples' reserve in elements that range from architecture to dress. I'm used to exotic places and people, but my experience in Morocco was different. Unlike Thailand and Mexico, where folks can be disarmingly welcoming and so much of life is lived out in the open (though to an outsider it can occasionally seem incomprehensibly foreign), Morocco remains behind a sheer veil, still mysterious and hidden.

The second is the way that cooks have woven the mystery and magic into their food through the use of spices. As though employing techniques of ancient Arab "scientists"—the alchemists—who sought to transform everyday materials into precious gold, Arab cooks combine spices from far-off lands to transform ordinary ingredients into precious sustenance. It is a sustenance that is much more than the simple sum of its parts.

Lanie: I'll admit it—I was scared to go to Morocco. I thought it was a bad idea. I mean, I was only 10 and on September 11, everybody freaked out and some of the kids at school said *ugly* things about anyone from a Muslim country. Which I told them was totally dumb since you can't generalize from one small group. But I was still scared. Like, would people yell at us or try to do stuff to us?

Besides just being generally scared, I was supposed to get my two days on the beach in Spain (Marbella—it was supposed to be *totally* cool with yachts and movie stars), but it turned out to be too cold to go swimming. So we went horseback riding instead, which *would* have been cool, except that the guy who was leading us was this Moroccan guy who spoke NO English and *almost* no Spanish. And he *did not* go slow. When my horse started slipping on a steep slope, I really freaked—I mean CRYING freaked. But I couldn't go back because we were *who-knows-where* up in the mountains and we couldn't talk to this guy. All I could think was: What if all Morocco is like this?

Anyway, Morocco wasn't nearly as "unusual" as I thought it might be, even though it was kind of hard to communicate. And when we got to know people—especially Bouchra, who cooked with us in Marrakech—it was kind of like everywhere else we visited. Except that you had to wash

your hands in front of everyone before you eat. They make a kind of *ritual* of hand washing in Morocco.

I have five favorite things from the trip:

(1) **Hot chocolate and churros.** The first thing we got to do when we landed in Madrid was drink that really thick, *really* chocolatey Spanish hot chocolate that you dip these long crispy fried donuty things in. TOTALLY, *totally* delicious.

(2) **Roses.** I'm not usually into flowers, but everywhere we went in Marrakech there were roses, sometimes regular (like in vases), but mostly rose petals floating in fountains or dishes. *Everywhere.*

(3) **Henna tattoos.** We walked across that main square in Marrakech many times (partly because we kept getting lost in all the small streets). There were these women here and there around the square covered with dresses and scarves from head to toe, only slits left open for their eyes, who painted henna (a kind of dye) tattoos, which my parents said I could get on my hands. (They wear off after a week or two, and besides it's *very* TRADITIONAL—my parents are all about traditional—for girls to get them on their hands before special occasions, like their weddings.) But I was kinda scared—the square was a wild scene (more about that below). When we went to this spice shop in the market part (*souk*) of the old town, there were two girls (no "costume") doing henna tattoos there. Go figure. Well, I *did it*—two girls working on me at the same time. And it took, like, *5 minutes!* And the tops of my hands were covered with all these whirligigs and scrolls and stuff. VERY, *very* cool. Then they told me I couldn't go swimming for a day (it has to dry completely), which was really a bummer, since I *really wanted* to go swimming.

(4) **Eating on the square (Djemaa el Fna).** This place is really *crazy*. First, there's all those women doing the henna tattoos, and they're wearing *all those clothes*, and they have little metal decorations all over them that make noise when they walk. Then there are all these groups of men

Mediterranean Coast Gazpacho

RICK: *Here's my prediction: You'll think gazpacho is phenomenal if you understand exactly what it is and you season it right. First, it's a soup but it's cold. And don't think it's just cold tomato soup, because there's a lot more to it than that. On our first trip to Spain, we traveled with one of our Mexican chefs from Frontera Grill. He proclaimed gazpacho to be "salsa soup." Tomatoes, peppers, onions, vinegar—makes sense, although it's smoother and not as spicy as salsa. My tip for you is to taste the finished soup carefully and adjust the vinegar and salt little by little. Without enough of either one, the tomatoes will taste flat—exactly what a lot of kids (Lanie included) don't like about tomatoes. Really ripe tomatoes make the best soup.*

✕   ✕   ✕   ✕   ✕   ✕

LANIE: *The worst part about gazpacho is trying to convince people that cold soup— at least THIS cold soup—is really good. (Not so hard if it's summer, and something cold and light seems PERFECT.) The best part about gazpacho is that you get to put in whatever garnishes you want. (If I were you, I'd toast the bread cubes—they're better crunchy.) I know it's a pain, but you should pay attention to the weight of the tomatoes (and the bread, if you can figure it out) so the soup turns out right.*

2 "large" eggs
2½ pounds ripe fresh tomatoes (7 to 8 medium round ones)
1 cucumber
3 slices (about 3 ounces total) cakey white bread—Pepperidge Farms white original, brioche or challah are good choices
1 small green bell pepper
1 garlic clove
1 cup tomato juice
½ cup olive oil
2 tablespoons vinegar, preferably red wine vinegar
Salt
½ small onion

····· **DO THIS FIRST** ·····

TOMATOES: With a small knife, cut out and discard "core" from top of tomatoes where stem once attached. Cut ¼ of them (usually 2) into ¼-inch slices. Cut slices into ¼-inch cubes. Scoop into a small serving bowl and set aside for garnish. Cut remaining tomatoes into 6 pieces each.

CUCUMBER: Cut in half. Slice one half into ¼-inch-thick slices. Cut slices into ¼-inch dice. Scoop into small serving bowl and set aside for garnish. Cut remaining half into 6 pieces.

BREAD: Cut crust off bread. Discard. Cut 2 slices into small cubes. Scoop into a small serving bowl and set aside for garnish. Tear rest of bread into large pieces.

GREEN PEPPER: Cut in half down through stem. Pull out and discard seed pod and stem. Cut each half into 3 pieces.

GARLIC: Peel. Cut the clove in half.

ONION: Cut off top and bottom and discard. Peel off papery outside layers and discard. Slice about ¼ inch thick. Cut slices into ¼-inch cubes. Scoop into small serving bowl and set aside for garnish.

garlic from sides of processor. Add drained tomatoes, olive oil, tomato paste and chopped onion. Add the remaining *1½ teaspoons* paprika, *1 teaspoon* cumin and parsley. Season with ½ teaspoon salt. Process until *nearly* smooth. Scrape into pan or deep skillet that is about 10 inches across (size is important here). Set over medium heat. Bring to a boil and cook 2 to 3 minutes. Remove pan from heat.

3. *Cook meatballs and serve.* Nestle meatballs into sauce in a *single* layer. Swirl pan gently to ensure all meatballs are covered with sauce. Set over medium heat with lid slightly ajar and cook 10 to 12 minutes, until meatballs are cooked through. Taste and stir in more salt if you think necessary. If sauce is very thick, add a little water. Spoon onto individual plates and serve.

SERVES 4

❊ Five Cool CDs to Play While Cooking Moroccan ❊

Not everything here is Moroccan, but it all has Arabic roots—which means it's pretty different from most anything we're used to, but it has a pretty cool groove.

1. Arabic Groove: My favorite North African/Middle Eastern CD because it's a compilation that's "total groove"— cool music from cultures all the way from Lebanon to Morocco that's all about rhythm. (You may notice influences from hip hop and R&B.)

2. Desert Roses and Arabic Rhythms: Another compilation that's all about cool dance, pop and world beat techno. Some of the songs are in English but all are unmistakably Arabic in rhythm. There are two volumes (my favorite is II).

3. Kenza: One of the latest albums from Kahled (the king of Rai, Algerian pop dance music). Great stuff that blends this super-popular dance music (we heard it everywhere in Morocco) with Western influences (Kahled records mostly in Paris and London).

4. Moroccan Street Music: A compilation CD that's the real stuff—simple, rhythmic melodies that we heard from street performers in Marrakech. You can't dance to it, but it has the allure of authenticity.

5. Best of Gipsy Kings or Moroccan Spirit: These two albums couldn't be more different. The first is great party music, sung in Spanish by a bunch of talented French guys in a traditional gypsy style that has deep Arabic roots. It's for anyone who can't quite get into the seriously Arab stuff. The second is sometimes a little mellow for me, but you can find some good groove in it, too. Done by world-beat guys who immersed themselves in Moroccan music before returning to the electronics of the European studio.

Preserved Lemon Chicken with Olives

RICK: *I didn't get to Morocco until I was well into my forties, though I had dreamed about visiting that exotic land since I was a kid. Just as I'd hoped, I was completely enthralled by the winding alleys in the ancient marketplaces called* souks: *the mysterious aromas that float from spice stalls no bigger than large closets, the "31 flavors" of olives and the fragrant lemons preserved in salt. So much of what I love about Morocco comes together in this dish. There they sometimes use the very expensive golden saffron in place of the intensely yellow turmeric. Red-brown olives such as Kalamatas are most traditional, but we sometimes like to use green ones such as gaetas or picholines.*

⁙ ⁙ ⁙ ⁙ ⁙ ⁙

LANIE: *I can tell you honestly: This dish has really* great *flavor!! Not too tangy or strong, even though the preserved lemons by themselves are a little strong (not sour, but saltier and stronger than green olives). The recipe's not too hard, but I have 2 warnings: (1) The golden sauce will turn any white spatula yellow. (2) You should read the recipe* at least twice *so you remember everything and don't screw it up like I did once. I guess the heat was more like medium-high and not "medium to medium-low" (like the recipe says). Besides, the chicken was SUPPOSED to cook solo for 20 minutes and I had just gotten that new Britney Spears CD. Well, my mom SAVED THE DAY, and she figured out how to save the chicken from the* black *pan and make a new "improvised" Moroccan Lemon Chicken sauce. Which came out so good even my dad couldn't be mad. For this dish to come out* really good, *you need chicken that still has skin and bones.*

3 garlic cloves
1 large preserved lemon—available at Moroccan or Middle Eastern groceries or make your own (opposite page)
¼ cup vegetable oil (use only 2 tablespoons if using thighs)
1 teaspoon powdered ginger
¼ teaspoon turmeric
¼ teaspoon ground black pepper
Salt
½ small onion
½ cup loosely packed fresh cilantro leaves, plus extra for garnish
4 large (about 2½ pounds total) chicken breast halves with bones
OR 8 (about 2½ pounds total) chicken thighs with bones
½ cup olives (pitted if you like, opposite page)

DO THIS FIRST

GARLIC: Peel.
LEMON: Rinse to remove excess salt. With spoon, scoop lemon pulp from peel. Cut peel into strips ¼ inch wide. Roughly chop pulp, removing seeds as you find them.
ONION: Cut off top and bottom and discard. Peel off papery outside layers and discard. Slice about ¼ inch thick. Chop slices finely.
OVEN: Position rack in middle of oven and turn on to 425°F.

1. *Make flavoring.* Turn on food processor. Drop garlic cloves one by one through feed tube. Turn off machine, remove lid and scrape garlic from sides. Add lemon

pulp, oil, ginger, turmeric, pepper and ½ teaspoon salt. Process until mixture is pretty smooth—about a minute.

2. *Cook chicken.* Scrape garlic mixture into medium-large (6-quart) heavy pot (preferably a Dutch oven) or very large (12-inch) deep skillet. Add chopped onion, cilantro and 2½ cups water. Stir, set over medium heat and let come to a boil. Nestle chicken pieces in the sauce. Place lid on pan slightly ajar and cook over medium to medium-low heat until *almost* tender when probed with a fork (about 20 minutes for breasts, 25 minutes for thighs). Use tongs or spoon to remove chicken to a baking sheet. Set chicken in oven and bake 15 minutes, until lightly browned.

3. *Finish sauce and serve.* Turn heat under sauce to medium-high. Add strips of lemon peel and olives. Cook—stirring frequently—until it begins to thicken, about 5 minutes. It should be thicker than chicken broth, but not as thick as cream of mushroom soup. Place chicken on a deep serving platter. Spoon sauce over top. Decorate with more cilantro leaves if desired.

SERVES 4

Basic Moroccan-Style Preserved Lemons

Scrub four (or more if you like) lemons with a stiff brush under cold running water—important because you're using the rind. Stand 1 lemon on end and cut it in half to within ½ inch of the bottom. Rotate it one-quarter turn and cut down through lemon again to within ½ inch of the bottom. (You now have a quartered lemon with all four quarters still connected at one end.) Now, holding the lemon slightly open, sprinkle about 1 tablespoon salt down over the quarters. Re-form the lemon and lay it in a wide-mouth glass jar or plastic storage container. Quarter and salt the remaining lemons in the same way, fitting them tightly into the jar or container. Sprinkle on another tablespoon of salt, press down on the lemons to release a little juice, then cover with fresh-squeezed (not bottled) lemon juice. Cover and refrigerate for 3 to 4 weeks until the lemon peel is completely tender. These keep indefinitely in the refrigerator.

How to Pit Olives

Pitting olives can be a pain, so most people buy them already pitted. Unfortunately, really good-tasting olives aren't usually pitted. If you've got olives with pits, it's best to lay them one at a time on a cutting board, hold a metal spatula, wide knife or cleaver flat on top of it, and then thwack it with your other hand. The flesh of the olive should break free from the pit so that you can tear the olive apart and remove the pit. The thwacked olive will look a little ragged, but it will be pitless.

Moroccan Beef or Lamb Kebabs

RICK: *Djemaa el Fna, the great square in Marrakech, is one of my favorite places on earth. Besides the musicians and snake handlers that delight or frighten tourists, the dramatic storytellers captivate huge groups for hours—even me, and I don't speak a word of Arabic. As the sun sets over this ancient desert town, cooks set up row after row of stalls, offering everything from couscous and vegetable "salads" to chickpea soup and the most wonderful kebabs (called* brochettes, *as in France, because Morocco was once a French colony) and merguez sausage. The kebabs are made from bite-size cubes of lamb (sometimes beef), simply seasoned with salt or with the addition of hot paprika and cumin. The meat cubes are typically threaded onto great-looking metal skewers and then seared to well-done over smoky charcoal. You can use a lot of different cuts of beef to make these: strip (New York) steak, rib eye, tenderloin, even chuck (though that can be a little chewy).*

❈ ❈ ❈ ❈ ❈ ❈

LANIE: *All I remember about eating these in Marrakech is the smoke. And the smell of all the stuff grilling—especially the sausages, which were ab-so-lute-ly delicious, but a lot more difficult to make than anything I would want to try. So try these kebabs instead, which are almost as good as the sausages. (Make them with beef instead of lamb, if you share my taste.) They're good with the Moroccan Roasted Pepper and Tomato Salad (page 164).*

1 small red onion
½ lemon
1½ pounds boneless beef top sirloin or boneless leg of lamb
12 fresh parsley sprigs
½ teaspoon ground black pepper
Salt
Fourteen to sixteen 6- to 8-inch bamboo skewers

⋯⋯ DO THIS FIRST ⋯⋯

ONION: Cut off top and bottom and discard. Cut in half from top to bottom. Peel off papery outside layers and discard. Slice halves about ¼-inch thick. Chop slices finely.
MEAT: Trim most of the fat from the meat—leaving a little fat keeps meat moist and adds flavor. Cut meat into ¾-inch cubes.
PARSLEY: Pull off leaves and discard stems. Finely chop. (See page 37.)
SKEWERS: Lay skewers in a long dish. Cover with water.

1. *Marinate meat.* Place chopped onion in large bowl. Squeeze juice of lemon into bowl. Add cubed meat, chopped parsley, pepper and 1 teaspoon salt. Mix well. Cover and refrigerate for 1 hour.

2. *Cook meat and serve.* Heat grill or grill pan over medium-high until quite hot. Thread about 8 pieces of meat onto each skewer. (Discard any marinade left in bowl.) Lay skewers on grill or pan so that they don't touch. (Grill in two batches if they don't fit easily.) Cook until well-browned underneath—3 to 4 minutes—then flip and cook about the same amount of time on the other side. Or, cook 4 inches below a preheated broiler on a baking sheet lined with foil. They take about the same amount of time per side.

SERVES 4 TO 6

❊ Grilling 101 ❊

There are three common ways to grill: a charcoal grill, a gas grill and a grill pan (not really grilling but very easy and better than no grill flavor at all). A charcoal grill is the hardest to use and makes the tastiest food. You have to light the coals and let them burn until they're covered with gray ash. We use one of those "chimney" starters to get the coals going and then dump them into the grill—a little tricky for a beginner. All you have to do with a gas grill is light it, pretty much like lighting a gas burner on the stove. The food from a gas grill is medium tasty because there's less "grilled" flavor.

Here are my six Grilling Commandments for working with a charcoal or gas grill:

(1) Make sure the grill grate (the thing you cook on) is very clean—a wire brush works best to clean it.

(2) Heat the grill grate thoroughly before putting food on it.

(3) Lightly oil the food (not the grate) before laying it on the grill grate—peppers are an exception, since they don't usually get oiled.

(4) Don't try to move food until it is well-browned underneath; before that, it will usually stick to the grill grate, and it'll rip if you try to move it.

(5) If the fire (or grill grate) is not hot enough, food will stick. If the fire (or grill grate) is too hot, food will burn. Be like Goldilocks: try to get it just right.

(6) Have a spray bottle filled with water to smother flare-ups that come from fat dripping on the charcoal or gas burner.

Using a grill pan—one of those ridged pans, usually made out of heavy metal—sears "grill marks" on the foot, but is otherwise considered "fake grilling." Some things actually taste better broiled, but broiling doesn't make those nice grill marks, which we all like and which do add a little taste of their own.

Paella—Spanish Rice with Chicken, Shrimp and Ham

LANIE: *I don't know why, but paella always sounds fancy or something. Paella (pie-ay-ya). Even though it's basically just tasty rice with stuff like chicken and shrimp in it. On our way to Morocco, we got to stop at this really cool town on the coast in Spain and we went to a restaurant that had, like, a hundred different things you could get in your paella. (In summer, they cook it outside on a big fire.) Saffron is the spice everyone talks about in paella. It's super-EXPENSIVE (my dad keeps it in the freezer)—little orange threads from inside crocus flowers. Not too strong . . . or delicious . . . or anything. I can't figure out why it costs so much.*

※　※　※　※　※　※

RICK: *Paella's a pretty big deal in Spain, especially along the Mediterranean coast, not because it's hard or uses a lot of special ingredients. It's a big deal because folks make it for special occasions—to bring people together at the paella pan. Lots of people in Spain use a paella pan that's 3 or 4 feet across—enough to feed 30 or 40—and everyone gathers round to help themselves. For me, saffron is the ultimate paella flavor. Not strong, but wonderful. Maybe it takes a while to appreciate. Traditional paella rice has a fat, short grain that cooks up firm, but tender. It is available in well-stocked grocery stores. You can get a similar texture from medium-grain rice, but rest assured that any rice will work in this recipe.*

3¼ cups chicken broth (use 2¾ cups if using the short-grain "paella" rice from Spain)
¼ teaspoon saffron, optional
Salt
¼ cup olive oil or vegetable oil
6 chicken thighs
1 large red bell pepper
2 garlic cloves
One 15-ounce can diced tomatoes in juice
1 big handful green beans OR 1½ cups frozen peas
2 cups rice
½ pound medium shrimp
¼ pound ham
1 lemon

······ DO THIS FIRST ······

RED PEPPER: Cut pepper in half down through stem. Pull out white seed pod in middle and pull off stem. Discard. Cut pepper into small pieces (about ½ inch).

GARLIC: Peel.

TOMATO: Pour the tomatoes and their juice into a blender or food processor, secure lid and blend until smooth.

GREEN BEANS: Break off and discard stem end and pointy end. Cut into small pieces (about ½ inch).

SHRIMP: Peel shell off each shrimp: Hold shrimp in one hand and pull off tiny legs with the other hand; next, peel off shell a few sections at a time.

HAM: Cut into small pieces (about ½ inch).

LEMON: Cut into 8 wedges.

OVEN: Position rack in middle of oven and turn on to 325°F.

1. *Heat broth.* Pour broth into medium (4- to 6-quart) saucepan. If using saffron, mash the little threads into a $1/4$ teaspoon measure; then add. Add salt (2 teaspoons for unsalted broth, $1^1/_2$ teaspoons for low-salt broth or 1 teaspoon for salted broth). Cover pan with lid and set over medium heat.

2. *Brown chicken.* Measure olive oil into a very large (12-inch) skillet or heavy pot (preferably a Dutch oven) 12 inches in diameter *that can go in the oven.* Set over medium-high heat. Dry chicken with paper towels. When oil is hot, carefully lay chicken in oil. When well browned underneath (4 to 5 minutes), turn over with tongs. Brown other side. Use tongs to transfer chicken to a plate.

3. *Cook flavorings.* Reduce heat to medium. Add pepper pieces to pan and cook—stirring occasionally—until it begins to brown, about 4 minutes. Crush garlic through press and add to browned peppers. Stir well, then add the pureed tomatoes and pieces of green beans. (If using frozen peas, add after you take paella out of oven.) Cook and stir until thick and pasty (about 4 minutes).

4. *Cook rice.* With pan still over heat, add the rice. Stir 3 or 4 times, then cook for 1 minute. Pour hot broth into rice. Scrape all rice kernels down into liquid. Stir once. When liquid boils, set timer for 10 minutes. Don't stir (stirring makes the rice gummy).

5. *Finish paella.* When the timer goes off, lay peeled shrimp, browned chicken and pieces of ham in a single layer on rice and gently press in. Set skillet in oven and bake 13 minutes. Take out of oven. "Fluff" rice with fork. If using frozen peas, add them. Cover with lid or piece of aluminum foil. Let stand 10 minutes to finish cooking rice. Either serve the paella straight from the skillet at the table or spoon onto individual plates. Serve with lemon wedges for each person to squeeze on paella.

SERVES 6

THAILAND
{with side trips to Japan and Hong Kong}

❀ ❀ ❀ ❀ ❀ ❀

Rick: When I was 14 years old, I took my first trip outside the United States, to Mexico. By the time my parents and I arrived at our Mexico City hotel at 10 o'clock at night, I was already completely, comfortably in love with a culture I'd previously had only secondhand experience with. Thirty years later, I had an equally passionate love-at-first-sight experience on New Year's Day 1999, visiting Bangkok with Deann and Lanie.

Such an instant love affair with Thai culture may seem unlikely, since that culture is so utterly foreign to Americans. There are few Thais in the United States (and almost no "Thailand Town" sections of American cities), the language is impossibly difficult for English speakers, and the country is on the opposite side of the globe.

Yet, when I arrived in Thailand, I resonated instantly with the pungent, earthy aromas that filled the streets around our hotel. And with the warmth and grace of the people, the sensuality of the colors and textures that surrounded us, and the flowers

that sprung and tumbled from every conceivable spot. My heart soared as I looked at temple spires ascending to the heavens, and watched gregarious, noisy groups of Thais sharing a meal of noodles, satay, or dumplings around a glaringly lit street stall. It all felt so good.

I doubt any of this would have happened so quickly without our friend Olivia Wu, who was born in Shanghai, raised in Bangkok, and college educated in the United States. For years, Olivia had encouraged us to visit Thailand with her, to meet her extended family and understand more fully why we loved her cooking. When my cousins

moved to the northern Thai city of Chiang Mai to teach in an English-speaking school, I knew a trip was imminent.

Crossing twelve time zones can cause wicked jet lag. The morning after we arrived, I felt punch-drunk as I stumbled out of our hotel. Walking the few blocks to a dock to catch a water "taxi" (noisy small barges that plow through the busy waters of the Chao Prya river avoiding the car-clogged Bangkok streets), I passed a food stand of little bananas grilling over charcoal. And another offering spicy Thai coffee with sweetened condensed milk. And another featuring two huge pots: one holding a stew that smelled of kaffir lime leaves and coconut milk, another filled with aromatic jasmine rice.

There's nothing luxurious about Bangkok's river taxis. Packed into the boat like sardines in a tin can, we breathed in river aromas and exhaust fumes as we counted stops to the Imperial Palace. That stop was filled with even more vendors than the one we'd left, and they were more formally organized into a small market. I wanted to taste the piles of fresh lychee fruits and the little banana-leaf wrapped packets of charcoal-grilled, coconut-flavored sticky rice. I wanted to buy a handful of satay skewers dipped in peanut sauce, some of that famous banana-leaf wrapped fish mousse, or a bowlful of earthy stew sold from one of those portable palm baskets with four willowy rattan handles that meet in an elegant point above the basket, mimicking temple spires. I wanted to buy bouquets of lotus blossoms or jasmine leis for Olivia, Deann and Lanie. This was the most sensuous place I'd ever been. Flowers, flavors, finesse and aromas triggered total infatuation.

Bangkok-Style Chicken Satay, recipe on page 194

What we saw that day was both thrilling and challenging: no bare legs or arms allowed in sacred places, shoes off in temples, never point your toes toward the Buddha, never touch a monk, bow with hands in prayer position to show gratitude, never shake hands. Everything was awkward and foreign, but no one made us feel foreign. Thailand is the land of smiles. And sweetness, and fierce spiciness, and brutal kickboxing (which always starts with meditation and prayer). This is the land of ornate vegetable carving so intricate it requires tools that rival those of a surgeon.

None of this, however, prepared me for Aw Daw Gaw Market. I've been to markets in many countries—markets where earthy subsistence reminds me of food's elemental role in our lives, markets where abundance overwhelms, markets where food is treated like jewels. This market combined it all—earthy, abundant and precious—then smacked it with emphatic, complex flavor. It was, in a word, thrilling. As a chef, I saw Aw Daw Gaw as elegant, exotic and awe-inspiring—the culinary equivalent of Cirque du Soleil.

Main Players: A chorus of raw rices, displayed as burlap-clad pillars, ranging from cheap to expensive, aromatic to plain, fluffy to sticky, one region or another. Youthful herbs, their aromas leaping into the air—cilantro, mint, holy basil, lemongrass and pungent sawtooth coriander. Eggplants from pea- to softball size, and greens with wiggling tendrils. Mounds of durian, that extravagant fruit so pungently aromatic (think tropical fruit blended with ripe, ripe French cheese) that it has been banned from some airplane cabins and hotel rooms. Earthy curry pastes, flooding the air with exotic spice and pungency. Luxuriously rich coconut milk freshly expressed from whirling extractors.

Most Stunning Costumes and Makeup: The tree limb of cascading green mangoes hanging over a tray of cream-colored, coconut-flavored sweet sticky rice. The burnished veneer of red-skinned grilled pork. The saffron yellow hue of turmeric root staining salads, satays and stews.

A Sampling of the Greatest Feats: The impossibly thin "crepe" folded over a *pad thai*–like stir-fry just as the crepe sets to a total crispness. Aromatic satay skewers grilled within millimeters of luminous coals to a perfect sear and doneness. Green papaya reduced to thin, long shreds (by rapid-fire assault with a sharp knife while being held in the cook's palm) and seasoned with mortar-pounded preserved crab, hot chile and lime. Rice noodle batter spread paper thin overly tautly-stretched, steam-heated cotton cloth, topped with a nugget of filling, then elegantly pleated into a dumpling as it sets.

I was smiling from ear to ear. And speechless. I hadn't developed a vocabulary to describe these sights and scents, flavors and techniques.

When we got back to the United States, I dedicated some time to learning more about the Thai kitchen. But dedication wasn't enough. I found myself perplexed in our local Thai market; I was confounded at the stove. How could anything so comfortably delicious be so difficult for me to re-create?

For the first time in many years, I faced exactly the difficulty that I see many of my students, cookbook readers and television viewers experience when I share with them my thoroughgoing knowledge of the Mexican kitchen: Really learning to cook a different cuisine was requiring about as much time and cultural immersion from me as learning to speak a different language. I could master a couple of dishes—like learning to say "how are you?" or "where's the bathroom?"—but I didn't know nearly enough to determine what to serve when, or how to authentically improvise when ingredients weren't available.

I loved Thai food so much (not to mention the people, terrain and aesthetic) that I knew we had to go back. Which we did every couple of years, until I began to feel a little more "fluent" in Thai cuisine.

I had my Thai cooking epiphany one January day in 2003 in the home of Khunying Aoy in Chiang Mai. My cousins Mike and Cheri Potter, who taught at the Chiang Mai International School, had gotten to know Khunying Aoy as the mother of several of their students. She was highly regarded at the school as a generous, hard-working parent and a knowledgeable Thai cook. Through Cheri, we inquired as to whether we could spend a day cooking with her and her family, and she graciously agreed. None of us understood what a special experience we'd been offered.

Khunying Aoy's house, on the outskirts of town, was a rustic, rural dream. Her husband, a renowned architect, had constructed the main part of the house using the skeleton of a century-old rice barn (the largest one ever made in Northern Thailand), which he'd taken apart board by board and rebuilt on their property. She'd done the lush, tropical landscaping (read: jungle control) that cradled the place— she'd even used part of their land for commercial flower production at one time. The environment was seductively green, punctuated with a multitude of orchids, bromeliads and heliconias.

My cousins hadn't realized that their students' mom was such a legendary Thai cook. Or that, as a young woman, she'd chosen to go to the Cordon Bleu in London rather than college, because she had a passion for the culinary arts. Or that her mother was widely celebrated for the classic Thai dishes she prepared and sold to restaurants in her native Bangkok. Or that she was connected to the royal court.

When we arrived, Khunying Aoy ushered us into the first kitchen, her everyday kitchen, the one frequently used by

the family's "Western" cook for the preparing of American fried chicken and Italian pasta when the kids wanted them. We were set up to make stuffed yellow chiles rolled in an egg "net," a dish typically served during warm weather. Ground pork was mixed with garlic, coriander root and cilantro, and stuffed into raw yellow chiles. After the chiles had steamed for a few minutes, we started making the egg nets: We dipped fingertips into beaten duck eggs (used for richness and consistency), then waved them over a hot pan as egg "threads" wove themselves into a net-like pattern. Each egg net was rolled around a warm, steamed chile just as the "net" turned crisp, creating an ethereal contrast to the soft meatiness within.

As we transitioned into preparing duck in red curry, I realized why some Thai dishes had presented hurdles for me. Khunying Aoy had been able to buy a wonderful barbequed duck at her favorite market, she'd gotten freshly pressed coconut milk, and she'd commissioned a curry vendor to make curry paste to her specifications. Those were not easy options for me in Chicago.

First she showed us how to cook the coconut milk down until the fat separates and how to infuse the goodness of curry paste and kaffir lime leaf into the reduced milk. As the kitchen filled with the quintessential curry aroma, she added the remaining ingredients—eggplants, cherry tomatoes, basil and duck—explaining how she'd made modifications to the dish while living in London. With each thoughtful mention of a substitution, I began to understand

the vigorous, adaptable character of Thai cooking more fully. I couldn't wait to get home and get cooking.

Then we progressed from the everyday kitchen to the huge Asian-style banquet kitchen outfitted with four wok stoves. There Khunying Aoy showed us how to make Thai-style crispy fried chicken wings with mushroom stuffing (most of which was carted off by the family's Asian cook to the noisy kids above us in a family room). Next came a simple stir-fry of a thick-leaf lettuce (harvested right outside the kitchen door) in oyster sauce—an example of the strong Chinese influence on Thai cooking. And lastly, grilled out by the lettuce patch were huge prawns basted with a sweet-sour-pungent glaze of tamarind, palm sugar and fish sauce.

We were ushered outside to the huge, beautifully set teak dining table the family had made from a felled teak tree that had literally floated into their life on the Ping River that skirts one side of their property. The cooks had arranged everything we'd made on a sideboard, along with steamed rice (Khunying Aoy's was a healthy, organic, half-polished variety) and the components for *mien khom*—edible leaves that you top with pinches of tiny dried shrimp, toasted coconut, peanuts, bits of lime, incendiary chiles and a sweet sauce, then wrap into packets and pop in your mouth. This classic Thai appetizer offers an explosion of thrilling flavors and, as Khunying Aoy pointed out, a perfect balance of the four natural elements—earth, wind, water

and fire. Though I couldn't intuitively tell which ingredient represented each element, I began to understand more fully the Thai notion that food always transcends mere momentary pleasure. Food is integral to the enhancement (or diminishing) of total well-being.

I'd noticed that several times during our "cooking class" Khunying Aoy had referred to a cookbook with beautiful pictures of finished dishes. I asked if it was a favorite. "Yes," she said. "My mother's recipes."

It took me a few minutes to comprehend that this new-looking cookbook hadn't been one her mother relied on, but one Khunying Aoy had *written* to honor her mother's mastery of the culinary craft. After her mother and father had tragically died in a plane crash in the early '90s, she dedicated several years to writing books that documented their passions, expertise and knowledge, as is the custom in Thailand. Khunying Aoy had had to immerse herself in the complexities of classic Thai food, which up until then she had not explored. After all, she'd been Cordon Bleu educated, a master of Western cuisine ("Caucasian" as she called it); with a mother so well recognized for her mastery of Thai classics, Khunying Aoy had chosen to make her mark with an entirely different cuisine. That is, until fate brought her back to her roots and a new-found passion for passing on the knowledge of a Thai culinary master, her mother.

"*Vithayatharn*," the Thais say. "Give away knowledge." It's a practice that always comes back to honor the giver.

Lanie: Thailand was definitely one of the most comfortable places I've ever visited. I know that sounds weird—it's *way* far away, I don't speak Thai, and I *certainly* wasn't raised on Thai food. But I *did* feel comfortable when I got there.

Maybe that's because we were with our good friend Olivia, who speaks Thai and could ask people directions and stuff, just like I can when we go to New York or somewhere like that. Maybe I felt comfortable because we visited Mike and Cheri, my dad's cousins, who live in Chiang Mai—and *don't* speak much Thai, *don't* eat that much Thai food, but

do have loads of Thai friends. They *l-o-v-e* the "Thai people" which is what the Thais call themselves when they speak English. Besides, Thais are really nice—always asking if everything is O.K., if you have what you need, if you know where you're going.

Or maybe I remember feeling so comfortable because Cheri took me to a "modern" shopping mall near their apartment, where all the kids hang out. *And* she bought me my first pair of platform shoes, *and* she took me to a Pizza Hut and Dairy Queen. That was the first time I'd had Dairy

Queen—*in Chiang Mai, Thailand!* Just think about it: *totally* w-e-i-r-d. But a fun memory.

My other favorite experiences were (1) eating stuff at Aw Daw Gaw market, (2) staying on the river in Bangkok, (3) the Night Market in Chiang Mai, and (4) hiking and elephant riding. First things first.

Yes, Aw Daw Gaw is a *very cool* market (as long as you stay away from the smelly durian fruit). They have great satay there and great *pad thai,* too, especially the kind wrapped in the thin omelet. And the coconut "tart" thingies that they make in the back of the market are VERY good. And those little rice noodle dumplings, too.

I actually like the Thai food courts in the big shopping malls a little better, and *not* just because I love shopping when I'm not eating. I had really good fried rice at MBK in Bangkok (kind of like the recipe we included here) and an iced coffee drink that tasted like a Frappuccino. And at Old Siam Square, there's a food court that's all desserts, which sounds *awesome,* except that a lot of Thai sweets are made out of duck eggs and beans, which doesn't exactly qualify as dessert for me. No chocolate. But there are these cool "tacos" (the shell is kind of a wafer cookie) filled with either (1) something like cotton candy or (2) meringue and coconut. Both of them are really, *really* good—like you could eat a ton of them.

The dessert food court has sweet coconut sticky rice (recipe on page 222), which they top with mango (totally delicious) or durian (totally not). You can imagine which my dad always gets. Well, once he took a serving of durian back to our hotel and *ate it in our room!* My mother and I had to lay on the bed with pillows over our faces trying to get away from the smell. And when he finished we had to open all the windows.

It was good we were staying at a hotel on the river where there was a breeze. In the morning, we always ate breakfast outside looking at the river (before it got too hot and humid). I ate omelets. My dad ate rice soup with fish sauce and chiles and those crispy garlic "chips" they put on practically everything in Thailand. (How anyone could eat that in the morning, I'll never understand.) What I remember most about breakfast in Bangkok, though, is watching those noisy, long skinny boats (they call them "long-tail" boats) delivering people from here to there, churning up the water and making tons of noise as they criss-crossed the river. That and the rice barges that float slowly along.

Bangkok is *huge,* but Chiang Mai isn't. Chiang Mai isn't nearly as crowded, except at the Night Market, which is this whole section of town where people set up hundreds of stalls *every single night.* It's jammed and *crowded,* but fun, because people are selling everything from t-shirts (favorite: Coca Cola written in Thai) to old "antique-y" stuff to CDs (with no labels—if you get my drift), which they play v-e-r-y loud.

We always went to the Night Market because Cheri and Mike's apartment building is right in the middle of it, and Cheri knows the vendors that have the coolest stuff. She took me to buy these batik beach wraps, awesome macramé belt wraps and some little books of handmade paper (gifts for my friends). And—as *usual*—I came across my mom, dad and Olivia waiting in line to buy food—a dish called *roti.* It's this huge, super-thin pancake/crepe that gets sprinkled with sugar and rolled up. You can get it with chocolate and bananas, too, which is why Cheri and I had decided to cruise by there.

You can go on these organized hikes and elephant rides around Chiang Mai which are really fun, unless you get on a really hard one. Like we did, even though we thought it was supposed to be easy. I was wearing white pants—completely the wrong choice, since I (and *everyone else* in our group) ended up slipping down muddy banks and falling into the river *more than once.* Half the time we couldn't even see a trail, because the jungle was so thick!

We were almost to the elephant camp when my mom slipped and twisted her ankle really bad—like it swelled up so she couldn't walk. Then, just like out of a movie, this mahout (elephant trainer/master) appeared, said something to our guide, and flew off running through the jungle. We all tried to support my mom from the sides as we inched her along toward the river, where the guide said the mahout would meet us. He neglected to tell us that the mahout would be riding an elephant—the "elephant ambulance," we like to call it.

Well, my mom got to ride to the elephant camp on that elephant. She looked like the Queen of Sheba as the elephant plodded through the shallow river water, tearing a path through all those unbelievable jungle vines. I walked with everyone else along the bank to the elephant camp. Which is where we got on elephants (that's another story!) and started on a SCARY, steep *downhill* ride to where our van was. Riding elephants (under *normal* circumstances and on *flat* ground) is totally one of my favorite Thai experiences. They're so huge—like riding a breathing boulder or something. You are painfully aware at every moment that if one rolled over on you, there'd be nothing left thicker than a CD. Which is what I thought might happen to me as we went down the hill.

The next day, Cheri had set up for us to cook with Khunying Aoy. I never know exactly what to expect when we do this, but I certainly *never* expect to be cooking with someone connected to the *ROYAL COURT.* When Khunying Aoy showed us around, we saw pictures of her and the QUEEN OF THAILAND visiting her in *her* house. That's when we found out that Khunying Aoy was a "Lady in Waiting."

When she started cooking, Khunying Aoy had several helpers with her in the kitchen. She was really nice, though, not at all stuck-up. Like you could imagine her being your mom. The first thing we made was duck in red curry. It smelled really, *really* good when Khunying Aoy cooked the coconut cream with the red curry paste and kaffir lime leaves. Truth is, it smelled so good I actually wanted to eat it, even though I don't really like duck very much. Or those tiny little eggplants they eat in Thailand (bitter). And it was *delicious,* especially spooned over jasmine rice.

What was REALLY FUN, though, was making the egg "nets" for stuffed chiles. They had already made the meat filling, so all we had to do was stuff it into these small pointed yellow chiles and cook them. When they were done, we dipped our fingers in beaten egg and waved them over a non-stick skillet—like making one of those funny kindergarten paintings where you drip paint on paper. But you

drip the egg from your fingertips over and over—crisscrossing—so it turns out like a net. Which we wrapped around the chiles. It wasn't as hard as it looked at first.

Now, about that non-stick skillet: Khunying Aoy is very modern, even though she makes very traditional Thai food. She uses lots of modern equipment, like non-stick skillets. And her freezer, which she uses a lot to make Thai food easier. And her blender, which she uses more than her big stone mortar. I liked hearing that.

And the dessert—well it wasn't chocolate—but it was *really* cool looking, *really* good. It was a specialty of Khunying Aoy's mother (she used to sell them to restaurants in Bangkok) and hardly anyone knows how to make them. My dad looked in a *lot* of cookbooks before he found the recipe. To make them, you first have to make a little "cup" out of banana leaf (folded up and tooth-picked at the corners). Then you add a layer of sweet bean "pudding," which I don't normally like, but this one was delicious,

made with jasmine (smelled *f-a-b-u-l-o-u-s*) and crunchy little bits of water chestnut. On top you put a layer of sweet coconut cream (more jasmine!) and one little red rose petal.

It wasn't until we were eating those little desserts that Khunying Aoy told us that SHE had written the cookbook that was sitting on the table. She'd written it for her mother because her mother, father and sister had been killed in a plane crash. She said it was to honor her mother's great cooking. I got really sad—which I never want to be, especially on vacation.

But then I thought: We had a lot of *fun* cooking her mother's red curry and stuffed chiles in egg nets. And EVERYONE seemed to LOVE eating EVERYTHING, especially her mother's special dessert. Thinking like that made me feel less sad. Even though Khunying Aoy's mother wasn't there anymore, she kind of was in a way. Isn't it awesome how food can make you feel closer to people?

Vietnamese Rice Paper—Wrapped Salad Rolls

LANIE: *The last time I made these, I couldn't stop feeling the noodles when they were soft. It's totally awesome to run them through your hands—kind of g-l-a-s-s-y and cool. I love salad rolls. They're sort of like Asian pasta salad burritos, with peanut dipping sauce. Who wouldn't like that? Even though the wrapper has a kinda weird texture in your mouth, kinda sticky-glassy-spongy. Plain mint leaves are a little strong for me, but the cool thing is you get to make your own. So put in whatever you want.*

❊ ❊ ❊ ❊ ❊ ❊

RICK: *These look like big egg rolls (they're sometimes called spring rolls), but they're always soft—not fried—so they seem light and healthy, especially with all the salady stuff inside. They are good for vegetarians, too, if you leave out the shrimp or replace it with tofu. This is a recipe based on one in my friend Mai Pham's book* Pleasures of the Vietnamese Table. *Make these right before you eat them or the rice paper will dry out and get tough. You can also use 8-inch rice paper wrappers but since they are smaller, you'll need to leave the ends open. Rice paper wrappers are a key ingredient here. I don't recommend using the ones made of wheat. The wrappers are available at Asian markets; a 12-ounce package contains about 16 wrappers.*

Half of an 8-ounce package dried rice vermicelli noodles—aka rice sticks

Eight 12-inch dried round rice papers—aka spring roll wrappers

About 8 ounces (16 medium) cooked peeled shrimp
OR 8 ounces cubed, cooked chicken, cooked pork or tofu

1 small bunch mint or cilantro

1 cup (about 3 ounces) bean sprouts (mung bean sprouts are most common)

1 small head Boston/Bibb or red leaf lettuce

Peanut Dipping Sauce (opposite page)

······ **DO THIS FIRST** ······

SHRIMP: Cut in half lengthwise down the back of each shrimp (making two crescents).

MINT OR CILANTRO: Pick off leaves. Discard stems. You need ½ cup or more leaves.

LETTUCE: Wash. Dry on paper towels. Cut 4 leaves in half lengthwise, down center rib.

1. *Cook noodles.* In a large tea kettle or medium (4- to 6-quart) saucepan, bring 2 quarts water to boil. Put noodles in a large heatproof bowl. Cover with the boiling water. Let stand until soft—about 5 minutes, depending on the thickness of the noodles. Set a colander in the sink. Pour in noodles to drain. Rinse noodles under cold water. Let drain in sink while getting other ingredients together.

2. *Set up ingredients.* On the back of the countertop, line up ingredients in the following order: rice paper rounds; halved shrimp or cubed chicken, pork or tofu; mint or cilantro leaves; cooked noodles; sprouts and cut lettuce leaves.

3. *Form rolls.* Lay a clean kitchen towel on counter in front of the ingredients. Set a baking sheet with sides next to the towel. Fill the baking sheet ²/₃ full with warm tap water. Submerge 1 rice paper round in the water until it becomes soft (about 20 seconds or up to as long as a couple of minutes). Carefully remove round and lay it flat on the towel—they are fragile. Lay 4 shrimp halves or cubes of chicken, pork or tofu on the rice paper in a line from side to side about 4 inches from the edge closest to you—leave about 1¹/₂ inches empty on each side. Top with a few mint or cilantro leaves, a small handful (loosely filled ¹/₂ cup) noodles and a few sprouts. Lay a lettuce leaf half on top, folding it if needed to get it to fit. Pick up the edge of the rice paper closest to you and tuck it over the filling. Hold the rice paper and filling in place with one hand while folding in the "flaps" of rice paper from each side. Then, continue rolling tightly until all rice paper is rolled around. Set roll aside. Make remaining rolls in the same way.

4. *Serve.* Serve whole or cut into several pieces with the Peanut Dipping Sauce for each person to dip into.

MAKES 8 ROLLS, ENOUGH TO SERVE 6 TO 8 AS A SNACK OR 3 OR 4 AS A LIGHT MEAL

Spring roll wrappers

Peanut Dipping Sauce

This may be more packed with flavor than what you're used to eating in some restaurants. We like it that way. If you want it spicy, add Asian hot sauce. (Our favorite is Sriracha.)

2 garlic cloves
¹/₂ cup hoisin sauce
¹/₂ cup smooth peanut butter
2 teaspoons tomato paste

Peel garlic and crush it through a garlic press into a small saucepan. Add the remaining ingredients and add 1 cup water. Stir to combine. Set over medium heat. Cook—stir almost constantly—for about 5 minutes to blend flavors. Allow to cool. Pour into serving bowl.

MAKES 1¹/₂ CUPS

Gomae—Japanese Sesame Spinach

RICK: *This very common Japanese spinach dish is typically covered with a creamy sesame sauce. But at Matsuya in Chicago, they dress the spinach with a simple soy-mirin mixture instead and sprinkle it with sesame seeds; we do the same in our recipe. Sweet mirin and salty/tangy soy balance spinach's stronger flavors, and tasty sesame seeds make it all delicious.*

✳   ✳   ✳   ✳   ✳   ✳

LANIE: *I think this was one of the first vegetable things I liked. I ate it at Matsuya, where we went for Japanese since before I remember. Anyway, we worked out something almost e-x-a-c-t-l-y like theirs—before it changed owners. Which means there is another way I'll eat spinach besides spinach salad with honey mustard dressing.*

1 teaspoon sesame seeds

One 10-ounce bag fresh spinach (for bundled spinach, buy 1 pound and cut off stems where leaves start)

3 tablespoons soy sauce

2 tablespoons mirin (sweet Japanese rice wine)—available at well-stocked grocery stores

1 teaspoon sugar

2 teaspoons Asian sesame oil

1. *Toast sesame seeds.* Set a small (6-inch) skillet over medium-low heat. Pour in the sesame seeds and stir 3 to 4 minutes until lightly browned and aromatic. Remove from the heat.

2. *Cook and cool spinach.* Look over the spinach and break off and discard any large stems. Rinse spinach well. Shake off as much water as possible. Place in a large bowl. (If using washed spinach, skip the rinsing and sprinkle with 1 tablespoon water.) Cover with plastic wrap. Poke 5 holes in the plastic. Microwave 2 minutes on high (100%) power to completely wilt spinach. (The spinach should be soft but not mushy and still bright green.) Spread the spinach in a thin layer on a large plate or baking sheet. Allow to cool to room temperature—10 to 15 minutes.

3. *Make sauce.* In a small bowl, combine the soy sauce, mirin, sugar and sesame oil with 1/4 cup water. Stir until sugar has dissolved.

4. *Serve.* Divide spinach into 4 portions. One at a time, gather each portion of spinach into your hands and squeeze firmly to release as much water as possible. Loosen up the ball of spinach and then form it into a tall mound (like a short fat cigar). Set each portion of the spinach in the middle of a small shallow bowl or small deep plate. Pour 1/4 of the sauce over and around each serving of spinach. Sprinkle with toasted sesame seeds and serve.

SERVES 4

Asian flavorings

❀ Seven Cool Things to Buy at an Asian Grocery ❀

Asian groceries are a treasure trove of treats, especially because many Asian groceries sell foods from many countries, from Thailand across to China and Japan. Here's our attempt to choose just seven of them.

Japanese Salty Snacks: These are mostly little rice cracker snacks that come in lots of little shapes, colors and sizes, but are frequently orange-ish and shiny, though some look like beans or something you might not recognize. Some packages have little dried fish added to the mix (can frighten the unsuspecting) or have powdered nori (seaweed) on them. Or they might taste spicy like my favorite little dried peas with a wasabi (Japanese green horseradish) coating on the outside. Dangerously delicious. Most people could eat them all day long.

Sesame/Cashew/Peanut Brittle: Mixed in with the candies are packages of sesame brittle, which is essentially hard caramelized sugar loaded with toasted sesame seeds. Very cool. Very delicious. Popular all over Asia (and Mexico), this candy also comes in cashew and peanut versions.

Any Version of "Pocky": These amazingly popular sweet snacks range from the original little cookie "sticks" dipped in chocolate to super-deluxe ones filled with white chocolate mousse. There's even a "Hello Kitty" strawberry-flavored version and one with a soft caramel pouch for do-it-yourself dipping. Kids love them. Adults sneak them.

"Fear Factor" Soft Drinks: Amaze and challenge your friends with canned "soft drinks" in flavors like Grass Jelly, Rice Glue Congee, Peanut Milk and Black Rice. Buy a bunch and open them at a party. You'll be surprised who'll like what. (Lanie likes the aromatic Grass Jelly; I love the porridge-like Black Rice drink with longan fruit,

lotus seed and coconut.) You'll never know 'til you try 'em. Also look for the carbonated soft drink in the hourglass-shaped bottle. There's a marble in the cap that you press into the top of the bottle to open it. Who knows why (but it's cool)? The flavor is a cross between Sprite and bubble gum.

Little Cakes: You have two very different choices here. There is one section of cookie-like "cakes" with sticky/jammy fruit fillings wrapped in shortbread-like pastry (we love the one with honeydew melon filling). And there's another section of "soft flour cakes" which we describe as looking and tasting sort of like limp rice crispy squares. But they taste really cool—chewy, sweet and delicious (plain or yogurt-flavored are often more natural tasting than fruit-flavored).

Bubble Tea: If you're lucky, you'll find a kit with English directions that'll contain quick-cooking tapioca balls, a drink mix and straws. Otherwise buy the big fat bubble tea straws and a package of regular-cooking bubble tea tapioca balls (simmer them in lots of water for 30 minutes, turn off the heat and let stand 20 minutes, then drain and toss with some sugar). Divide the cooked, cooled bubble tea balls among tall glasses, fill with any cold fruit drink (or practically anything else liquid) and drink with the straws.

Mochi: Sticky Japanese rice is pounded into a paste (and often flavored), then formed into a little "cake" around a filling. Far too often to suit Lanie's taste, the filling's made from sweet red beans. So, if you're like Lanie, look for one of the other fillings. Like the oh-so-popular-in-America ICE CREAM! (Not all that popular in its native Japan.) Find regular-filled mochi with sweet snacks, ice cream-filled mochi in the freezer case. The tender chewy texture is what makes these so, so popular in Japan.

Thai Chicken-and-Rice Soup

RICK: *You may think the whole idea of "rice soup" sounds plain. Well, this one is certainly not. Khao Tom (the Thai name for the soup) is one of the reasons to go to Thailand. It's on every breakfast (!) buffet, because, like its Chinese cousin congee, it's a good way to start your day. It tastes like a delicious savory hot cereal—you can even make it spicy. I ate my favorite Khao Tom on the Thai island of Phuket, where a whole egg was poached into it. There, the chicken wasn't stir-fried with flavorings as it is in this recipe; I learned that trick from the Thai Cooking Class cookbook I bought in Bangkok. The crisp fried garlic or onion (available already fried in jars in Asian groceries) adds fabulous sweet toastiness. Green onions or cilantro add fresh aroma.*

The last four garnishes—fish sauce, red chile flakes, sugar and hot-sour fresh chiles in vinegar—are always on the Thai table—something like our salt and pepper. Fish sauce (look for it in the international section of the grocery store) is like very flavorful Thai salt. The hot-sour fresh chiles in vinegar and the dried chile flakes are there to blast whatever you want. And then there's a bowlful of sugar (can you believe it?) to balance all that spiciness. Makes our salt and pepper seem a little puny, doesn't it?

❈ ❈ ❈ ❈ ❈ ❈

LANIE: *I love rice, but I'm not sure I'd say this soup has anything to do with the rice I know. It cooks so long that it gets a kind of different texture—if you get my drift. Think: extremely soft tapioca or cream of wheat. This is, like, my dad's favorite thing. Not that I think it's bad or anything. Maybe I just need to eat it a few more times before I can say I love it—but NOT for breakfast. Honestly—I don't know how you could eat it for breakfast.*

½ cup rice (long grain jasmine rice is aromatic and authentic, but any rice will work)

1 tablespoon vegetable oil

3 garlic cloves

A small piece of fresh ginger (should be at least 1 inch long)

6 to 8 ounces boneless, skinless chicken (1 to 1½ breast halves or 2 to 3 thighs)

½ teaspoon ground white pepper

3 tablespoons fish sauce

FOR THE GARNISHES (CHOOSE ANY OR ALL TO SUIT YOUR TASTE)

Several tablespoons Thai-style crisp-fried garlic or red onion/shallot (available in Asian markets)

Small handful of chopped green onions or cilantro leaves

Small bowl of fish sauce

Small bowl of red chile flakes—ones bought in Asian markets are toasted

Small bowl of sugar

1 or 2 fresh green or red hot chiles—like serranos—cut thinly crosswise, floating in white vinegar

······ **DO THIS FIRST** ······

GARLIC: Peel. Crush through garlic press into a small bowl.

GINGER: Grate the cut side of the ginger through the finest holes of a grater until you have ½ teaspoon. Add the grated ginger to the bowl with garlic. Wrap and refrigerate remaining ginger for another use.

CHICKEN: On an easy-to-clean surface, cut into ½-inch pieces. Clean cutting surface well.

1. *Cook rice.* Measure 7 cups water into medium (4- to 6-quart) saucepan. Set over high heat. Add the rice. When the water boils, reduce heat to medium-low. Set lid on pan, slightly askew to allow some steam to escape. Simmer 40 minutes—stir as little as possible, but don't let it stick to the bottom of the pan—until rice is translucent and broth is creamy, like a super-thin cream of wheat.

2. *Stir-fry flavorings.* Set another medium (4- to 6-quart) saucepan or small soup pot over medium-high heat. Add the oil. When hot, add the garlic-ginger mixture. Stir for 30 seconds, then immediately add the pieces of chicken. Stir almost continuously until chicken turns white—about 2 minutes. Add the white pepper and fish sauce and stir-fry for another minute.

3. *Finish soup.* Pour the rice "broth" in the chicken mixture. Simmer 10 minutes to finish cooking chicken and allow flavors to mingle. Add water if necessary to keep that thin cream of wheat consistency.

4. *Serve.* Ladle into bowls and serve. Top with fried garlic or onion and chopped green onion or cilantro (if you have chosen to use them). Set out fish sauce, chile flakes, sugar and fresh chiles in vinegar for everyone to add to their taste.

MAKES ABOUT 6 CUPS, ENOUGH TO SERVE 4 GENEROUSLY

Bangkok-Style Chicken Satay

RICK: *Satay is great, gutsy Thai street food. Morning, noon and night you can find skinny charcoal grills in Thailand topped with a searing single layer of satay skewers—chicken, pork, lamb, sausage. It's the charcoal flavor that makes them so good, plus the fact that you're standing on a sidewalk or in a market, dipping and munching, and your head is filled with all kinds of aromas and activity. On top of that, there's the flavor of the red curry marinade, the spicy peanut-coconut milk dipping sauce and the sweet-sour cucumber "salad" that's almost always served with it. A memorable light meal that's quite easy to make. When grilling satay over charcoal or gas, we find it best to fold a long piece of aluminum foil in half lengthwise to lay under the part of the skewers that doesn't have any chicken—it keeps the skewers from burning.*

❈   ❈   ❈   ❈   ❈   ❈

LANIE: *When you realize that you have to make the satay, the sauce AND the salad, it looks like a long list of ingredients. It's not hard, though, and the cooking goes pretty fast. And satay is something most everyone loves. Like, REALLY LOVES. We sometimes cook these on a grill pan inside in winter. Which is okay, but it's not a real grill. If you want, you can make "satays" out of pork tenderloin or shrimp or just about any kind of meat—even tofu for the vegetarians. You just have to cut everything (except shrimp) into strips—think 4 inches long, 1 inch wide and about ½ inch thick. You'll have leftover sauce, which is fine since it keeps for several weeks in the refrigerator.*

- 1½ teaspoons ground turmeric—yellow spice available at most any grocery store
- 1 to 1½ teaspoons Thai red curry paste (depending on how spicy you want it)—available at many groceries and Asian markets or make your own (page 199)
- 1 teaspoon sugar
- 2 tablespoons vegetable oil
- Salt
- 4 (about 1⅓ pounds) large boneless skinless chicken breast halves (or an equivalent weight of chicken "tenders"—make sure they're not torn up)
- Sixteen 8-inch bamboo skewers
- Satay Sauce (opposite page)
- Thai Cucumber Salad (page 196)

Thai red curry paste

> ······ **DO THIS FIRST** ······
>
> **CHICKEN:** For breasts, lay chicken on an easy-to-clean surface. Pull long "tenderloin" off underneath side of each chicken breast half (if there is one). Cut large remaining piece lengthwise into 3 strips. (The pieces should be about the same size as the "tenderloin" you pulled from the underside.) Place in a large bowl. Wash cutting surface well. (If using only "tenders," simply place in bowl.)
> **SKEWERS:** Place in a long pan, like a loaf pan, and cover with water. Let stand while meat is marinating.

1. *Marinate meat.* In a small bowl, mix together turmeric, curry paste, sugar, oil and ½ teaspoon salt. Spoon over chicken strips and mix until chicken is evenly coated. Cover and refrigerate 1 hour.

2. *Skewer meat.* Thread each chicken strip onto a wet skewer. Lay on a large plate.

3. *Grill and serve.* Heat grill (or grill pan) over medium-high heat until quite hot. Lay skewers on grill. Cook until well browned underneath—about 3 minutes—then flip and cook about the same amount of time on the other side. Serve with Satay Sauce for dipping and with Thai Cucumber Salad.

MAKES 16 SATAYS, ENOUGH TO SERVE 6 TO 8 AS AN APPETIZER, OR 4 AS A MAIN DISH

Coconut milk

Satay Sauce

One 14- to 16-ounce can unsweetened coconut milk
1 to 2 tablespoons Thai red curry paste—available in Asian markets, or
   make your own (page 199)
1 cup roasted peanuts without skins
   OR ½ cup natural smooth peanut butter
¼ cup sugar—dark brown sugar is best
2 tablespoons Thai fish sauce—available where curry paste is sold

Measure all ingredients into a food processor. Secure the lid. Process until smooth. Remove top and blade, scraping as much sauce as possible back into container. Scrape into a small saucepan. Set over medium heat and stir with a whisk until mixture boils. Remove from heat and allow to cool. If not using right away, cover and refrigerate for up to 3 weeks.

MAKES 2½ CUPS

Thai Cucumber Salad

⅓ cup vinegar—either distilled white or cider vinegar
2 tablespoons sugar
Salt
1 medium cucumber—hothouse cucumber is a good option here
1 small hot green chile (like Thai or serrano chile), optional
3 tablespoons roasted peanuts
A small handful of cilantro leaves

Measure vinegar into a glass measuring cup. Add sugar and ½ teaspoon salt. Stir. Microwave on high (100%) power for 45 seconds. Stir until sugar has dissolved. Allow to cool. Use vegetable peeler to "zebra" peel cucumber—every ½ inch—if peel seems tough. Cut cucumber in half lengthwise, then slice each half crosswise ⅛ inch thick. Scoop into a bowl. Break off and discard stem from chile, then slice across very thinly (page 43). Add chile to the bowl, along with vinegar mixture. Stir to combine. Cover and refrigerate up to several hours if not using right away. Chop peanuts. Serve cucumber salad sprinkled with peanuts and cilantro leaves.

MAKES 1½ CUPS

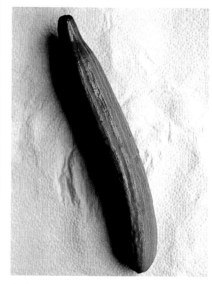

Hothouse cucumber

Thai Red Curry with Duck {or Pork or Chicken}

LANIE: *For me this is the perfect balance of SWEET and SPICY. In case you didn't know already, coconut milk is the sweet part of this dish (rich and totally y-u-m-m-y) and the curry paste is the spicy part. You don't really have to follow the recipe except for the coconut milk/curry-paste-sauce part. You can make it with pretty much whatever meat (or no meat, even tofu if you happen to like it). And with the vegetables—add whatever. If ours didn't have to be a "family decision," I'd make red curry with barbeque pork—the kind you can buy in Chinatown—and potatoes and carrots. (I'll add green beans to the list, since I know my dad will read this.)*

✄   ✄   ✄   ✄   ✄   ✄

RICK: *The smell of this classic Thai dish is incredible when you swirl the curry paste into the reduced coconut "cream." The recipe is exactly what Khunying Aoy taught us, though she used her own homemade curry paste and toasted the coriander and cumin in a wok to bring out more flavor. But I agree with Lanie: You should feel free to customize your red curry, since there is no such thing as one "authentic" curry— in Thailand, cooks add all kinds of different ingredients to it. But try not to leave out the aromatic kaffir lime leaf.*

This is an easy recipe once you get all the ingredients—it's really good even when you shop at a regular grocery store rather than an Asian market.

······ DO THIS FIRST ······

DUCK: Pull off and discard skin. Pull meat from bones. Discard bones. Tear meat into coarse shreds.

BARBECUE PORK: Slice ¼ inch thick.

FRESH PORK: On easy-to-clean cutting board, slice ¼ inch thick. Wash cutting surface well.

CHICKEN BREAST: On easy-to-clean cutting board, slice into ½ inch wide strips. Wash cutting surface well.

KAFFIR LIME LEAF OR LIME RIND: If dry, soak in hot tap water for 10 minutes. Break fresh or reconstituted dry leaf into several pieces. If using rind, slice into thin slivers.

EGGPLANT OR GREEN BEANS: For golf-ball-size Thai eggplants, cut into quarters. (If you are using the pea-size eggplants, they do not need cutting up.) For American eggplant, cut into roughly 1-inch cubes. For green beans, break off stem and pointy bottom end; cut into quarters.

Two 14- to 16-ounce cans coconut milk (not "lite")

3 tablespoons red curry paste, available in most well-stocked groceries and Asian markets or make your own (page 199)

½ teaspoon ground cumin

½ teaspoon ground coriander

½ teaspoon ground nutmeg

1 Chinese-style roast duck
OR 1 pound Chinese-style barbecue pork, fresh pork tenderloin or boneless skinless chicken breast

1 or 2 fresh or dried kaffir lime leaves
OR a 2-inch piece chopped lime rind— use vegetable peeler to take it off

1 teaspoon sugar (Khunying Aoy says to use Thai golden palm sugar—way more flavor)

2 tablespoons Thai fish sauce (available where red curry is sold)

4 ounces little Thai eggplants (about 1 cup pea-size Thai eggplants or about 3 golf-ball-size Thai eggplants)
OR about ⅓ of a medium American eggplant
OR about 1½ cups cut green beans

¾ cup cherry tomatoes

1 loosely packed cup basil leaves (Thai basil tastes like Thailand, but you can also substitute a small handful of cilantro or just leave out)

1. *Make sauce.* Spoon the top half (the thick part) of both cans of coconut milk into a wok or small (3- to 4-quart) saucepan. Set over medium heat and boil until clear oil begins to separate out—about 5 minutes. Add the curry paste and cumin, coriander and nutmeg. Stir for 3 to 4 minutes, until mixture is very aromatic. Add remaining coconut milk (the watery part) and bring to a boil.

2. *Cook meat and vegetables.* Add shredded duck, pork slices or chicken strips and bring to a boil. (If using raw pork or chicken, let cook 5 to 6 minutes—meat will give off liquid, but sauce should thicken again.) Add kaffir lime leaf pieces or lime rind, sugar, fish sauce and eggplant or green beans. Stir well. Simmer over medium-low until vegetable pieces are tender—about 5 minutes. Add tomatoes and basil. Let return to a simmer and it's ready. Serve with rice.

SERVES 4

Kaffir lime leaves

❄ Five Cool CDs to Play While Cooking Asian ❄

If you want to buy Thai pop music from Amazon.com or CDUniverse.com, you won't find much. I would give you the names of the two hottest pop stars' albums that I brought back from Thailand (my cousin's market-vendor friend chose them for us), but the album cover is written in Thai, which I don't read. So here's a good "starter" choice from Thailand, followed by the 2004 hippest pop offerings from Japan and other stuff.

1. Rough Guide to the Music of Thailand: *A fun mix of everything from classical to pop. Listening to this CD is like walking through the Night Market in Chiang Mai: You hear a little of everything. If you're into funky-weird, you may want to order* Thai Elephant Orchestra. *Yes. Elephants playing music, mostly drums and gongs.*

2. A Best: *Ayumi Hamasaki is a superstar in Japan and this is a "best of" album. Girls love listening to it; guys like watching Ayumi videos. I don't mean to offend, but she's a little like the Britney Spears of Tokyo. Pop/dance music.*

3. First Contact: *Orange Range's most successful album to date. Definitely Japanese rock, not pop. If you like Blink 182 or Good Charlotte, you'll probably like these guys.*

4. Love Notes: *I love* The Gospellers, *an acapella group of young Tokyo hipsters, because their music is fun (in a pop sort of way), their harmonies are rich and their choice of songs is a little unexpected. We're not talking dance music or anything—but great to put on while cooking.*

5. Facts and Fictions: *This CD by the Asia Dub Foundation takes us to the very vibrant Southeast Asia music scene. When you want to push past Putamayo's Asian Groove CD or the soundtrack to* Bend It Like Beckham, *you'll be ready for this Asian Underground group. Pure D&B and dance music from the Indian/ Pakistani tradition—it nods toward hip hop, not New Age.*

Homemade Thai Red Curry Paste

Sure, making curry paste is for the dedicated adventurer, but some of you will want to try it. By far the best curry paste is made by pounding all of the ingredients in a granite Thai mortar (its shape and size and the very hard stone it's made from, are perfect for the task). You can also make it in a food processor: just *double* all the ingredients and pulse the processor, regularly scraping down the ingredients that stick on the sides, until you have as smooth a paste as possible (you'll see some chile seeds). Ingredients will probably require a trip to an Asian grocery. Since the typical Thai dried chile used for this paste isn't widely available here (it's 5 or 6 inches long), we've combined the common, small, very hot Thai dried chile with paprika (a ground mild chile) for very good results.

Thai granite mortar

10 small (1½-inch) dried red Thai chiles
1 tablespoon mild paprika
½ cup roughly chopped red shallots—peel before chopping
2 tablespoons roughly chopped garlic—peel before chopping
½ teaspoon grated lime rind (green part only)
2 tablespoons thinly sliced lemongrass—use mostly white end
¼ teaspoon black pepper
2 tablespoons grated fresh ginger—peel before grating
¼ teaspoon ground turmeric

Break the stems off the chiles (if they have stems). Shake out and discard the seeds (most will come out—don't worry about the rest). Place chiles in a mortar. Add the remaining ingredients. Pound the mixture for a full 20 minutes. (That's how long it takes to get a smooth, fluffy paste—you may have to take a break every few minutes, but don't skimp on the time.) Scrape the mixture into a small jar. If not using immediately, cover tightly and refrigerate. It will keep for several weeks.

MAKES ABOUT ½ CUP

Street Vendor Pad Thai

RICK: *I couldn't believe it when I discovered that* pad thai *just means "Thai stir-fry." No wonder we found so many variations when we went to Bangkok to visit our friend Olivia's family. At the amazing Aw Daw Gaw food market there, a woman works wonders with a 3-foot-wide flat steel griddle on which she makes a rustic flat omelet, then folds it over sprouts, preserved radish and soft rice noodles infused with sweet-tart sauce, and calls it* pad thai. *Of the dozens we tried, hers was my favorite. For this recipe (which is* almost *as good as the market vendor's—but a lot easier), you can use a large griddle, a very large skillet or a wok. Also, you can double or triple the sauce recipe and keep it in a tightly closed bottle in the refrigerator for up to a month, ready for an emergency* pad thai *fix. A little less than 1 cup of it is what you need for each batch. "Pickled radish," used by many Thai cooks, is really sweet pickled daikon radish (sometimes the package won't say pickled). It adds an authentic taste, but isn't essential.*

✵ ✵ ✵ ✵ ✵ ✵

LANIE: *This is DELICIOUS pad thai! Which is predictable since I LOVE anything with noodles. Think of these as sweet-and-sour (perfect!) noodles with a bunch of other stuff that, in my opinion, you hardly taste—except the peanuts. Also good cold for lunch the next day. Note: The cooking goes quickly, so have everything set up by the stove!*

······ DO THIS FIRST ······

NOODLES: Put noodles in a large bowl. Cover with hot tap water. Let soak 20 to 30 minutes (no more) while preparing other ingredients and sauce, until noodles are soft enough to be pliable. Drain.

TOFU: Drain and cut into ½-inch cubes. Spread on paper towels to dry.

PICKLED RADISH: If radish didn't come shredded, shred it through the large holes of a grater.

EGGS: Crack into a bowl and beat lightly.

GREEN ONION: Cut off and discard root end. Peel off and discard withered outer layers. Cut green part into 2-inch lengths; discard white part or use in another dish.

GARLIC: Peel. Cut cloves in half.

PEANUTS: Roughly chop.

LIME: Cut into 8 wedges.

---

6 ounces dried thin (about ¼ inch wide) rice noodles

About 12 ounces extra-firm tofu

⅔ cup shredded Thai pickled radish

3 cups (about 10 ounces) loosely packed mung bean sprouts, divided use

4 "large" eggs

3 green onions

FOR THE SAUCE

2 garlic cloves

¼ cup Thai fish sauce—plus a little more for serving

2 tablespoons sugar—use dark brown sugar if not using tamarind

1½ tablespoons ketchup

½ teaspoon chile flakes—plus more for serving

1½ to 3 tablespoons tamarind (see box) OR 3 tablespoons rice (or white or cider) vinegar

FOR FINISHING THE DISH

2 tablespoons vegetable oil

About ⅔ cup roasted skinless peanuts

1 lime

1. *Set up ingredients.* Set drained noodles, cubed tofu, shredded pickled radish, *half* of the sprouts, beaten eggs and green onion pieces by the stove.

2. *Make sauce.* In a blender, combine the garlic, fish sauce, sugar, ketchup, chile flakes, tamarind (or vinegar) and ½ cup water. Blend until smooth.

3. *Cook dish.* Set large griddle, wok or very large (12-inch) skillet over medium-high to high heat. When hot, add the oil. Very gently slide in tofu and radish. Stir slowly and continuously with a metal or wooden spatula 3 to 4 minutes, until tofu browns lightly. Add the *half* of the sprouts by the stove and stir-fry 1 minute longer. Drizzle eggs over everything. Count to 10, then stir gently 3 or 4 times. Count to 10 again and stir to break up egg once more. (Repeat if egg is not set.) Add green onions and noodles to pan. Drizzle sauce over everything. Stir gently for 1 to 3 minutes, until noodles are soft and have absorbed the sauce.

4. *Serve.* Divide among 4 plates. Sprinkle with remaining sprouts and the chopped peanuts and serve with lime wedges, extra fish sauce, chile flakes and sugar for anyone who wants them.

SERVES 4

Tamarind

❊ Tamarind ❊

Tamarind is a fat brown pod that has the most amazing flavor. Rich and caramely (a hint of molasses), fruity (like a dried apricot or date) and, above all, very tangy. No, not just tangy: sour. Like a lemon shouting at the top of its lungs. It's the special rich sourness that folks all over the world have fallen in love with, using tamarind to season favorite Mexican drinks and candies, favorite Indian curries, and favorite Thai noodle dishes like pad thai.

Tamarind pods grow by the hundreds on tall, frilly-leafed tamarind trees anywhere that has a near-tropical climate. You pick the pods and break off their brown, bark-like outer shell (it'll crack off in pieces), revealing an eerie web of light-colored strings that grasp the dark-brown tamarind "pulp" where all the flavor is.

You can buy tamarind pods in Mexican, Indian and Asian groceries and some regular well-stocked groceries. Before you buy, crack a pod open to make sure that the pulp inside isn't rock hard—it should be pliable like fruit leather. In Indian and Asian markets you can also buy tamarind concentrate—some watery, some thick. But it's not so fresh and full of flavor.

Here's what you do with fresh tamarind pods: Peel the barky exterior from 8 ounces fresh tamarind pods. Pull off the whitish strings. Put the pulp in a bowl and cover with 1 cup boiling water. Let stand 1 hour. Use your finger-tips to work the embedded seeds free from the pulp. Pour the pulpy liquid into a strainer set over a bowl and work the pulp through the strainer with your fingertips or the back of a spoon, leaving seeds behind. Yields about ¾ cup.

❋ Knife Basics ❋

Basic facts: (1) There is an appropriate knife for every task. My 3 essential knives are a chief's knife, a paring knife and a serrated (bread) knife. **Chef's knives** are large and are used for slicing and chopping fruits, vegetables, meat, chicken and fish. The slight curve in the cutting edge of the blade makes this knife useful for mincing ingredients like garlic and herbs, using the "rock-and-chop" technique described below. (My favorite chef's knife shape for general home cooking is called "Santoku" and it has a 7-inch blade. The cutting edge of this Japanese-inspired shape has less curve than is common in most Western-style chef's knives. The blade's wide enough to scoop up what you've chopped.) A **paring knife** is used for peeling and for tasks where a chef's knife blade is too large (like cutting the core out of an apple or picking the seeds out of a lemon). A **serrated knife** is essential for cutting bread and cake. A chef's knife has a tendency to mash, rather than cut through, bready or cakey foods. (2) Cooks get more frequent, serious cuts with dull knives than with sharp ones, since the greater force needed to use them causes the cook to have less control. I sharpen my knives with a sharpening steel or stone every time I use them. For a detailed explanation of this, go to the internet site of world-famous chef Jacques Pépin (jacquespepin.net).

Basic Techniques for Using a Chef's Knife: (1) Grasp the knife's handle firmly in your "writing" hand. For best control, "choke" up on the handle so that your thumb is firmly planted on one side of the blade's end. Your index finger can rest on the top edge of the blade, as is common for Japanese cooks, or wrap around to the side of the blade opposite your thumb. Grasp the food you're going to cut with the fingertips of your other hand, fingertips curved in slightly. Now, rotate your fingers (and the food) so that your knuckles face toward the knife blade. Start slicing, always slicing away from you in long strokes (letting the sharp blade do the work) rather than trying to "hatchet" through the food using brute downward pressure. Using long strokes will always produce more uniform slices than short "sawing" strokes. After a couple of slices, reposition your "holding" hand and continue slicing. If cutting an ingredient into cubes, simply lay a slice on the counter, slice into strips, then rotate the strips a quarter of a turn and slice into cubes. That's how chefs make that beautiful little dice. (2) To mince ingredients like garlic, herbs and ginger, first slice the ingredient thinly, then "rock-and-chop": Hold the knife in your "writing" hand as described above. With the extended fingers of your other hand, hold the top of the knife firmly in place

about an inch from the tip itself. Starting with the point down and the handle raised, rock the blade across the ingredient, then back to the point-down/handle-up position. Keeping the point down in roughly the same place, move the handle a little to the right and rock the blade back and forth again. Move the handle a little more to the right and rock again. Keep going until you've rocked-and-chopped across the ingredient, then rock-and-chop back toward the left, always pivoting with the knife point in roughly the same place. As you feel comfortable with the technique, you'll quickly mince your ingredient, rocking-and-chopping back and forth a few times.

Teriyaki Chicken *Donburi*

RICK: *The shiny, deep-flavored sweet-saltiness of good teriyaki is just about every-one's favorite. It's easy to make your own teriyaki sauce, and homemade is better than most of what you can buy. (We tasted 9 different ones from the store—thick and thin, simple and complex, tasty and odd, some you wouldn't even recognize as teriyaki sauce.) Teriyaki chicken piled on a bowl of rice (they call this* donburi *in Japan) with thin-cut shreds of nori (the seaweed they use for sushi) or with broiled green onions, is pure comfort food to me.*

❊　❊　❊　❊　❊　❊

LANIE: *Though I've eaten this practically since I was born, I remember it most from this soba noodle shop in Japan where we sat on tatami mats on the floor around low black tables. To me, a lot of the food they eat in Japan tastes weird, so I was relieved when I got my "donburi" bowl of teriyaki chicken and rice. It's really easy to make—especially if you have the teriyaki sauce (which you should make in* big *batches and keep in the refrigerator). Don't freak when the sauce you brush on the chicken runs off, because it soaks in as the chicken cooks. And don't leave the kitchen while the chicken is cooking—you have to make sure the thighs don't brown too much or get done too fast. (If the chicken thighs are small, you may want to omit the final 5-minute baking, but don't omit the broiling.)*

8 boneless, skinless chicken thighs
(about 2 pounds)
12 green onions
About 1 cup teriyaki sauce, store-bought
or homemade (page 204)
About 4 cups Basic Asian White Rice
(page 209)

⋯⋯ DO THIS FIRST ⋯⋯

OVEN: Position rack in upper third of oven and turn on to 425°F.
GREEN ONIONS: Cut off and discard root end. Peel off and discard withered outer layers.

---

1. *Bake chicken.* Line baking sheet (with sides) with foil. Lay chicken and green onions in a single layer on the foil. Divide teriyaki sauce into 2 bowls. Brush chicken and green onions heavily with teriyaki sauce from one bowl. Bake 10 minutes, remove from the oven and brush heavily again with sauce from the same bowl. Bake 5 minutes, then remove and brush heavily once more. Bake 5 minutes, remove and brush heavily again. Turn oven to broil. Turn the green onions over. Broil chicken and green onions 5 to 8 minutes longer or until

chicken is a rich mahogany-brown with dark splotches and is no longer pink when you cut into the thickest part. Throw away brushing sauce.

2. *Serve.* Scoop rice into bowls or onto plates. Cut chicken and green onions into bite-size pieces and place on top of mounds of rice. Drizzle with sauce from other bowl. Serve.

SERVES 6

Basic Teriyaki Sauce

This is an easy teriyaki sauce that we concocted. It's quick to make and you can find all the ingredients at the grocery store. The classic is equal parts sake (Japanese rice wine), mirin, soy sauce and sugar: Mix together ½ cup of each, set over medium heat and simmer until reduced to half the original quantity—takes about 15 minutes. The sake—look for it where top-quality wine is sold—gives the sauce a distinctly "Japanese" flavor that I love. The version below is a crowd pleaser that we can whip up at a moment's notice. Leftover teriyaki sauce can be refrigerated for several months.

½ cup mirin (sweet Japanese rice wine)
1 cup soy sauce
½ cup sugar
2 tablespoons corn syrup

In a small saucepan, combine all ingredients. Bring to a boil, then simmer over medium heat for 5 minutes to thicken slightly. Allow to cool and store in a covered jar in the refrigerator.

MAKES 2 CUPS

Sweet-and-Sour Stir-fry

RICK: *As a kid, I loved sweet-and-sour anything when we went to Chinese restaurants. When I grew up, I figured sweet-and-sour was just for kids. But when we went out with a Chinese family in Hong Kong, even the adults ordered it. So I developed this version from a cookbook Deann brought home after living in Taiwan.*

This recipe offers the perfect balance of sweet (sugar, ketchup) and tangy (vinegar, soy). And everyone seems to love this combination of vegetables. If you're cooking for big meat eaters, you may want to double the quantity of pork (double the soy-cornstarch marinade, too). Or you can substitute boneless, skinless chicken thighs, cut into 1-inch pieces; cook them a couple of minutes longer than the pork. Careful set-up before stir-frying is important.

✕　✕　✕　✕　✕　✕

LANIE: *Stir-fry prep takes longer than the actual stir-frying. And when you finally do start stir-frying, it's a little like one of those games at camp when you have to do one thing really fast after another. After you've done it once, though, you'll get the hang of it. The flavors in this dish are not exotic, they're just good. And you don't have to use exactly the vegetables we call for—use what you like. Then serve it with rice.*

FOR THE SAUCE AND MARINADE

2 garlic cloves

A small piece of fresh ginger (should be at least 1½ inches long)

¼ cup sugar—dark brown sugar is best

¼ cup vinegar—rice vinegar or white vinegar is best

4 tablespoons soy sauce, divided use

2 tablespoons ketchup

1 tablespoon cornstarch

FOR THE STIR-FRY

8 ounces raw pork tenderloin

2 tablespoons vegetable oil, divided use

1 medium onion (red onion is delicious here)

1 medium red bell pepper

6 ounces (about 2 heaping cups) snow peas or sugar snap peas

¼ head green cabbage

½ cup cilantro leaves

····· **DO THIS FIRST** ·····

GARLIC: Peel. Crush through garlic press into a small bowl.

GINGER: Grate the cut side of the ginger through the finest holes of a grater until you have 1 teaspoon. Add the grated ginger to the bowl with the garlic. Wrap and refrigerate the remaining ginger for another use.

PORK: On an easy-to-clean cutting board, cut into ¼-inch slices. Place in a small bowl; wash cutting surface well.

ONION: Cut off top and bottom and discard. Cut in half from top to bottom. Peel off papery outside layers and discard. Slice halves about ¼ inch thick. Break up into strips.

RED PEPPER: Cut in half down through stem. Pull out seed pod and stem from each side; discard. Slice pepper into ¼-inch strips.

PEAS: Snap off stem end and pull off the string that runs down one side of each pea and is attached to its stem. (Some peas will not have it.)

CABBAGE: Cut out and discard the hard triangular core on one side. Slice cabbage crosswise ⅛ inch thick. You should have 3 packed cups.

1. *Make sauce.* Into the bowl with the garlic and ginger, measure the sugar, vinegar, *2 tablespoons* of the soy sauce and the ketchup.

2. *Marinate pork.* To the sliced pork add the cornstarch and the remaining *2 tablespoons* of the soy sauce. Stir well to dissolve the cornstarch and coat the meat.

3. *Stir-fry vegetables.* Set wok or very large (12-inch) skillet (non-stick works best) over high heat. When very hot, add *1 tablespoon* of the oil. Swirl wok or skillet to coat evenly. Immediately add the sliced onion. Stir with a spatula to coat with oil. Add the strips of red pepper and stir to coat. Add the prepared peas. Cook—stirring with a spatula nearly continuously—until the onion looks a little soft, about 2 minutes from when the onions went in. Add the sliced cabbage. Stir continuously until the cabbage begins to wilt, about 2 minutes more. Scrape vegetables from the wok or skillet onto a serving platter. Wipe out with paper towels and set it over high heat again.

4. *Stir-fry pork.* When very hot, add the remaining *1 tablespoon* oil. Swirl wok or skillet to coat evenly. Add the meat and its marinade. Stir with a spatula to coat with oil, then spread out flat in wok. Wait 10 seconds or so, then start slowly turning and stirring meat until browned—about 2 minutes (or a little more).

5. *Finish dish.* Immediately add the vegetables and sauce to the pan. Cook—stirring continuously—until sauce boils, thickens slightly and the vegetables are hot, about 1 minute. Add the cilantro and toss a few more times. Scoop onto a serving plate.

SERVES 4

How to Care for a Steel Wok, Cast-Iron Skillet or Steel Crêpe Pan

These basic pieces of kitchen equipment typically have a "raw" surface that needs to be "seasoned" to seal out the raw metal taste and to make them more stick resistant. Once seasoned, they need to be washed in a special way, dried thoroughly and kept seasoned.

When you buy any of these in the raw state (some now come pre-seasoned), start the seasoning process by setting the pan over medium heat. When thoroughly hot, pour some vegetable oil in a soup bowl, wad up 3 or 4 sections of paper towel, dip in the oil until most of the wad is saturated, then carefully rub the oily paper towel wad evenly over the inside of the pan. Return the paper towel wad to the oil. Immediately wad up some clean paper towels and wipe out the excess oil. Leave the pan over the heat for a couple of minutes, then repeat with the oily wad of paper towels followed by the clean(er) wad. In a couple of minutes, do it all again, then turn off the heat. Let the pan cool and then it is basically ready to use, though it will cook better if you go through the whole procedure of multiple oilings and wipings a couple more times. Letting it cool periodically between oilings is important for creating that stick resistant surface.

The maintenance process is simple: wash the pan with hot water (not soap) as soon as it's used, dislodging sticky bits with something like a Scotch Brite pad—nothing so abrasive that it scrubs through the seasoned surface you've created. Set it over medium heat until all the water has evaporated, then rub a lightly oiled paper towel over the inside surface. Let cool and put away.

Bacon-and-Egg Fried Rice

RICK: *This is what I usually end up making when we're all hungry, tired and haven't been to the store in a while (seems we usually have bacon, eggs, rice and hot sauce in our house). Only one hitch: Good fried rice needs to be made with cold rice or it comes out greasy and sticky. So, whenever we make rice, I cook up more than we need (and always bring home leftovers from Asian restaurants), so it's ready when we are. (You can also freeze leftover rice to use for fried rice.)*

The flavors in this recipe aren't super-traditional—I made it up when Lanie was little using traditional techniques and simple flavors. I start by slow-cooking onion and red pepper to sweetness with the bacon, then finish everything over much higher heat in typical fried rice fashion. Soy sauce makes it taste Chinese, while basil and fish sauce (my new favorites) make it taste Thai.

⌗　⌗　⌗　⌗　⌗　⌗

LANIE: *It's my kind of dinner when the main dish is a little sweet—like this one. Sweet red peppers, sweet cooked onions, sweet bacon. Plus it's a little salty, too— bacon and soy sauce or fish sauce. Sounds like my favorite caramel corn (Garret's on Michigan Avenue—don't miss it if you come to Chicago): kinda sweet, kinda salty. You'll find that making fried rice is really easy, even though you do have to cut up an onion, which always makes me a little dizzy.*

4 thick bacon slices (4 ounces total)
1 large red bell pepper
1 medium onion
3 "large" eggs
3 tablespoons vegetable oil
4 cups cold cooked rice
1 to 2 cups (½ to 1 ounce) pretty tightly packed whole fresh basil leaves—no stems (basil gives the dish a Thai flavor—can leave out)
5 tablespoons soy sauce
    OR 4 tablespoons fish sauce mixed with 1 tablespoon sugar
2 to 4 teaspoons hot sauce, optional

····· DO THIS FIRST ·····

BACON: Cut into ½-inch-wide pieces.
PEPPER: Cut in half down through stem. Pull out seed pod and stem from each side; discard. Slice pepper into ¼-inch strips.
ONION: Cut off top and bottom and discard. Cut in half from top to bottom. Peel off papery outside layers and discard. Slice halves about ¼-inch thick.

1. *Cook bacon, pepper and onion.* Set wok or very large (12-inch) non-stick skillet over medium heat. Add the pieces of bacon. Cook—stirring regularly—until you see lots of rendered fat but bacon is not brown, about 6 minutes. Add the sliced pepper and onion. Cook—stirring regularly—until soft, about 8 minutes. Onion should brown a little.

2. *Cook eggs.* Crack the eggs into the wok or skillet and break their yolks. Stir every 15 seconds or so until eggs have just set, about 2 minutes.

Rice cooker

3. *Finish fried rice.* Immediately raise heat under wok or skillet to medium-high. Measure in oil and add rice and basil (if using). Stir almost continuously as the rice crackles and starts to brown, 4 to 5 minutes. *Evenly* drizzle soy (or fish sauce mixture) and hot sauce (if using) over rice. Stir several times, then spoon fried rice on plates and serve.

SERVES 4

Basic Asian White Rice

In Asia, rice varies from the stickier, softer short-grain types (Calrose is a common brand here) to the more separate, firmer grains of the Thai jasmine rice (I buy it when I shop at Asian markets). You can also use regular grocery-store long grain white rice, if that's what is available. Before cooking the rice, most cooks in Asia rinse it several times until the water runs clear, then soak it for 10 minutes and drain—all to ensure that excess starch on the outside of the grains won't make the rice gummy. Our recipe is written to bypass rinsing and soaking. (Most American rice cooks beautifully without the soaking.) If you want to take this traditional step, though, use only 2½ cups water and cook the rice 10 minutes; remove it from the heat and let stand, covered, for 10 minutes before serving.

2 cups white rice

Measure 3 cups water into a 2-quart saucepan with a lid. Add the rice. Set over medium-high heat. Bring to a boil. Reduce heat to medium-low. Cover and cook 20 minutes. Remove from heat. Let stand, covered, 5 minutes before serving. If using for fried rice, scoop onto baking sheet and allow to cool completely; if not using right away, cover and refrigerate.

MAKES ABOUT 4 CUPS

Why We LOVE Our Rice Cooker

Three reasons an electric rice cooker is essential in our kitchen:

* *It cooks rice perfectly and evenly—the rice never sticks or burns.*

* *It keeps the rice warm and ready-to-eat for a long time, so you don't have to time the rest of the meal around the rice.*

* *The bowl comes out and is really easy to clean.*

*If you use the **water** measuring marks on the inside of the rice cooker bowl, make sure to measure the **rice** using the little cup that comes with the cooker—it's closer to ¾ cup than 1 full cup.*

Another "rice cooker plus": You can use the steaming basket insert to steam-heat corn tortillas: Wrap them in a clean kitchen towel, put them in the basket and steam them over a little water in the rice-cooking bowl.

Our Favorite Homemade Sushi Maki Rolls

LANIE: *I'm sure I don't have to tell you about sushi. I mean practically* everyone *today loves sushi, though* not *everyone knows that sushi doesn't* have *to have RAW FISH in it. And—get this!—when we learned to make sushi in Japan, we just dumped the sushi rice on a platter, scattered all the fillings (no fish) on top and everyone just scooped up portions. They call it "scattered sushi"—none of that green nori-seaweed paper anywhere in sight. (Not that I don't like it—I do... more or less.) Sushi maki rolls are NOT HARD TO MAKE—and I think they're more fun than "scattered sushi." You should just put out the stuff and show your friends how to make their own. Honestly, they* can *do it.*

✄   ✄   ✄   ✄   ✄   ✄

RICK: *Sushi is a huge "category." It can (and is most commonly thought to) include exquisitely fresh exotic fish and seafood on top of or in the middle of vinegared rice. But sushi can also be deliciously wacky "modern" combinations that occasionally feature downright questionable ingredients: like the corned beef sushi, chicken nugget sushi and grilled hamburger sushi that we got in Tokyo—delivered to our table by a conveyor belt that snaked through a very modern restaurant. Bottom line: Sushi basically includes sticky, vinegary rice with fillings or toppings. Maki rolls (as opposed to nigiri sushi) are rice-and-filling wrapped in nori (the special ground-up seaweed that's dried into crispy sheets—roasted is my favorite). Really good grocery stores often have the very fresh "sushi-quality" tuna (or other fish) that you can cut into long french-fry shapes and use as a raw filling, but the fillings listed below (no raw fish) are great, especially when you're serving people who are raw-fish challenged.*

2½ cups short-grain rice (sometimes called sushi rice—Botan Calrose Rice is a common brand)

⅓ cup rice vinegar

2 tablespoons sugar

Salt

½ seedless (hothouse) cucumber (or 1 Japanese cucumber)

A ¼-inch-thick slice of ham (6 to 8 ounces)

1 ripe avocado

1 package (2 ounces) radish sprouts (aka *kaiware*) or pea shoots

About 1 cup cooked, shelled crabmeat, optional

6 pieces (8-by-7 inches) sushi nori (see Rick's introduction)

Soy sauce, pink pickled ginger, wasabi and/or sesame seeds

1. *Cook, season and cool rice.* Measure 2½ cups water into 2-quart saucepan with a lid. Add the rice. Set over medium-high heat. Bring to a boil. Reduce heat to medium-low. Cover and cook 20 minutes. While cooking, mix together the vinegar, sugar and 1½ teaspoons salt in a small bowl. When the rice is done, scoop it into a large bowl. Sprinkle evenly with about *one-third* of the vinegar mixture. Use a sushi paddle or wooden spatula to stir rice up from the bottom, gently mixing and tossing to cool the rice and evenly distribute the vinegar. (All through the sprinkling and mixing, I fan the rice with a piece of paper to cool it quickly.) Never press the rice down. Sprinkle on *half* of the remaining vinegar mixture and repeat the mixing. Sprinkle on the remaining vinegar mixture and mix a final time.

2. *Prepare fillings.* Peel cucumber and cut lengthwise into 4 slices (easiest to slice a little off one side first, then roll onto cut side to make cucumber stable for slicing). Cut slices in half across the middle. Cut these half slices into $1/4$-inch-thick strips. (They will look like french fries.) Place on a large platter (the start of the "fillings" platter). Slice the ham into $1/4$-inch-thick strips. Add to platter. Cut avocado in half—start at the pointy stem end (the top) and circle around pit. Twist sides in opposite directions and pull apart. With a large spoon scoop out pit and discard. Scoop avocado flesh from the skin in a single half. Discard skin and slice each half into 8 strips. Add to "fillings" platter. Add radish sprouts (or pea shoots) and crabmeat if desired.

3. *Form maki rolls.* Have a small bowl of water on hand to wet fingers. Lay sushi mat on counter, flat-side up and lines running side to side. Lay 1 piece of the nori on the mat, rough side up. Line up long side (8-inch side) of nori with the edge of the mat closest to you. Scoop 1 cup of the rice onto the nori. Wet hands and use fingertips to gently spread out rice to cover nori, leaving 1 inch uncovered at front, $1/2$ inch on either side and about $1/3$ of the sheet of nori uncovered at the back. (The rice should look "fluffy"—you will see the nori peaking through.) Use dampened side of hand to press a shallow "trench" for filling from side to side

about $1/3$ of the way back. Use a finger to smear a little wasabi if you like it spicy—beware: too much makes your nose burn—down the "trench." Sprinkle with sesame seeds. Choose 2 or 3 filling ingredients to lay in the trench. (It doesn't take much of any one, but be careful to distribute it from side to side.) Spread the fingertips of both your hands (like claws) and use to hold the filling in place. Scoop thumbs under the mat to lift it and hold the mat and nori together with thumbs and index fingers. Begin rolling mat, nori and rice up over filling, pressing the filling with your fingertips. It's important to keep the filling in the middle as you begin rolling. When the mat comes over the top, pull out your fingertips and continue rolling until the mat touches the other side. Peel back the mat and continue rolling the nori until it completely wraps the roll. Now, grip the mat firmly around the roll to compact it and make it round. Remove mat and wrap in plastic and refrigerate until ready to serve. Continue making the other 5 rolls.

4. *Serve sushi.* One at a time, unwrap the rolls from the plastic. Using a sharp, dampened knife, cut each roll into 6 or 8 slices, dampening the knife between cuts. (Use the sushi mat, rolled firmly around the roll, as a cutting guide.) Arrange on a platter, rice side up. Pour a little soy sauce into small dishes for each person to dip his or her sushi into. Scoop pickled ginger and sesame seeds into small serving bowls. Scoop or squeeze out wasabi into a small dish. Set all out on a table. Serve sushi, passing wasabi, sesame seeds and ginger for those who want it.

MAKES 6 MAKI ROLLS (EACH CUT INTO 6 TO 8 PIECES),
ENOUGH TO SERVE 4 AS A LIGHT MEAL OR 8 TO 10 AS AN APPETIZER

Pickled ginger, wasabi and sesame seeds

Wasabi powder and paste

Chinese Potsticker Dumplings

RICK: *When Deann lived in Taiwan and taught English literature in a local university, she ate once a week at a stand that served these wonderful little meat-filled dumplings with the crispy, golden-brown bottoms. Her love for these inspired our whole family to fall in love with them, too, whether they're called Chinese potstickers or Japanese gyoza (they're basically the same). This recipe is based on one from Pei Mei's Chinese Cook Book Deann brought back from Taiwan 30 years ago and now looks all splattered and, shall we say, "well used." (Which is what all favorite cookbooks should look like.) The filling is easy, but forming the pleated "crescent-shaped" dumplings takes a little practice. When we visited Japan, we watched gyoza makers make one after another until we felt we could do it, too—and explain the technique to you. If you want to fry them all at once, you'll need a 12-inch skillet (use 1½ tablespoons oil and about ⅔ cup water).*

✕ ✕ ✕ ✕ ✕ ✕

LANIE: *I basically wouldn't try these unless I had someone to help me—which is exactly what happened one day when my mom was trying to show us how to form them. My cousins, aunts and uncles showed up (with friends, I might add), and before long everyone was forming them (without our even asking!). And then we fried them and ate them and everyone was really happy. Great tasting party food, especially since you can make up your own dipping sauce. NOTE: They sell a little plastic dumpling "former" in Asian markets, which works okay. You lay the wrapper in the press, wet it, plunk in the filling and fold it over to seal. They don't look quite as good as hand-formed ones but they're easier to make.*

⋯⋯ DO THIS FIRST ⋯⋯

GARLIC: Peel. Crush through a garlic press into a large bowl.

GREEN ONIONS: Cut off and discard the root ends. Peel off and discard any withered outer layers. Cut crosswise into ¼-inch pieces. Add to the bowl with the garlic.

GINGER: Grate the cut side of the ginger through the finest holes of a grater until you have a generous teaspoon. Add the grated ginger to the bowl with garlic. Wrap and refrigerate the remaining ginger for another use.

CABBAGE: Remove and discard any wilted outer leaves. Slice crosswise very thinly. You should have 3 cups.

2 garlic cloves

2 green onions

A small piece of ginger (should be at least 1½ inches long)

1 pound lean ground pork, chicken or turkey

⅓ of a small head Napa cabbage

2 tablespoons soy sauce

2 tablespoons sesame oil

Salt

About 40 round dumpling wrappers (aka *gyoza* wrappers or dumpling skins)

3 tablespoons vegetable oil, divided use

About 2 cups Potsticker Dipping Sauce (page 217)

Dumpling skins

1. *Make filling.* To the bowl containing garlic, green onions and ginger, add the meat, sliced cabbage, soy sauce, sesame oil and 1½ teaspoons salt. Mix well.

2. *Form dumplings.* Set out a tray or a couple of large plates for finished dumplings. Set out a cup of water. Set out dumpling wrappers and cover with a damp towel to keep moist while forming dumplings. Remove 1 wrapper and lay it in the palm of one hand. Dip the index finger of the other hand in the cup of water. Use finger to moisten the wrapper evenly. With a small spoon, scoop 1 tablespoon filling into the center of the wrapper. Fold up sides to meet, enclosing the filling. Press edges together to ensure a complete seal. Pleat sealed edge of dumpling in 5 or 6 places to pull dumpling into a crescent shape—pinch pleats firmly to seal. Set dumpling upright on a tray or plate (sealed edge pointing upward). Gently press each dumpling downward to flatten its bottom, making it stable. Cover with a damp towel. Continue making dumplings until all the filling is used.

3. *Fry-steam and serve.* Set a large (10-inch) skillet (with lid at hand) over medium heat. Measure in *1 tablespoon* of the vegetable oil. When hot lay ⅓ of the dumplings (not packed tightly) in the pan. Fry until golden brown—about 3 minutes. Dribble ½ cup water into the skillet around the edge (will spatter a little). Cover and cook until most of the liquid evaporates—about 6 minutes. Uncover and fry 2 to

3 minutes longer to evaporate all the water and to crisp the bottoms again. Use a spatula or tongs to remove dumplings to a serving platter, laying them on their side, so you see the browned bottom. Keep dumplings warm in 150°F oven while cooking the rest. Wipe out the skillet and set back on the heat. Add *1 tablespoon* of the oil. When hot, fry-steam the second batch and add to the plate in the oven. Repeat with the remaining *1 tablespoon* oil and fry-steam the remaining dumplings. Serve dumplings with dipping sauce (or dipping sauce ingredients for all to mix to their liking). It is common for each person to have a little bowl for their own dipping sauce.

MAKES ABOUT 40 DUMPLINGS, ENOUGH TO SERVE 4 TO 6 AS A LIGHT MEAL OR 8 TO 10 AS AN APPETIZER

Potsticker Dipping Sauce

At the potsticker stand where Lanie's mom used to eat these in Taiwan, there were bottles or jars of soy sauce, sesame oil, vinegar and chile paste so that each person could mix his or her own personalized dipping sauce. You, too, can just set out the ingredients, provide some small bowls and have everyone give it a try. You might want some guidelines, though, so you don't overdo it, say, with the vinegar or chile paste. Here are my favorite proportions.

¼ cup soy sauce
1½ teaspoons sesame oil
1 tablespoon vinegar
½ teaspoon chile paste (available in Asian markets)

Mix all the ingredients together and you should have enough for 4 people. You may like it better after adding a tablespoon or so of water, a teaspoon of sugar or a little grated ginger. Feel free to play around with the seasonings and proportions until you have your own "signature" dipping sauce.

MAKES ABOUT ⅓ CUP

Chinese Celebration Hot Pot

RICK: *Our Chinese friend Olivia said it perfectly when she gave me this recipe: "Erling [Olivia's son] and I began to entertain with this hot pot more and more in the last few years. It is really a wonderful way to be with friends (and do minimal prep), to have this wonderful communal cauldron of soup on a cold winter's day and a circle of dear faces sitting around, lingering, steam mossing the window glass. The routine was clinched when Yaohan [supermarket] opened nearby because we could buy pre-sliced, thin, thin beef for the hot pot. Now, many Chinese, Korean and Japanese stores carry pre-sliced beef, and sometimes other meats, just for this meal. The democratic, do-your-own element of the meal is also emphasized by the simplicity of equipment. You can get fancy with it—a copper pot, a restaurant-power burner—but I recall so fondly my student days, when we just turned on a yard-sale electric skillet, filled it with stock and made a feast. The ritual varies hugely throughout Asia, especially within China—lamb in the northwest, seafood and vegetables in the south. Without question, napa cabbage and tofu at the end are critical for they absorb the final, complex flavors of the soup so well."*

✄   ✄   ✄   ✄   ✄   ✄

LANIE: *Don't even THINK about making hot pot 'til you decide how you're going to serve it. (The broth has to stay at a simmer at the table so that people eat and cook at the same time.) My mom has this real brass hot pot she brought back from Taiwan (she was teaching English there). But other than an adventure in Chinatown (or a trip to Amazon.com—search "Mongolian Hot Pot"), who's going to have that? Read Olivia's note (above) about the electric skillet—or set two stacks of bricks on a baking sheet, put a Sterno in between and set your serving pot on top.*

SHOPPING NOTE: Buy pickled mustard greens and preserved bean curd in (Chinese) Asian markets. It's a good idea to buy bean thread noodles and thin-sliced beef there, too.

······ DO THIS FIRST ······

GREEN ONIONS: Cut off and discard the root ends. Peel off and discard any withered outer layers. Cut 3 of the green onions into 2-inch lengths. Slice the remaining one thinly and scrape into a small serving bowl.

(continued on next page)

FOR THE BROTH

2 quarts chicken or beef broth (doesn't have to be homemade)

½ cup pickled Chinese mustard greens (press into cup to measure—optional for some Chinese cooks)

3 fresh ginger slices about the size of a quarter

4 green onions

FOR THE SAUCE

½ cup fermented bean curd

1 tablespoon sugar

¼ cup rice wine, mirin (sweet Japanese rice wine), sherry or water

¼ cup soy sauce

½ cup vegetable oil

¼ cup sesame oil

¼ cup rice vinegar

FOR THE MEAT, VEGETABLES AND NOODLES

1¼ pounds uncooked shrimp (or 1 pound boneless, skinless fish cut in cubes or shrimp balls available in Asian groceries)

1 pound thinly-sliced raw beef

1 pound thinly-sliced raw turkey

1 very small head (about 12 ounces) Napa cabbage

4 ounces (6 cups lightly packed) spinach (preferably baby leaves or big leaves with stem broken off and leaves cut in half)

1 pound silken or soft tofu

4 ounces bean thread (aka glass or cellophane noodles)

(continued on next page)

FOR THE FINAL TOUCHES
½ bunch cilantro
Hot sauce (like Sriracha Vietnamese hot
sauce or even Tabasco)
Salt

SHRIMP: Peel shell off each shrimp: Hold a shrimp in one hand and pull off tiny legs with the other. Next, peel off the shell a few sections at a time, discarding the shell as you go. Scoop onto large serving platter and refrigerate.

CABBAGE: Cut 1 inch off the bottom and discard. Separate leaves. Cut larger leaves into 3 pieces lengthwise. Cut leaves crosswise in 1-inch pieces. Scoop into a large bowl.

SPINACH: Rinse well in a colander and pile on top of cabbage.

TOFU: Cut into ½-inch cubes. Scoop into a small bowl.

BEAN THREAD: Place in a bowl and cover with very hot tap water. Soak 10 minutes and then drain.

CILANTRO: Bunch leaf end of sprigs together. Cut across the bunched leaves with a sharp knife, slicing them thinly. Stop cutting when you only have stems left. Discard stems. Scoop into a small bowl.

1. *Simmer broth.* Measure broth and 2 quarts water into a large (7- to 8-quart) pot. Set over high heat. When broth boils, turn down to medium-low. Set a cover on the pot slightly askew and let simmer *gently* while making sauce and setting up meats, vegetables and garnishes. Set mustard greens, ginger and 2-inch green onion pieces near pot.

2. *Make sauce.* In a small bowl, whisk together the fermented bean curd, sugar, ¼ cup water, rice wine or sherry (or additional water), soy sauce, vegetable and sesame oils and vinegar. Scrape into a serving bowl.

3. *Set up meats, vegetables and garnishes.* On the platter with the peeled shrimp, make mounds of the beef and turkey. Set out on the table along with the bowl of cabbage pieces and spinach. Set the bowls of cubed tofu, drained bean thread, chopped cilantro and thinly sliced green onion on the table along with the sauce and hot sauce.

4. *Serve.* Add the ginger, mustard greens and 2-inch green onion pieces to the simmering broth. Set timer for 10 minutes. Set table with soup bowls (ones that hold 2 cups are best), soup spoons and either hot pot baskets (little wire baskets with long handles), chopsticks or fondue forks. In the center of the table, set up your "hot pot": either (1) a traditional Chinese hot pot with lit Sterno in the center or (2) a plugged-in electric skillet or (3) a heavy pot over a portable burner or on a heavy rack over lit Sterno. Have a heatproof trivet next to the hot pot. When

Bean thread

timer rings, fish out mustard greens and ginger from the broth and discard. Taste and season broth with about 2 tablespoons salt, depending on the saltiness of the broth you started with. Carry pot of hot broth to the trivet. Using a ladle or small saucepan, fill "hot pot" (or your version) *half* full with broth; return original pot with remaining broth to stove, re-cover it and keep it at a gentle simmer. Adjust heat under the "hot pot" so broth simmers. Call the guests to the table. Have each guest scoop some sauce into their soup bowl (say, 2 tablespoons to start with) and top with cilantro, green onion and hot sauce (if desired). Instruct the guests to cook shrimp, beef and turkey in simmering broth a piece or 2 at a time, holding with chopsticks, fork or little basket; when cooked, dip into the sauce and eat. (If broth in "hot pot" gets low, add more from the broth on the stove.) When the meats are all gone, refill broth from the kitchen. Add the vegetables, tofu and bean threads to make a final soup. Cover pot and cook until the cabbage is tender—8 to 10 minutes after soup boils. Ladle soup into each guest's bowl over remaining sauce (or add more sauce if it is all gone).

SERVES 8 TO 10

Meat, poultry and seafood for hot pot

Alternative Hot Pot Sauce Without Fermented Bean Curd

1 cup soy sauce

⅓ cup sesame oil

2 tablespoons honey or sugar (may need more)

2 tablespoons rice wine, mirin (sweet Japanese rice wine) or sherry

2 to 3 teaspoons Chinese chile-garlic sauce or other hot sauce

Mix all ingredients together with ⅓ cup water. Taste and add more honey or sugar if you think necessary. Scrape into serving bowl.

MAKES ABOUT 2 CUPS

Final soup ingredients

Thai Coconut Sticky Rice with Mango

RICK: *In Thai markets, there are always fruit vendors selling sweet, rich, coconut sticky rice that they scoop into little bags and top with cut-up fruit, usually mango, but sometimes the* very pungent *durian which Lanie thinks smells so much like overripe cheese she won't even walk near it. When we got back from Thailand, I was so in love with this simple, delicious dessert that I immediately started developing a foolproof recipe—one just right for our home. I combined suggestions from my favorite* Thai Cooking Class *cookbook, from our Chiang Mai friend Yui, from Jeffrey Alford and Naomi Duguid's* Seductions of Rice, *and from a beautifully written cookbook called* It Rains Fishes *by Kasma Loha-Unchit.*

In Thai kitchens, sticky rice is typically cooked in a conical bamboo steamer. (You can use any kind of wide, flat steamer. Or, you can build a makeshift steamer: Upend 3 custard cups in a wide, deep pan filled with about ½ inch of simmering water. Put a pie plate on top of the custard cups, cover with a lid, and steam the rice in there. Also, they frequently put long dried pandanus *leaves (available in Thai markets) in the coconut milk as it simmers, adding a delicious, slightly smoky taste. To be completely Thai, scoop the thick "cream" off a second can of coconut milk, mix in a little salt and spoon it on top of the dessert at serving time. And serve it on a square of banana leaf!*

⁘ ⁘ ⁘ ⁘ ⁘ ⁘

LANIE: *As desserts go, this one is really easy—a little time consuming (you have to soak the rice), but easy. And it's* g-o-o-d: *think of it as Thai-flavored rice pudding with a great chewy/sticky/sweet texture. Not everyone will think it has "coconut" flavor since it's made from coconut* milk *not coconut . . . coconut. Even if your mangoes aren't completely sweet and ripe, it won't matter much, because the rice is sweet.*

1½ cups long-grain Thai sticky rice (aka glutinous rice—only available at Asian, especially Thai, grocery stores—no other rice works for this)
One 13- to 15-ounce can coconut milk
½ cup sugar
Salt
2 to 3 ripe mangoes (depending on size)

DO THIS FIRST

RICE: Pour into a large bowl. Measure in 4 cups hot tap water. Let stand 2 hours.

MANGOES: Peel mangoes; discard peels. Stand peeled mango on end and slice fruit off pit on 1 flat side. (Start slicing down about ½ inch away from center axis so you don't cut right into the large pit.) Rotate mango to other side and slice off fruit. Slice large pieces into 3 long strips. Slice smaller pieces of fruit off edges of large, flat, clinging pit. Transfer all the fruit to a plate; discard pit. Repeat with remaining mangoes.

1. *Cook rice.* Pour soaked rice into a colander. Rinse under running water until water runs clear. Set up steamer. Pour about 2 inches of water into the bottom of a steamer. Wet a clean kitchen towel (not terrycloth), wring out and lay in the steamer. Pour rice onto towel. Set over high heat. When water boils, cover pot and reduce heat to medium. Steam for 25 minutes, until the rice is tender. It will be sticky-chewy but not chalky inside. (Don't let steamer run out of water—put a coin in the pot to jangle around, letting you know there's still water.)

2. *Make coconut seasoning.* When the rice is nearly ready, combine coconut milk, sugar and 1 teaspoon salt in a small (3- to 4-quart) saucepan. Set over medium heat. When mixture simmers, stir for 3 to 4 minutes.

3. *Finish and serve.* When the rice is done, dump the contents of the steamer basket into a bowl and peel off towel, or pick up the corners of the towel, carry the rice to a bowl and dump it in. (Watch out for steam—it's very hot.) Dribble about 1 cup of the coconut mixture over the rice. Mix to distribute thoroughly. Let the rice mixture stand to cool and thicken. Serve scoops of rice drizzled with a little of the remaining coconut mixture and topped with mango slices.

SERVES 6

APPENDIX

Conversion Charts

WEIGHT EQUIVALENTS

The metric weights given in this chart are not exact equivalents, but have been rounded up or down slightly to make measuring easier.

AVOIRDUPOIS	METRIC
¼ oz	7 g
½ oz	15 g
1 oz	30 g
2 oz	60 g
3 oz	90 g
4 oz	115 g
5 oz	150 g
6 oz	175 g
7 oz	200 g
8 oz (½ lb)	225 g
9 oz	250 g
10 oz	300 g
11 oz	325 g
12 oz	350 g
13 oz	375 g
14 oz	400 g
15 oz	425 g
16 oz (1 lb)	450 g
1½ lb	750 g
2 lb	900 g
2¼ lb	1 kg
3 lb	1.4 kg
4 lb	1.8 kg

VOLUME EQUIVALENTS

These are not exact equivalents for American cups and spoons, but have been rounded up or down slightly to make measuring easier.

AMERICAN	METRIC	IMPERIAL
¼ t		1.2 ml
½ t		2.5 ml
1 t		5.0 ml
½ T (1.5 t)		7.5 ml
1 T (3 t)		15 ml
¼ cup (4 T)	60 ml	2 fl oz
⅓ cup (5 T)	75 ml	2½ fl oz
½ cup (8 T)	125 ml	4 fl oz
⅔ cup (10 T)	150 ml	5 fl oz
¾ cup (12 T)	175 ml	6 fl oz
1 cup (16 T)	250 ml	8 fl oz
1¼ cups	300 ml	10 fl oz (½ pt)
1½ cups	350 ml	12 fl oz
2 cups (1 pint)	500 ml	16 fl oz
2½ cups	625 ml	20 fl oz (1 pint)
1 quart	1 liter	32 fl oz

OVEN TEMPERATURE EQUIVALENTS

OVEN MARK	F	C	GAS
Very cool	250–275	130–140	½–1
Cool	300	150	2
Warm	325	170	3
Moderate	350	180	4
Moderately hot	375–400	190–200	5–6
Hot	425–450	220–230	7–8
Very hot	475	250	9

Internet Mail-Order Sources for Food,
Cooking Equipment and Music

Most everything needed to prepare the dishes in this book can be purchased at a well stocked grocery store—in fact, we sourced everything except a couple of special ethnic items at the Jewel chain store near our house. Some of you, however, may find internet mail-order sources easier and more efficient. Here are my favorite sites.

Best Overall Site for Food and Equipment: **ethnicgrocer.com**

Best Site for Mexican Ingredients and Equipment: **mexgrocer.com**. They have all the dried chiles and masa "flour" for making tortillas (their tortilla making kit is great).

Best Site for Peruvian Ingredients: **grantangolandia.com**

Best Site for French Ingredients and Equipment: **igourmet.com**. They have a wonderful selection of cheese, including Reblochon for *tartiflette*.

Best Site for Moroccan Ingredients and Equipment: **tagine.com**. They have good preserved lemons.

Best Site for Asian Ingredients and Equipment: **www.asiafoods.com**. Their sushi set will get you started fast. They offer good brands of fish sauce and Thai red curry paste.

Best Sites for Nearly All the Recommended Music: **amazon.com** and **cduniverse.com**

ACKNOWLEDGMENTS

This book is the result of extraordinary generosity offered by people all over the world. We are forever grateful to all of you for enriching our lives so liberally. *France:* Josette, Thierry, Robin, Stephanie and Julien Coussement; Bob and Jewel Hoogstoel. *Morocco:* Bouchra Benjelloun (and her mother and family); Rafih Benjelloun. *Mexico:* Toni Sobel; Andrés, Laní and Javier Méndez. *Thailand:* Olivia Wu, Khunying Aoy, Mike and Cheri Potter. *Oklahoma:* Levita Anderson; LuAnn, Gracie and Lane Tucker. *Italy:* Faith Willinger. *Ireland:* Darina Allen. *Peru:* Isabel Alverez. *Japan:* Elizabeth Andoh. *New York:* Leslie Stoker, our editor and publisher at Stewart, Tabori & Chang, without whose vision we wouldn't have been able to share with cooks of all ages these delicious insights from around the world; Steve Tager, director of marketing at STC; Laura Lindgren, our very talented designer. *Chicago:* Kirsten West, our research assistant and test kitchen director; Jennifer Fite, publicist and personal assistant; Nick Cary who helped me cook practically everything in this book (LB) and Stella Ryan, who was always willing to help when I needed extra hands (LB). A special, special thanks to Christopher Hirsheimer, who came into our home to capture our cooking in photographs, and ended up capturing our hearts along the way. And, as always, none of this would ever have come about without the loving and brilliant Doe Coover, our literary agent.

INDEX